The Recreation and
Entertainment Industries

THE RECREATION AND ENTERTAINMENT INDUSTRIES

An Information Sourcebook

by

Norman F. Clarke

McFarland & Company, Inc., Publishers
Jefferson, North Carolina and London

British Library Cataloguing-in-Publication data are available

Library of Congress Cataloguing-in-Publication Data

Clarke, Norman F.
    Recreation and entertainment industries : an information
sourcebook / Norman F. Clarke.
        p.   cm.
    [Includes index.]
    ISBN 0-89950-464-7 (lib. bdg.: 50# alk. paper) ∞
    1. Leisure industry — United States — Bibliography.   2. Leisure
industry — Canada — Bibliography.   3. Leisure industry — Great Britain —
Bibliography.   4. Leisure industry — United States — Directories.
5. Leisure industry — Canada — Directories.   6. Leisure industry —
Great Britain — Directories.   I. Title.
Z7164.L53C57   1990
[GV188.3.U6]
016.338′4779 — dc20   89-43641
                                                            CIP

Manufactured in the United States of America

McFarland & Company, Inc., Publishers
  Box 611, Jefferson, North Carolina 28640

790.013
C599r

249647

To

Pat

my associate in all things

and

Carl, Marilyn, and
the LRS Computer Gang

Table of Contents

Introduction

Few will challenge the assertion that recreation and entertainment are among the largest consumer industries worldwide today. The truth may be that if all aspects of recreation and entertainment were viewed as a single unit, this giant industry would be the largest and the fastest growing segment of today's economy.

People in the industralized world seem consumed by the search for new and expanded forms of recreation and entertainment. Even with workers spending as much as 48 hours per week to earn the same living which in 1975 required only 40, recreation and entertainment still expand from 5 to 10 percent each year.[1]

As the result of this seemingly inexhaustible drive for more and varied recreation and entertainment, the manufacturers, retailers, and servicers in the recreation and entertainment industries have enjoyed phenomenal success and income from marketing new products and services. For example, portable video equipment and vcrs have led to new dimensions in independent motion picture production and distribution. Resorts, on the decline in the 1970s and early 1980s, have been revitalized by condominium development, timesharing, and the evolution of whole recreation communities, e.g. Vail, Colorado. And who would have imagined 20 years ago that a group of professional participants, the Professional Golfers' Association of America, would be investing in the creation of "tournament quality" golf courses throughout the United States.

Yet, until recently, recreation and entertainment were not recognized as major GNP-producing industries. Wall Street was aware of Brunswick Corp., Warner Communications, Inc., Resorts International, Coleman Co., Inc., and Coleco Industries because they were publicly traded firms. Brokerage houses and venture capitalists were knowledgeable about the investment potential of resorts and amusement real estate development, motion picture, theatrical, and sports enterprises, and new computerized games and toys. But, for the most part, the industries were undervalued, underestimated, and overlooked for a number of reasons:

First, recreation and entertainment are perceived as part of a larger, all-encompassing, loosely defined industry called "leisure." Lately, the definition of the leisure industry has been further confused by the outgrowth of a new set of government and private agencies specifically designated to promote recreation and entertainment ventures under the equally nebulous term "tourism."

Second, most recreation and entertainment enterprises are small and privately owned. They tend to lack the name recognition of the major product-producing, publicly owned stock corporations. However, as massive amounts of money flow into the recreation and entertainment coffers, this small, private image has been changing.

Third, many recreation and entertainment companies "produce" a service or a production, not a trade name product. Thus the trademark identification so important to marketing and consumer recognition is virtually unknown or nonexistent outside the recreation or entertainment industry.

Fourth, despite the fact that recreation and entertainment activities are constantly in the public eye, few people understand the organization or the inner workings of the businesses.

Fifth, there is the misconception that recreation and entertainment enterprises are largely tax-supported establishments. Many facilities such as golf courses, campgrounds, and amusement centers are perceived to be controlled or largely underwritten by government agencies and taxes when in fact they are mainly private or quasi-public, non-profit enterprises.

For the student, business person, or investor seeking information on the recreation and entertainment industries, other problems exist. One is that while excellent general business reference books have been produced, e.g. Daniells,[2] none is industry-specific for recreation and entertainment industries sources. Two recent business sourcebooks are of some help and reflect the growing interest and concern with providing bibliographic and institutional access to specific business information. They are the *Encyclopedia of Business Information Sources*[3] and *Small Business Sourcebook*.[4] Both contain industry-specific information; however, the number of sources cited is still limited by their effort to achieve breadth in the number of businesses covered.

A number of reference works on specific sports, performing arts, and recreation activities have been published by Bowker, Gale, Greenwood, Libraries Unlimited, McFarland, Oryx, and Scarecrow, but these are generally exhaustive bibliographies of published materials past and present rather than information biblio-directories or sourcebooks. Further they provide only incidental information on the business, economic, and industry aspects and virtually nothing on industry sources.

One reason for the lack of business information sourcebooks specifically on the recreation and entertainment industries may be the absence of agreement in determining what the recreation and entertainment industries are, or even if such industrial entities exists. Alvin Epperson, in his book on private and commercial recreation,[5] argues that recreation and entertainment industries do have an interrelationship and presents a history of the efforts by various government, international, and professional agencies to consistently define industries such as leisure, tourism, recreation, and entertainment. His conclusion is that there "continues to be a serious problem in the industry in terms of definition."[6]

Thus, a publication which proposes to provide information sources on the recreation and entertainment industries must, first, be industry specific; second, focus on information sources by being a sourcebook, not a bibliography; and third, define the recreation and entertainment industries and describe their information unity.

In the absence of consensus among researchers and compilers of data as to what constitutes the "Recreation and Entertainment Industries," this author has chosen to utilize the four-digit categories found in the United States government's *Standard Industrial Classification Manual*[7] as the basis for defining specific recreation and entertainment industries. *The Recreation and Entertainment Industries: An Information Sourcebook* has been organized into 30 industries using specific sic class numbers to define their parameters.

Other decisions which have prescribed the resources included in this sourcebook are:

First, the industries represent for-profit and non-profit establishments if operated as business enterprises dealing primarily with a consumer public via:

Centers, e.g. amusements, fitness, lodging.
Product lines, e.g. goods, vehicles, toys.
Productions, e.g. events, motion pictures, music.
Retail and distribution outlets.
Agents and service organizations.

Second, the sourcebook is a collection of citations with annotations to publications, databases, and associations. All are treated as information sources of equal importance.

Third, the geographical scope of the book is the United States, Canada, and Great Britain. International sources which include information on these three areas have been included.

Fourth, the book focuses on the industries and their enterprises and related organizations, rather than on people and professionals, except when these persons in their own right are enterprises, e.g. a ski instructor, a musician, or a professional golfer. Thus, while resources about professional sports clubs, hockey schools, and agencies scheduling musical events are included, publications on participation and players, the activity and its rules, or titles and records usually are not.

Fifth, the publication is intended primarily for the business community, students, and librarians seeking a thorough approach to the information structure of the recreation and entertainment industries. Because the business researcher seeks specific types of information, each industry chapter has been subdivided by one or more of the following categories:

Directories: Lists of companies and agencies producing, distributing, and servicing the consumer public. Directories provide the researcher with knowledge of the extent and geographical scope of the industry and its components. In addition, they can provide data on sales and employment, products and services, names of key company personnel, and other specific company and agency information.

Resources not included: product directories, though they are listed under an industry or trade periodical when produced as a "special" issue.

Management: Information on planning, establishing, operating, and preparing business strategies. Such source materials are essential elements in the full understandings of any industry.

Resources not included: tools of the trade, e.g. travel schedules and timetables, price lists, mechanical handbooks, organizational manuals, and technical bulletins.

Industry: Industry surveys, financial statistics, and ratio analyses. This material is the heart of industry research, particularly the information on the companies in the industry, their organization, and their financial and investment status.

Market: Consumer profiles and surveys, marketing statistics, and market analyses. The key to developing a marketing strategy is knowledge of consumer purchasing habits and preferences and demographic and financial data on a market area.

Periodicals: Trade and industry, association, and product newsletters, magazines, and research or statistical journals. The trade and industry periodical is today a primary resource for news, information, financial and marketing data, opinion, and analysis on industries and companies.

Resources not included: popular consumer magazines, unless they contain ongoing and significant industry articles and data.

Databases: Online or member-access bibliographic, directory, news, statistical, or full-text computerized data storage and retrieval systems accessible directly from the producer, via telelink from a vendor, or available on compact disc (CD-ROM). The online database is fast becoming the primary source for current information, referral, and data in the recreation and entertainment industries because of the immediacy of access to a variety of statistical, directory, and scheduling sources essential to day-to-day work and management activities.

Bibliographies/Indexes: Systematically organized compilations of citations, usually subject-oriented, to books, articles, etc., on recreation and entertainment subjects. A major handicap for the researcher in utilizing the data contained in periodicals is the fact that so few recreation and entertainment trade and industry journals are currently indexed in traditional library indexes. Many business people find it necessary to develop a personal program of ongoing reading and filing of these publications. The alternative is a bibliography or index. In this category, less emphasis has been placed on current information and more on identifying bibliographies and indexes which will provide a broad and varied sweep of all types of industry publications. Included under this heading are bibliographies with limited references to business but of significance for their information on recreation and entertainment fields.

Associations: Trade and professional groups organized to enhance, set standards, train, certify or sanction, compile statistics, conduct industry-oriented research, and provide and publish information for their members or the general public. These associations may be the most important, yet least used, information resource in the recreation and entertainment industries. Their prolification in recent years astounded this writer. Even more amazing to this reference librarian has been their general willingness, when approached, to provide industry and marketing data for use by business students. I have been liberal in including many associations which though not officially tied to a specific recreation or entertainment industry appear to be important because of their industry relationships.

Resources not included: fan clubs, hobby societies, and strictly social groups unless their purpose was to enhance or establish standards for the industry.

Finally, three other decisions have influenced the contents of this publication:

First, the publication is not a bibliography presenting a complete and exhaustive list of publications and resources; rather, it seeks to be a "sourcebook," a comprehensive guide to information resources in print, online, and via organizations, needed for in-depth company, industry, and marketing intelligence.

Second, entries, with a few exceptions representing classic studies or compilations, are in print or currently active. This decision reflects the bias of the author towards the most recent or relied-upon sources.

Third, prices have been included in the citations as guides to cost with the realization that prices change. Prices are given in American dollar equivalents as a means of universally measuring cost. The word "membership" in place of price data indicates that the publication is available only through membership in the organization.

Notes

1. U.S. Bureau of Labor Statistics. "Annual Percentage Change in Earning and Compensation." Published in *USA Today*.

2. Daniells, Lorna M. *Business Information Resources,* Rev. ed. Berkeley CA: University of California Press, 1985.

3. Woy, James, ed. *Encyclopedia of Business Information Resources,* 6th ed. Detroit MI: Gale Research, 1986.

4. Elster, Robert J., ed. *Small Business Sourcebook,* 2nd ed. Detroit MI: Gale Research, 1986.

5. Epperson, Alvin F. *Private and Commercial Recreation.* New York: Wiley, 1977.

6. *Ibid.,* p. 21.

7. U.S. Office of Management and Budget. *Standard Industrial Classification Manual,* 2nd ed. Washington DC: U.S. Government Printing Office, 1987.

1. The Fitness Industry

SIC Code: 7991.

Enterprises providing organized health, physical, and recreation activities indoors. For enterprises whose primary emphasis is manufacturing, selling, and/or servicing fitness equipment see Chapter 8, The Sporting Goods Industry.

Directories

1. Association of Physical Fitness Centers. *Roster of Reciprocal Centers*. Rockville MD. Annual. Membership. Lists facilities open without charge to members of other APFC centers giving name, address, and phone. Arrangement is geographical.

2. International Physical Fitness Association. *IFPA Membership Roster*. Flint MI. Annual. Membership. Lists member clubs, giving name, address, and phone.

Management

3. American Entrepreneurs Association. *Aerobic Dance Studio*. Los Angeles, 1984. 108p. $34.50. Guide to establishing and operating a small business. Legal, management, marketing, operations, and financial procedures. Supplier addresses and a bibliography. Looseleaf format.

4. _____. *Physical Fitness Center*. Los Angeles, 1984. 108p. $45.

Guide to establishing and operating a small business. Legal, management, marketing, operations, and financial procedures. Supplier addresses and a bibliography. Looseleaf format.

5. Bannon, Joseph J., and Busser, James. *Sport Club Management*. Champaign IL: Management Learning Laboratories, 1985. 258p. $39.95. Textbook for center managers. Chapters on operations, equipment, and office and management procedures and techniques. Sound recording included.

6. Wendy Fink Associates Inc. *Winning with Wellness: A Step-by-Step Guide for Racquet and Fitness Clubs*. Wellesley MA: Wendy Fink Associates Inc., 1985. 192p. $165.00. Plan for health and physical fitness activities. Distributed by the International Racquet Sports Association.

Industry

7. Association of Physical Fitness Centers. *APFC Facility Survey*. Rockville MD. Annual. Membership. Statistics on member clubs, personnel, usage, finance, and amenities.

Market

8. Biedermann, James H. *Analysis of Personal Motivation for Health Club Membership in Northern Ohio*. Med Thesis, University of

1

Toledo, 1984. 106p. Survey of members of 14 clubs.

9. Game Plan, Inc. *Why People Join: A Market Study for Racquet and Fitness Clubs.* Boston: International Racquet Sports Association, 1985. 102p. Membership. Survey and statistical analysis of members of racquet and fitness clubs by various demographic and attitude categories.

10. Marcum, Stephanie. *Influence of Nursery Factors on a Woman's Decision to Join a Health Club.* PhD Thesis, Texas Woman's University, 1986. 91p. Study to determine the relation between on-site child care, environmental features, play equipment and activities, and nursery personnel and the decision to join. Results indicated a relationship.

11. Warnick, Rodney B. *Marketing Factors in the Evaluation of Exercise/Fitness Programs.* PhD Thesis, Pennsylvania State University, 1983. 203p. Study of 478 participants enrolled in 22 exercise/fitness classes sponsored by Citiparks Department of Pittsburgh, Pennsylvania. "Importance-performance Grid" developed as part of study was determined to be helpful in determining marketing strategies for selected target markets being recruited for the classes.

Periodicals

12. Association of Physical Fitness Centers. *APFC Quarterly.* Rockville MD. Quarterly. Membership. News articles, product information, and statistical data about the industry.

13. *Fitness Industry.* North Miami FL: Industry Publishers. 9 issues. Controlled distribution. Features home and institution physical fitness equipment and tanning units. Articles on fitness center operation, new products and supplies, fitness methods, and merchandising.

14. *Fitness Management.* Los Angeles: Leisure Publications. Bimonthly. $15. Emphasis on exercise programs, equipment, and supplies. Articles on financial and operations management, facilities, and marketing. "Directory" supplement in each January issue.

15. International Racquet Sports Association. *Club Business.* Boston. Monthly. Membership. Emphasis is on racquetball clubs, but because of extensive involvement of this type of club in fitness programs, contains a wealth of information on equipment and its use in the programs operated by the clubs.

Associations

16. Association of Physical Fitness Centers. Jefferson St., Suite 202, Rockville MD 20852. (301) 424-7744. Association of owners of centers and suppliers. Compiles statistics. Conducts research. Provides seminars. Publishes standards, handbooks, directory, periodicals.

17. International Physical Fitness Association. 415 W. Court St., Flint MI 48503. (313) 239-2166. Association of physical fitness centers. Purpose is to facilitate transfer of membership between clubs. Publishes directory.

18. International Racquet Sports Association. 132 Brookline Ave., Boston MA 02215. (617) 236-1500. Association of racquetball, tennis, and fitness clubs and racquet sports manufacturers and suppliers. Compiles statistics. Conducts research.

Provides management counsel, seminars, trade shows. Publishes handbooks, statistics, directory, periodical. Formed by merger of National Tennis Association, Indoor Tennis Association, and National Court Clubs Association.

2. The Skiing Industry

SIC Code: 7999.

Enterprises providing opportunity for skiing. For enterprises whose primary emphasis is manufacturing, selling, and/or servicing skiing equipment see Chapter 8, The Sporting Goods Industry. For enterprises whose primary emphasis is professional skiing competition see Chapter 22, The Professional Tournaments Industry.

Directories

19. Enzel, Robert G. *White Book of Ski Areas: United States and Canada.* Washington, DC: Inter-Ski Services. Annual. $13.95. Ski areas and resorts giving name, address, phone, location data, facilities, season, elevation, costs, and special services. Arrangement is geographical by region and state.

20. Fehr, Lucy M. *Cross-Country Skiing: A Guide to America's Best Trails.* New York: Morrow, 1979. 198p. Out of print. Somewhat out of date but still the most comprehensive guide to cross country ski areas. Each listing gives name, address, phone, location, and facilities. Arrangement is geographical.

21. Mead, Robin. *European Ski Resorts.* London: Batsford; New York: Hippocrene, 1985. 178p. $14.95. Guidebook to the major ski areas and resorts. Each resort is described including data on location, facilities, and cost.

22. National Ski Areas Association. *Membership Directory.* Springfield MA. Annual. $300. Gives members and supplier associate members on separate lists. Each listing gives name, address, phone, and owner or contact. Associate members are listed alphabetically and by product category.

23. *Skiers Directory.* New York: CBS Magazines. Annual. $3.95. Lists resorts and ski areas, both alpine and cross country, and equipment suppliers. Each listing gives name, address, phone, location directions, cost, and facilities. Arrangement is geographical. Includes calendar of ski events.

Management

24. Cone and Company. *NSAA Media Relations Handbook.* Springfield MA: National Ski Areas Association, 1983. 72p. $50. Guide to establishing a media relations program. Suggestions on dealing with media. Examples of publicity and press releases.

25. Cross Country Ski Areas of America. *Cross-Country — USA Manual.* Brattleboro VT. 1v. $100. Guide to establishment and operation of a ski center. Information on design, construction, maintenance, operations, management, financial records, marketing, publicity, instruction, and operations forms. List of manufacturers and suppliers with data on products and services. Looseleaf format.

26. Laventhol and Horwath. *Ski Area Financial Management Series.* Springfield MA: National Ski Areas Association, 1976–77. $100. Guide to ski area bookkeeping systems and practices. Following titles published: *Uniform Systems of Accounts; Essential Elements of Internal Control;* and *Internal Control of Food and Beverage Operations.*

27. Goeldner, Charles R. *How to Conduct a Skier Study.* Boulder CO: University of Colorado Business Research Div., 1983. 67p. $25. Includes procedures, questions, and forms. Chapters on methodology, the questionnaire, sampling, data collection, coding, tabulation, and analysis.

28. Lucas, Christopher A., and _____. *Ski Area Marketing.* Boulder CO: University of Colorado Business Research Div., 1987. 115p. $25. Survey and analysis of ski area marketing policies and practices of members of the National Ski Areas Association in 1985–1986.

29. National Ski Areas Association. *Compensation and Benefits Survey.* Springfield MA. Biennial. $50. Survey of close to 150 ski areas. Statistics and analysis by type of employment.

30. _____. *Personnel Reference Employee Handbook.* Springfield MA, 1986. 100p. $50. Examples from several ski area employee handbooks. Information on hiring, labor relations, and legal concerns.

31. _____. *Ski Area Accident Investigation Manual.* Springfield MA, 1985. 51p. $25. Step-by-step guide to handling accidents from first report to final resolution. Designed to prepare all ski area personnel to react properly to emergencies.

32. National Ski Areas Association Special Taskforce on Snowmaking. *Snowmaking Management Outline.* Springfield MA, 1984. 21p. $15. Outlines practices currently recommended. Information on snowmaking units, subsystems, energy sources, water and air supply, and proper utilization of personnel. Training videotape accompanies the manual.

33. Nelson, Janet. *101-Plus Great Ski Marketing Ideas: Marketing & Promotion Techniques for the Ski Industry.* Springfield MA: National Ski Areas Association, 1985. 1v. $100. Case studies. Information on attracting new skiers, target marketing, building midweek business, and providing services. Forty new case studies have been published for the 1986 insert. Looseleaf format.

Industry

34. Cross Country Ski Areas of America. *Cross-Country Ski Area Operations Survey.* Brattleboro VT. Annual. $50. Statistical analysis of the industry. Information on types of operations, revenue, sales, fees, skiers, lessons, and grooming patterns.

35. Duea, Karen. *Ski Rental Shop Survey.* Boulder CO: University of Colorado Business Research Div., 1983. 38p. $25. Survey of 50 establishments by type of shop, inventory policy, and financial categories.

36. Goeldner, Charles R., et al. *Colorado Ski Industry Characteristics and Financial Analysis.* Boulder CO: University of Colorado Business Research Div. Annual. $30. Statistical study conducted annually since 1979. Data for ski areas by state includes facilities, usage, and financial. Analyses impact of areas on state and communities in which located.

37. _____. *NSAA Economic Analysis of North American Ski Areas.* Boulder CO: University of Colorado Business Research Div. Annual. $55. Statistical study conducted annually since 1967. Data and statistics for regions of the United States and Canada includes financial statement information, employee statistics, usage, facilities, and ratio analysis.

Market

38. Brand Group. *Market Research Report: Skier Attitudes, Perceptions and Behavior.* Springfield MA: National Ski Areas Association, 1984. 29p. $10. Data which identify "hard-core" skiers from "casual" skiing participants. Recommendations for marketing to the frequent-skiing group.

39. Kottke, Marvin W. *NSAA End of Season National Business Survey.* Springfield MA: National Ski Areas Association. Annual. $15. Examines annual changes and trends of skiers. Analyzes the effects of length of season, lift capacity, night skiing, snowmaking, and other factors on the skiing decision process.

40. National Ski Areas Association. *National Ski Opinion Survey.* Springfield MA, 1986. 24p. $150. Reports on demographics, psychographics, and habits of United States alpine skiers by age, income, marital status, etc. Compiled from 6000 questionnaires completed at 13 ski areas nationwide.

41. Opinion Research Corporation. *Growth Potential of the Skier Market in the National Forests.* Washington DC: U.S. Forest Service, 1980. 31p. Out of print. Tele-phone survey conducted in 1978. Analyzes demand for skiing areas on United States Forest Service lands. Charts and tables.

Periodicals

42. American Ski Federation. *ASF Washington Letter.* Washington DC. Monthly. Membership. Information on national and state legislation affecting ski areas, skiing equipment, and manufacturing and retailing of skiing products.

43. Cross Country Ski Areas of America. *CCSAA Newsletter.* Winchester NH. Bimonthly. $25. Official association publication. News and articles on the association, its activities, and industry developments. Reports on area management, trail design and grooming, media promotion activities, legislation and regulation, and new area developments.

44. National Ski Areas Association. *NSAA News.* Springfield MA. Bimonthly. Membership. Official association publication. News and articles on the association, its activities, and industry developments. Reports on new area developments, research, products, trends, and technical standards.

45. *Ski Area Management.* Woodbury CT: Beardsley. Bimonthly. $22. Endorsed by the American Ski Federation, the Cross Country Ski Areas of America, and the National Ski Areas Association as the ski operator's "bible." Articles on management, operations, and marketing. Information on equipment, products, and maintenance. Special columns each issue: "X-Country Connection," "On-Line," "B77 Standard," "Ski School," and "New Products." Special reports: "Economic Study" and "Lift Construction Index" in each January issue.

Bibliographies/Indexes

46. Goeldner, Charles R., and Duea, Karne. *Bibliography of Skiing Studies,* 7th ed. Boulder CO: University of Colorado Business Research Div., 1984. 130p. $15. Recognized as the most comprehensive bibliography of recent references to the ski industry, operation of ski areas, and the economic impact of skiers and skiing. Canadian as well as United States publications and sources. Divided into public and private studies and thesis-dissertation section. Alphabetical arrangement by title under each. Author and subject index.

Associations

47. American Ski Federation. 207 Constitution Ave., N.E., Washington DC 20002. (202) 543-1595. Federation of associations and corporate members from the ski industry. Purpose is to monitor federal and state ski area and product legislation. Conducts research. Publishes periodical.

48. Cross Country Ski Areas of America. RD2 Bolton Rd., Winchester NH 03451. (603) 239-6387. Association of owners and operators of cross country ski areas and individuals owning related businesses. Compiles statistics. Conducts research. Provides management counsel, seminars. Publishes standards, handbook, statistics, periodicals.

49. National Ski Areas Association. 20 Maple St., P.O. Box 2883, Springfield MA 01101. (413) 781-4732. Association of ski areas and related individuals and organizations as associate members. Compiles statistics. Conducts research. Provides management counsel, seminars, trade shows. Publishes handbooks, statistics, directory, periodicals.

3. The Skating Industry

SIC Code 7999.

Enterprises providing opportunity for ice and/or roller skating. For enterprises whose primary emphasis is manufacturing, selling, and/or servicing skating equipment see Chapter 8, The Sporting Goods Industry. For enterprises whose primary emphasis is professional skating competition see Chapter 22, The Professional Tournament Industry.

Directories

50. Roller Skating Rink Operators Association. *Membership Directory*. Lincoln NE. Annual. Membership. Lists rinks, suppliers, manufacturers, and other associated businesses. Each listing gives name, address, phone, and contact.

Management

51. American Entrepreneurs Association. *Roller Skating Rink and Skateboard Park*. Los Angeles, 1984. 196p. $39.50. Guide to establishing and operating a rink or park. Chapters on legal, management, marketing, operations, and financial procedures. Supplier addresses and a bibliography. Looseleaf format.
52. Roller Skating Rink Operators Association. *Roller Skating Business Fact Book,* Rev. ed. Lincoln NE, 1986. 42p. Membership.

For the prospective or beginning rink operator. Basic management decisions required for starting a skating center business. Information on site selection, rink design, equipment, staffing, and operations.

Market

53. National Family Opinion Research. *Roller Rink Usage Study*. Lincoln NE: Roller Skating Rink Operators Association, 1984. 24p. Membership. Survey of potential skaters and current users. Focuses on use and potential use in relationship to demographics, particularly households.

Periodicals

54. Ice Skating Institute of America. *ISIA Newsletter*. Wilmette IL. Monthly. Membership. Official association publication. News and articles on management, instruction, competitions, and association activities.
55. Roller Skating Rink Operators Association. *Roller Skating Business*. Lincoln NE. Bimonthly. Membership. News and data on management, operations, promotional activities, products, personnel, security, and other concerns of the rink owner and/or manager.
56. _____. *RSRDA Newsletter*. Lincoln NE. Monthly. Membership.

Official association publication. News, tips on management and finance, legal and legislative information, current music charts, and announcement of coming events.

Associations

57. Ice Skating Institute of America. 1000 Skokie Blvd., Wilmette IL 60091. (312) 256-5060. Association of rink owners and managers, industry builders and suppliers, and amateur, professional, and teacher skaters.

Compiles statistics. Conducts research. Provides management counsel, seminars, trade shows. Publishes standards, handbooks, statistics, directory, periodicals.

58. Roller Skating Rink Operators Association. 7700 A St., Lincoln NE 68510. (402) 489-8811. Association of rinks and persons and organizations associated with the industry. Compiles statistics. Conducts research. Provides management counsel, seminars. Publishes standards, handbooks, statistics, directory, periodicals.

4. The Bowling Industry

SIC Code: 7993.

Enterprises providing opportunity for bowling. For enterprises whose primary emphasis is manufacturing, selling, or servicing bowling equipment see Chapter 8, The Sporting Goods Industry. For enterprises whose primary emphasis is professional bowling competition see Chapter 22, The Professional Tournament Industry.

Management

59. American Bowling Congress. *ABC Constitutions, Specifications, Rules & Suggested League Rules.* Greendale WI. Annual. Free. Required and suggested constitutions, rules, procedures, specifications for equipment, tournament rules, and sanctioning of state and local bowling associations and leagues. Includes American Bowling Congress constitution and rules.

60. American Entrepreneurs Association. *Bowling Center.* Los Angeles, 1984. 163p. $39.50. Guide to establishing and operating a center. Legal, management, marketing, operations, and financial procedures. Supplier addresses and a bibliography. Looseleaf format.

61. Holnick, Catherine S., ed. *Bowling Proprietor.* Arlington TX: Bowling Proprietors' Association of America, 1981. 88p. Membership. Center operations manual. Information on management, equipment, rules and leagues, promotion, and operating resources.

62. National Bowling Council. *Management Handbook Series.* Washington DC. Irregular. Membership. For bowling proprietors. The following titles have been published: *Public Relations Handbook; Marketing Primer;* and *Sales Promotion Handbook.*

63. National Duckpin Bowling Congress. *NDBA Rules.* Baltimore-Linthicum MD: Duckpin Congress Tournaments. Annual. Free. Rules and tournament guidelines, sanctioning and league operations, world records, and directory of duckpin lanes in the United States.

64. Women's International Bowling Congress. *WIBC Playing Rules.* Greendale WI. Annual. Free. General, league, and tournament rules, sanctioning of tournaments, awards, handicaps, and suggested mixed league rules.

Market

65. National Bowling Council. *Bowling: An In-depth Profile of a Dynamic Market.* Washington DC, 1984. 16p. Free. Diagrammatic picture of bowling America. Graphs portray bowling frequency by age group, education, occupation, family status, household size, and geographic region. Typical bowler is profiled.

Lacks details but is still valuable as an overview.

66. ____. *Market Studies.* Washington DC. Irregular. Membership. The National Bowling Council periodically contracts with national research agencies to conduct limited-scope marketing studies. Currently available are: *Bowling: 1984 Perceptions and Motivations; Understanding Casual Bowlers; Understanding Junior Bowlers; Understanding League Bowlers;* and *Understanding Non Bowlers.*

Periodicals

67. American Bowling Congress. *Bowling.* Greendale WI. 11 issues. Membership. Official association publication. For the male bowler in an ABC sanctioned league. For the bowling proprietor, news of products, league operations, rules, and tournaments.

68. Billiard and Bowling Institute of America. *Bowlers Journal.* Chicago: Bowlers Journal. Monthly. $15. Official association publication. Emphasis on news about the bowling world and bowlers. Articles on management, marketing, and teaching. Monthly column on marketing. Special reports: "Annual Recap of Bowling" in each January issue; "ABC Tournament" in each February issue; "WIBC Tournament" in each March issue; "BBIA Convention" in each April issue; and "BPAA Convention" in each May issue. Special issue: *Bowling and Billiard Buyers Guide* (Each January, $5).

69. Bowling Proprietors' Association of America. *Bowling Proprietor.* Arlington TX. Monthly. Membership. Official association publication. Articles on management and operation of alleys, information on laws and regulations, and new equipment and products. "BPAA Annual Meeting Report" in June issue.

70. National Duckpin Bowling Congress. *Duckpin News.* Baltimore MD: The Duckpin News. 3 issues. Membership. Official association publication. News articles on bowlers, tournaments, equipment and products, industry data, and new alleys.

71. Women's International Bowling Congress. *Woman Bowler.* Greendale WI. 10 issues. Membership. Official association publication. For the woman bowler in a WIBC sanctioned league. For the bowling proprietor, news of league operations, rules, and tournaments.

Associations

72. American Bowling Congress. 5301 S. 76th St., Greendale WI 53129. (414) 421-6400. Association of male bowlers. Purpose is bowling rule-making and league and tournament sanctioning. Compiles statistics. Provides seminars. Publishes standards, handbooks, periodical. Certifies leagues, equipment. Sanctions competitions.

73. Billiard and Bowling Institute of America. 200 Castlewood Dr., North Palm Beach FL 33408. (305) 842-4100. Association of manufacturers and suppliers of billiard and bowling equipment and products. Provides management counsel to bowling proprietors. Publishes directory, periodical.

74. Bowling Proprietors' Association of America. P.O. Box 5802, Arlington TX 76011. (817) 460-2121. Association of alley owners. Conducts research. Provides management counsel, seminars, trade shows. Publishes handbooks, periodical.

75. Bowling Proprietor's Association of Canada. 335 Nugget Ave., E., Suite 11, Scarborough, Ontario, Canada M1S 4J3. (416) 292-3433. Association of bowling centers.

76. National Association of Independent Resurfacers. P.O. Box 444, Hazelton PA 18201. (717) 454-6685. Association of companies and individuals engaged in maintenance of bowling alleys in the United States. Conducts research. Provides seminars. Publishes standards, handbooks, directory.

77. National Bowling Council. 1919 Pennsylvania Ave., Washington DC 20006. (202) 659-9070. Federation of bowling associations in the United States. Compiles statistics. Conducts research. Provides management counsel, seminars. Publishes handbooks, statistics.

78. National Duckpin Bowling Congress. Fairview Ave., Baltimore-Linthicum MD 21090. (301) 636-BOWL. Association of bowlers and bowling alleys in the United States. Compiles statistics. Conducts research. Provides management counsel, seminars. Maintains library. Publishes standards, handbooks, periodical.

79. Women's International Bowling Congress. 5301 S. 76th St., Greendale WI 53129. (414) 421-9000. Association of female bowlers. Purpose is bowling rule-making and league and tournament sanctioning. Compiles statistics. Provides seminars. Publishes standards, handbooks, periodical. Certifies leagues. Sanctions competitions.

5. The Racquet Sports Industry

SIC Code: 7999.

Enterprises providing opportunity for playing racquet or handball sports. For enterprises whose primary emphasis is manufacturing, selling, and/or servicing or racquet sports equipment see Chapter 8, The Sporting Goods Industry. For enterprises whose primary emphasis is racquet sports competition see Chapter 23, The Professional Tournament Industry.

Directories

80. International Racquet Sports Association. *IRSA Membership Directory*. Boston. Annual. $10. Lists member clubs giving name, address, phone, executives, and facilities. Arrangement is geographical.

Management

81. American Entrepreneurs Association. *Tennis and Racquetball Clubs*. Los Angeles, 1984. 1v. $45. Guide to establishing and operating a small business. Legal, management, marketing, operations, and financial procedures. Supplier addresses and a bibliography. Looseleaf format.

82. Blackburn, Lois H. *Handbook for Planning and Conducting Tennis Tournaments*. Princeton NJ: United States Tennis Association Center for Education and Recreational Tennis, 1986. 95p. $2. Planning, policies, rules, decisions, scheduling, and recognition procedures.

83. Gimmy, Arthur E. *Tennis Clubs and Racquet Sport Projects: A Guide to Appraisal, Market Analysis, Development and Finance*. Chicago: American Institute of Real Estate Appraisers, 1978. 94p. $15. Data on tennis and other racquet sports operations with emphasis on appraisal, market analysis, and development. Information on market, financing, site, and management considerations. Case studies and example forms.

84. International Racquet Sports Association. *Club Location: A Site Analysis*. Boston, 1984. 25p. $50. Procedures, examples, and diagrams.

85. _____. *Financial Management Manual*. Boston, 1985. 50p. $35. Procedures, forms, and examples.

86. _____. *IRSA Guide to Sales and Marketing*. Boston, 1984. 48p. $35. Articles and procedures on market, advertising, and promotions.

87. _____. *Member Retention Manual*. Boston, 1986. 100p. $195. Suggestions for continuing member involvement in club activities.

88. _____. *Uniform Reporting System*. Boston, 1983. 25p. $50. Procedures and forms.

89. United States Tennis Association. *Friend at Court*. Lynn MA: H.O. Zimman, 1985. 45p. $2. Rules, tournament regulations, officiating techniques, decisions, penalties, "knotty problems," and "The Code."

90. _____. *Rules of Tennis and Cases and Decisions.* Lynn MA: H.O. Zimman. Annual. $1. Updated rules with official rulings and decisions.

91. _____. *Tennis Courts: Construction, Maintenance, Equipment, Guideline Specifications.* Lynn MA: H.O. Zimman, 1986. 153p. $9.95. Recommendations and standards compiled and written by the United States Tennis Association's Facilities Committee in cooperation with the U.S. Tennis Court and Track Builders Association. Frequently updated.

92. United States Tennis Association Education and Research Center. *Financing Public Tennis Courts.* Princeton NJ, 1979. 80p. $2.50. For persons involved in financing public facilities, the procedure outline is valuable to persons doing cost analysis and promotion for private investment.

93. _____. *Lighting Outdoor Tennis Courts.* North Palm Beach FL: Tennis Foundation of North America, 1978. 56p. $2.50. Old, but still the only publication on this topic. Descriptions of the various types of illumination systems available.

94. Wendy Fink Associates Inc. *Winning with Wellness: A Step-by-Step Guide for Racquet and Fitness Clubs.* Wellesley MA: 1985. 192p. $165. For fitness and racquetball clubs. Program for health and physical development. Distributed by the International Racquet Sports Association.

Industry

95. International Racquet Sports Association. *Profiles in Success.* Boston. Annual. $150. Survey of IRSA members. Statistics, charts, and mathematical and narrative analysis of finance, operations, rates, salaries, and ownership. Former title: *Facts and Figures Report.*

Market

96. Game Plan, Inc. *Why People Join: A Market Study for Racquet and Fitness Clubs.* Boston: International Racquet Sports Association, 1985. 102p. $150. Survey and statistical analysis of members of racquet and fitness clubs by various demographic and attitude categories.

Periodicals

97. American Platform Tennis Association. *Platform Tennis News.* Upper Montclair NJ. 5 issues. Membership. Official association publication. News of tournaments, the association, and new products.

98. International Racquet Sports Association. *Club Business.* Boston. Monthly. Membership. Official association publication. Articles on management, finance, equipment, statistics, and racquetball. Information on regulations affecting racquet sports and fitness clubs.

99. *National Racquetball.* Clearwater FL. Monthly. $18. For club owners, managers, professionals, and amateurs. Emphasis on play and tournaments but includes extensive information on new clubs, play and fitness organization, and the industry. Indexed in *Real Estate Index.*

100. *Racquetball Industry.* North Miami FL: Industry Publications. Bimonthly. $12. Emphasis is on products and merchandising but contains articles on court operations. Special reports: "Tennis Industry National Buying Show" in each January/February issue; "Annual Court Club Construction" in each March/April issue; "Sporting Goods Manufacturers Show" in each September/October issue; and "Racquet Research" in each November/December issue.

101. Tennis Foundation of North America. *Net Friend News.* North Palm Beach FL. Bimonthly. Membership. Official association publication. Information, suggestions, examples for the promotion of tennis, and news of the industry.

102. *Tennis Industry.* North Miami FL: Industry Publications. 11 issues. $22. Emphasis on products, merchandising, and shop operations. Special columns on court building, racquet survey, racquet research, and court operations.

103. United States Tennis Association. *Tennis USA.* New York: Family Media. Monthly. Membership. Official association publication. Primarily news and announcements for the tennis player but is essential to owners and managers for rules and tournament information.

104. _____. *World Tennis.* New York: Family Media. Monthly. $16. For the tennis player. For the tennis court operator, news of the industry, equipment, rules, and tournaments. Special reports: "Tennis Camp Directory" in each January issue; "Top Tennis Resorts" in each March issue; "Equipment Directory" in each April issue; "Tennis Shoe Guide" in each June issue; "Racquet Review" in each November issue; and "World Tennis's Vacation Guide" in each December issue. Indexed in *Magazine Index, Readers' Guide.*

Bibliographies/Indexes

105. Lumpkin, Angela. *Guide to the Literature of Tennis.* Westport CT: Greenwood, 1985. 235p. $29.95. Contains references to some tennis industry information, but primarily articles and books on the game.

106. Peele, David A. *Racket and Paddle Games: A Guide to Information Sources.* Detroit MI: Gale Research, 1980. 300p. $62. Emphasis on games, not industry. Data on associations and racquet sports camps. Detailed, annotated bibliography of audiovisual materials, books, and periodicals. Each type of racquet game has its own chapter. Chapter on "Recommended Purchases." Author, title, subject, and association indexes.

Associations

107. American Platform Tennis Association. P.O. Box 901, Upper Montclair NJ 07043. (201) 783-5325. Association primarily of individuals and tennis clubs but includes owners of private courts. Provides management counsel, seminars. Publishes standards, handbooks, periodical. Sanctions competitions.

108. International Racquet Sports Association. 132 Brookline Ave., Boston MA 02215. (617) 236-1500. Association of racquetball, tennis, and fitness clubs and racquet sports manufacturers and suppliers. Compiles statistics. Conducts research. Provides management counsel, seminars, trade shows. Publishes handbooks, statistics, directory, periodical. Formed by merger of National Tennis Association, Indoor Tennis Association, and National Court Clubs Association.

109. Tennis Foundation of North

America. 200 Castlewood Dr., North Palm Beach FL 33408. (305) 848-1026. Association of manufacturers, suppliers, builders, and architects. Conducts research. Publishes handbooks, periodical.

110. United States Tennis Association. 1212 Avenue of the Americas, New York NY 10036. (212) 302-3322. Association of amateur tennis clubs. Serves as rulemaking and sanctioning body for tennis. Compiles statistics. Provides seminars. Publishes standards, handbooks, statistics, periodicals. Sanctions competitions.

111. U.S. Tennis Court and Track Builders Association. 223 W. Main St., Charlottesville VA 22901. (804) 971-2800. Association of contractors, manufacturers, and suppliers. Provides management counsel. Certifies businesses.

6. The Golf Industry

SIC Codes: 7992, 7999.

Enterprises providing opportunity for playing golf. For enterprises whose primary emphasis is manufacturing, selling, and/or servicing golf equipment see Chapter 8, The Sporting Goods Industry. For enterprises whose primary emphasis is golf competition see Chapter 22, The Professional Tournament Industry.

Directories

112. *Benson and Hedges Golfer's Handbook.* London: Macmillan. Annual. $50. Lists courses in the United Kingdom and Europe giving name, address, facilities, length of course, fees, and membership. Arrangement is geographical with club name index.

113. *Golf: Where to Play and Where to Stay.* Macclesfield, England: McMillan Martin. Annual. $10. Lists 2,000 golf courses in the British Isles giving name, address, phone, location, number of holes, fees, visitor policy, and name of professional and/or manager. Arrangement is geographical.

114. *International Golf Directory.* Glendale CA: Ingledue Travel. Semiannual. $75. Lists courses, clubs, and resorts worldwide giving name, address, phone, type, number of holes, fees, and membership policy. Arrangement is geographical.

115. Williams, Gwen. *Unique Golf Resorts of the World.* Corona del Mar CA, 1985. 271p. $34.95. Directory based upon the author's definition of "unique." Each listing gives name, address, and description of golf facilities.

Management

116. Beard, James B. *Turf Management for Golf Course.* Minneapolis MN: Burgess, 1982. 642p. $52.75. Written by turfgrass expert. Articles on building the golf course, greens and bunkers, pests and stress, and course use management.

117. Hawtree, F.W. *Golf Course: Planning, Design, Construction, and Maintenance.* London: E&FN Spon, 1983. 212p. $33. Architect's handbook on the design, construction, and landscaping of courses. British orientation. Extensive diagrams.

118. Heuer, Karla L. *Golf Courses: A Guide to Analysis and Evaluation.* Chicago: American Institute of Real Estate Appraisers, 1980. 128p. $15. Introduction to golf courses and their property, organization, and operation. Chapters on market analysis, development, site analysis and valuation, improvements and operations with extensive statistics and financial statement examples, and valuation procedures.

119. Jarrett, Albert R. *Golf Course & Grounds: Irrigation & Drainage.* Englewood Cliffs NJ: Reston, 1984. 246p. $32.95. Chapters on design, construction, drainage, watering systems, erosion, with plans, diagrams, and charts.

120. National Golf Foundation. *Golf Driving Range Manual.* Jupiter FL, 1987. 45p. $25. Guide to planning, developing, building, and operating various types of driving ranges.

121. _____. *Golf Operations Handbooks and Golf Facility Development Guide.* Jupiter FL, 1985, 1v. $85. Guide to all facets of golf course operations including maintenance, club activities. Looseleaf format.

122. _____. *Miniature Putting Course Manual.* Jupiter FL, N.d. 24p. $25. Guide to planning, building, operating, and maintaining a putting course with standards and equipment recommendations.

123. _____. *Par-3 and Executive Golf Course Manual.* Jupiter FL, N.d. 30p. $25. Guide to planning, building, operating, and maintaining a "short" golf course separately or as part of a resort or real estate community, with standards and equipment recommendations.

124. _____. *Planning and Building the Golf Course.* Jupiter FL, 1984. 48p. $11.50. Guide to designing and constructing regulation 9- and 18-hole golf courses. Guidelines and diagrams for planning, variations in course design, and watering systems.

125. _____. *Planning the Golf Clubhouse.* Jupiter FL, 1986. 169p. $30. Written by architects. Diagrams, sample floor plans, site plans, cost information, and essay on choosing the "right" architect.

126. _____. *Planning and Conducting Competitive Golf Events.* Jupiter FL, 1984. 84p. $25. Reprint of a 1973 publication on organizing, promoting, and conducting competitive tournaments. Specifics on rules and awards.

127. _____. *Professional Golf Shop.* 3rd ed. North Palm Beach FL 1982. 107p. $25. Guide to establishing, financing, and operating a golf sports shop primarily as part of a golf course or club. Data on manufacturers, suppliers, and management forms.

128. Sherman, William. *Buying or Leasing a Golf Course,* 2nd ed. Palm Beach Gardens FL: Pro Golfers' Association of America, 1986. 85p. $45. Information on investing in courses, investment requirements, lease transaction analysis, and other aspects of buying or leasing.

129. United States Golf Association. *Decisions on the Rules of Golf by the United States Golf Association and the Royal and Ancient Golf Club of St. Andrews, Scotland.* Far Hills NJ. Annual. $25. Up-to-date interpretations of the rules with the "Complete Rules" and index to the rules and interpretations. Looseleaf format.

130. _____. *Golf Handbook.* Far Hills NJ. Annual. $10. Regulations, policy statements, and other information from official USGA publications. Looseleaf format.

131. _____. *USGA Golf Handicap and Course Rating System and Golf Committee Manual.* Far Hills NJ, 1987. 82p. $3. Rules, forms, and directions for determining handicaps of men and women players, rating difficulty of holes, and other policies.

Industry

132. Golf Course Superintendents Association of America and National Golf Foundation. *Course Golf Course Maintenance Report.* Lawrence KS. Biennial. $90. Statistics on facilities, capital expenditures, expenses, inventory, maintenance costs, rounds played. Also data on course size, types of grass, irrigation systems. Based upon a sample of 2,300 facilities.

133. National Golf Foundation. *Golf Course Operations Survey.* Jupiter FL, 1986. 95p. $80. Data collected from 3,800 private, daily fee, municipal, executive/par 3, and resort courses. Statistics include memberships, fees, rounds played, facilities, and operations. Separate sections cover pro shops, carts, driving ranges, club repair, and lessons.

134. _____. *Golf Facilities in the U.S.* Jupiter FL, 1986. 18p. $120. Statistical summary of data contained in the NGF's "Golf Facilities" database of over 12,000 courses. Data by state subdivided by private, daily fee, and municipal courses. A "per capita golf supply" is also given for each state for both the private and public market.

Market

135. Market Facts, Inc. *Golf Participation in the U.S.* Jupiter FL: National Golf Foundation, 1986. 21p. $120. Survey of 35,000 individuals nationwide projects the number of golfers in the United States and then examines them in terms of age, sex, income, occupation, and education. Develops profile of new, frequent, and infrequent golfer.

136. National Golf Foundation. *Golf Consumer Profile.* Jupiter FL, 1986. 63p. $175. Follow-up questionnaire study of the NGF/Market Facts, Inc., "Golf Participation" report. 1200 respondents to a 10-page questionnaire are analyzed by types, reasons for playing, frequency of playing, purchasing behavior, and "media habits." Includes narrative book, "cross tabs" and "data tables."

137. _____. *Golf Projection 2000.* Jupiter FL, 1987. 87p. $50. Seven research papers presented at "Golf Summit '86." Topics include: demand, golfer profiles, non-golfer profiles, market segmentation, consumer psychology, target marketing, course development crisis, and positioning for success. Slide presentation also available for an additional $250.

138. Qualitative Decision Center, Inc. *Qualitative Exploration into Ways of Encouraging Growth of the Game of Golf.* Jupiter FL: National Golf Foundation, 1982. 80p. $35. Study of individuals who perceive benefits from playing golf. Attempts to explain "why" they desire to play, in terms useful to persons promoting golf course use.

Periodicals

139. Association of Golf Club Secretaries. *Golf Club Management and Equipment News.* Wokingham, England: Pressprint. Bimonthly. Membership. Official association publication. Articles on course planning and design, clubhouse management, and golfing equipment.

140. British Golf Greenkeeper Association. *Golf Greenkeeping & Course Maintenance.* Wetherby, England: Wharfdale. Monthly. Membership. Official association publication. Articles on the association, the industry, and new products.

141. Canadian Golf Superintendents Association. *Greenmaster.* Toronto, Canada. 8 issues. Membership. Official association publication. Articles on research, products, and practical methods for maintaining courses and turf.

142. *Executive Golfer.* Irvine CA: Pazdur. Bimonthly. $19.95. Primarily for business executive golf enthusiasts, but contains introductory and directory information on opportunities for playing golf worldwide, especially on private, membership courses. Special issue: *Private Country Club Guest Policy Directory* (each June, $15).

143. Golf Course Association. *GCA News*. Minneapolis MN. Irregular. Membership. Official association publication. News of the association and its members.

144. _____. *Golf Course Management Letter*. Minneapolis MN. Irregular. Membership. Official association publication. Articles of interest to owners and managers of daily fee courses.

145. Golf Course Superintendents Association of America. *Golf Course Management*. Lawrence KS. 12 issues. $30. Official association publication. Articles and news reports on all aspects of course management from soil to security. Reports on golfing rules and club operations as well as foreign courses.

146. _____. *News Line*. Lawrence KS. Irregular. Membership. Reports on meetings of the association, elections, by-law changes, and other news involving members.

147. *Golf Industry*. North Miami FL: Industry Publishers. Bimonthly. $12. Emphasis on golf products, sportswear, and retail operations, including pro-shop and golf course operations. Special reports: "PGA Merchandise Show" in each December/January issue; "Ladies Golf Products" in each February/March issue; and "Market Report" in each August/September issue.

148. *Golf Shop Operations: A Golf Digest*. Trumbull CT: Golf Digest — Tennis. Bimonthly. $18. Articles on marketing, new products, and store operations. Periodic surveys of sales. Valuable for the pro-shop operator but primarily oriented to the golf sports shop. Former title: *Pro Shop Operations*.

149. National Golf Foundation. *Wedge*. Jupiter FL. Monthly. Membership. Official association publication. Functions as the National Golf Foundation's market report. Reports on business news of interest to the golf industry. Carries a listing of golf courses opened, under construction, and in the planning stages.

150. Professional Golfers' Association of America. *PGA Magazine*. Palm Beach Gardens FL. Monthly. $12. Official association publication. Articles and news for the tour and course professional. Information on course operations and management, new equipment, and supplies. Especially valuable with PGA Tour's involvement in the development of Tournament Players Courses. Former title: *Professional Golfer*.

151. Professional Putters Association. *Putt-Putt World*. Fayetteville NC. Quarterly. Membership. Official association publication. News of events, people, and courses. Tournament results. Course management and operations.

152. *Southern Golf — Landscape & Resort Management*. Clearwater FL: Brantwood. Bimonthly. $9. For owners and managers of courses and resorts in the Sunbelt. Articles on course and turf maintenance, general management, pro shop, and equipment.

153. United States Golf Association. *Golf Journal*. Far Hills NJ. 8 issues. Membership. Official association publication. For golfer, tournament administrator, course pro, and superintendent. Articles on rules,

"Great Golf Holes," and the golf business world.

154. _____. USGA *Green Section Record*. Far Hills NJ. 6 issues. Membership. For course superintendents, greenskeepers, agronomists, turf suppliers, and club committees. Theoretical and practical articles on green and turf maintenance. Information on new products and equipment.

Database

155. National Golf Foundation. *NGF Golf Facility Database*. Jupiter FL. Updated continuously. Membership. Directory. Records on over 12,000 golf facilities in the United States. Each entry includes name, address, type (private, daily fee, municipal), size (regulation, executive, par 3), and number of holes. Service based on membership category. Not online.

Bibliographies/Indexes

156. Kennington, Don., ed. *Sourcebook of Golf*. Phoenix AZ: Oryx, 1981. 255p. $20. British-oriented narrative bibliography and sourcebook to all facets of golf in the United States, Canada, and Great Britain. Chapters on the history of golf and golf clubs, golfers, how to play, essays, fiction and humor, the golf business, reference, periodicals, and associations.

157. Murdoch, Joseph. *Golf: A Guide to Information Sources*. Detroit MI: Gale Research, 1979. 232p. $62. Chapters on all facets of the game of golf. Part 1: Books. Part 2: other sources, e.g. periodicals, golf courses, instruction. Has author, title, and subject indexes.

Associations

158. American Society of Golf Course Architects. 221 N. LaSalle St., Chicago IL 60601. (312) 372-7090. Association of professional architects who specialize in designing and redesigning golf courses.

159. Association of Golf Club Secretaries. Saltergate Lane, Bamford, Sheffield, England S30 2BH. (04) 335-1306. Association of secretaries (managers) of courses. Compiles statistics. Provides management counsel. Publishes directory, periodical.

160. British Golf Greenskeepers Association. 7 Tenterden Close, Knaresborough, North Yorks, England HG5 9BJ. (042) 376-3851. Association of individuals and suppliers. Provides management counsel. Publishes handbooks, periodical.

161. Canadian Golf Superintendent Association. 698 Weston Rd. Suite 32, Toronto, Ontario, Canada M6N 3R3. (416) 767-2550. Association of course managers and greenkeepers. Publishes periodical.

162. Golf Course Association. 8030 Cedar, Suite 226, Minneapolis MN 55420. (612) 854-8482. Association of public and private (daily fee) courses, suppliers of products and services to member courses. Conducts research. Provides management counsel. Publishes handbooks, periodicals.

163. Golf Course Builders of America. 4361 Northlake Blvd., Palm Beach Gardens FL 33410. (305) 694-2977. Association of builders and suppliers worldwide.

164. Golf Course Superintendents Association of America. 1617 S. Andrews Dr., Lawrence KS 66044. (913) 841-2240. Association of golf course maintenance superintendents and suppliers. Publishes handbooks, periodical.

165. National Golf Club Advisory Association. 34 Sheen Rd., Richmond, Surrey, England TW9 1AW. Association of over 800 private golf clubs. Provides legal counsel to members.

166. National Golf Foundation. 1150 S. U.S. Highway One, Jupiter FL 33477. (305) 744-6006. Association of golf courses, golf architects, course builders, manufacturers and suppliers, and other golf associations. Is the research and publication arm of golf in the United States. Compiles statistics. Conducts research. Provides management counsel, seminars. Publishes handbooks, periodical.

167. Professional Golfers' Association of America. 100 Avenue of the Champions, Palm Beach Gardens FL 33410. (305) 626-3600. Association of club and tournament professionals and apprentices. Provides seminars. Maintains library. Publishes periodical. Certifies professionals. Sanctions competitions.

168. Professional Putters Association. P.O. Box 35237, Fayetteville NC 28303. (919) 485-7131. Association of persons competing in national putting tournaments sanctioned by the PPA, "putt putt" golf course owners, managers, and suppliers. Compiles statistics. Publishes periodical. Sanctions competitions.

169. Scottish Golf Union. 54 Shandwick Place, Edinburgh, Scotland EH2 4RT. (031) 226-6711. Association of golfers and golf clubs and courses. Governing body for amateur golf in Scotland.

170. United Golfers' Association. 663 E. 105th St., Chicago IL 60628. (312) 785-8513. Association of golf clubs with predominately black membership. Compiles statistics. Provides seminars.

171. United States Golf Association. Golf House, Far Hills NJ 07931. (201) 234-2300. Association of regularly organized (18 hole) golf courses. Serves as the governing body for golf in the United States. Conducts research. Provides management counsel. Annual convention. Maintains library. Publishes standards, handbooks, periodicals. Sanctions competitions.

7. The Membership Club Industry

SIC Code 7997.

Enterprises providing recreation through membership. For enterprises whose primary emphasis is fitness or sports see Chapter 1, The Fitness Industry; Chapter 5, The Racquet Sports Industry; or Chapter 6, The Golf Industry. For enterprises whose primary emphasis is entertainment see Chapter 25, The Night Club Industry.

Directories

172. National Club Association. *Who's Who in the Private Club Industry.* Washington DC. Annual. Membership. Lists owners, managers, and associated personnel with addresses of clubs. Began publication in 1987.

Management

173. Barbour, Henry O. *Private Club Administration.* Washington DC: Club Managers Association of America, 1968. 630p. $19.95. Old, but still recognized as a major resource for private club management. Contains topics not addressed in detail by other publications, e.g. club charters and by-laws, boards, club committees, legal responsibilities, and budget planning.

174. Club Managers Association of America. *Club Management Operations.* 3rd ed. Dubuque IA: Kendall/Hunt, 1986. 317p. $29.95. Written, edited, and published under the auspices of the CMAA. Chapters on office and financial management, personnel, food, beverage, labor cost control, insurance and security, member relations, and talents and techniques for running a successful private club.

175. _____. *Compensation and Benefit Survey.* Bethesda MD, 1986. 84p. Membership. Statistics on salaries, benefits, bonuses, work-related expenses, and professional activity compensation for various positions.

176. _____. *Job Descriptions in the Private Club Industry.* Bethesda MD, 1986. 85p. $20. Gives descriptions from manager to janitor giving title, work activities, compensation.

177. _____. *Membership Surveys.* Bethesda MD, N.d. 90p. Membership. Contains chapters on effective surveying methods and examples of operations, food service, entertainment, and youth surveys.

178. _____. *Promotion Handbook.* Bethesda MD, 1984. 32p. $10. Techniques for involving members in activities, promotion of events, and party or activity preparation and planning.

179. _____. *Uniform System of Accounts for Clubs.* Bethesda MD, 1982. 40p. $9.95. This publication represents more than six decades of development in establishing a common language for club accounting. Includes examples and explanations for several types of balance sheets, income and expense statements, and other financial records.

180. White, Ted E. *Club Operations and Management.* Boston: CBI, 1979, 253p. $18.95. Old, but still considered relevant. Chapters on organization, management, finance, personnel, membership. Now available through Van Nostrand Reinhold, New York.

Industry

181. Club Managers Association of America. *Operational Profile of Private Clubs.* Bethesda MD, 1983. 60p. $50. Statistics on club membership and fees, club revenues, facilities, taxes, payroll, and related financial data organized and averaged for use in comparison with other clubs.

182. Pannell Kerr Foster, Inc. *Clubs in Town and Country.* New York. Annual. $5. Current and retrospective statistical analysis of operating, financial, and membership data on country clubs.

Periodicals

183. Alliance of British Clubs. *Alliance Bulletin.* Stockport, England. Monthly. Membership. Official association publication. News of the association and the individual clubs.

184. *Club Industry.* Brookline MA: Sportscape. Monthly. $36. For fitness, racquet, corporate, hotel, and other membership clubs. Articles on management, marketing, operations, club profiles, and in-

dustry trends as well as equipment reviews. Special features each issue and a special report: "Finance, Management, and Operations" in each April issue.

185. Club Managers Association of America. *Club Management.* Fulton MO: Commerce. Monthly. $10. Official association publication. Subtitled: "The National Magazine for Executives of Town and Country Clubs." Articles on developments in the industry, planning, control, inventory, purchasing, management, personnel training, and promotion.

186. _____. *Outlook.* Bethesda MD. Monthly. Membership. Official association publication. News of the association and the industry.

187. National Club Association. *NCA Newsletter.* Washington DC. Monthly. Membership. Official association publication. Brief reports on the association, current data on regulations, new developments, and people in the industry.

188. _____. *Perspective for Private Clubs.* Washington DC. 10 issues. Membership. Official association management publication. Articles on management, operation, and promotion of clubs. Data on laws and regulations and new developments and materials.

Associations

189. Alliance of British Clubs. P.O. Box 32, Stockport, Cheshire, England SK1 1ER. (01) 480-4262. Association of registered clubs. Compiles statistics. Conducts research. Provides management counsel. Maintains library. Publishes periodical.

190. Club Managers Association of America. P.O. Box 34482, Bethesda MD 20817. (301) 229-3600.

Association of private club managers. Compiles statistics. Conducts research. Provides instruction, management counsel. Maintains library. Publishes standards, handbooks, periodicals.

191. National Club Association. 1625 Eye St., N.W. Suite 609, Washington DC 20006. (202) 466-8424. Association of private clubs. Compiles statistics. Conducts research. Provides management counsel, seminars. Publishes directory, periodicals.

8. The Sporting Goods Industry

SIC Codes: 3949, 5091, 5941, 5999, 7999.

Enterprises manufacturing, selling, and/or servicing equipment used in sports recreation. For enterprises whose primary emphasis is manufacturing, selling, and/or servicing recreation vehicles see Chapter 9, The Recreational Vehicle Industry, or Chapter 10, The Boat Industry. For enterprises whose primary emphasis is manufacturing, selling and/or servicing games or toys for the home see Chapter 11, The Home Amusements Industry.

Directories

192. American Fishing Tackle Manufacturers Association. *Super Outdoor Market.* Arlington Heights IL: Annual. Membership. Trade show directory for the American Fishing Tackle Manufacturers Association. Each listing gives name, address, products, company personnel, and manufacturers representatives.

193. *Camping Caravan and Sports Equipment Trades Directory.* London: Camping and Sports Equipment. Annual. $80. Lists British manufacturers, wholesalers, distributors, and servicers of camping and sports equipment giving name, address, phone, contact, and products or services. Arrangement is classified, suppliers by products, and manufacturers by trade names.

194. *Canadian Sporting Goods and Playthings Directory.* West Hill, Canada: Lloyd. Annual. $35. Lists Canadian manufacturers, exporters, importers, agents, wholesalers, distributors, and servicers. Each listing gives name, address, phone, contacts, and products or services. Arrangement is classified by product and trade name.

195. National Association of Sporting Goods Wholesalers. NASGW *Membership Directory.* Chicago IL. Annual. Membership. Lists members of the association giving name, address, phone, key executive, territory, warehouse size, inventory, number of accounts and salesmen, sales, inventory, and whether catalog is available. Includes list of manufacturer members giving name, address, phone, and products. Arrangement is alphabetical.

196. National Golf Foundation. *Directory of Golf Product Manufacturers.* Jupiter FL. Annual. Free. Lists members of the association giving name, address, phone, contact, and products. Arrangement is alphabetical.

197. National Sporting Goods Association. NSGA *Buying Guide.* Mount Prospect IL. Annual. $15. Lists 10,000 manufacturers, sellers, and servicers of retail sporting goods giving name, address, phone, contact, and products or services. Arrangement is alphabetical with trade name and product indexes.

198. *Nationwide Directory of Sporting Goods Buyers.* New York:

Salesmen's Guide. Annual. $95. Lists retail stores with sales in excess of $100,000 giving name, address, phone, contact, executives, and sales volume. Arrangement is geographical with alphabetical name index.

199. *Shooter's Bible.* South Hackensack NJ: Stoeger. Annual. $13.95. Lists manufacturers and suppliers of sports firearms and accessories giving name, address, phone, and catalog description of guns and other materials produced. Arrangement is alphabetical.

200. *Sporting Goods Directory.* St. Louis MO: Sporting News. Annual. $30. Lists manufacturers, wholesalers, agents, and industry associations giving name, address, phone, and products or services. Arrangement is alphabetical with product/service index.

201. Tackle Representatives Association, International. *TRAI Roster.* Arlington Heights IL. Annual. Membership. Lists members giving name, address, phone, and manufacturers represented.

202. World Federation of the Sporting Goods Industry. *WFSGI Membership Directory.* Zurich, Switzerland. Semiannual. Membership. Federation of associations and associate member companies giving name, address, phone, telex, and executives. Separate alphabetical lists for members and associate members.

Management

203. American Entrepreneurs Association. *Backpacking Shop.* Los Angeles, 1984. 150p. $39.50. Guide to establishing and operating a small business. Legal, management, mar-

keting, operations, and financial procedures. Supplier addresses and a bibliography. Looseleaf format.

204. _____. *Golf-ball Retrieval.* Los Angeles, 1984. 115p. $34.50. Guide to establishing and operating a small business. Legal, management, marketing, operations, and financial procedures. Supplier addresses and a bibliography. Looseleaf format.

205. _____. *Roller Skate Rental Shop.* Los Angeles, 1984. 115p. $29.50. Guide to establishing and operating a small business. Legal, management, marketing, operations, and financial procedures. Supplier addresses and a bibliography. Looseleaf format.

206. _____. *Sporting Goods Store.* Los Angeles, 1986. 160p. $55. Guide to establishing and operating a small business. Legal, management, marketing, operations, and financial procedures. Supplier addresses and a bibliography. Looseleaf format.

207. Chapman Design. *Store Planning Workbook for Sporting Goods Retailers.* Mount Prospect IL: National Sporting Goods Association, 1983. 66p. $65. Guide to designing a sporting goods store, including floor arrangement, lighting, fixtures, and colors.

208. ComSource, Inc. *Advertising and Promotion Guide for Sports Retailers.* Mount Prospect IL: National Sporting Goods Association, 1984. 87p. $70. Covers promotion planning, media selection, creative advertising, budgeting, and target marketing. Monthly planning calendar for advertising.

209. Ellman, Edgar S. *Complete Guide to Writing an Employee Policy Handbook for the Sporting Goods Retailer.* Mount Prospect IL: National Sporting Goods Association, 1983. 126p. $60. Covers policy and store practice, sections on job descriptions, hiring, relations, discharging, and complaints.

210. Howe, Jon. *Study of State Laws and Practices Governing School Employees Selling Sporting Goods.* North Palm Beach FL: Sporting Goods Manufacturers Association, 1981. 72p. Membership. Addresses the problem of conflict of interest.

211. Macdonald, Janet W. *Running a Tack Shop Business.* London and New York: J.A. Allen, 1986. 86p. $12.50. Guide to establishing, financing, and operating a horse and rider supply shop. British orientation.

212. National Golf Foundation. *Professional Golf Shop,* 3d ed. North Palm Beach FL, 1982. 107p. $25. Guide to establishing, financing and operating a golf sports shop primarily as part of a golf club course. Data on manufacturers and suppliers, management forms, and names and addresses of sporting goods bodies.

213. National Sporting Goods Association. *NSGA Operating Guide for Retail Sporting Goods Stores.* Chicago. 1v. Membership. Instructions and forms for setting up a basic bookkeeping system. Looseleaf format.

214. Quinton, Jack. *Retail Advertising: The How and Why.* Chicago: National Sporting Goods Association, 1979. 158p. Membership. Early association guidebook (see ComSource, Inc., above). Offers additional approaches to effective store advertising.

215. Trophy Dealers and Manufacturers Association. *Getting Started in the Awards Business.* Fresno CA, 1986. 4p. Free. Guide to starting a business, the market, capital requirements, the industry, and the association.

216. U.S. Bureau of Alcohol, Tobacco, and Firearms. *Federal Regulation of Firearms and Ammunition.* Washington DC: U.S. Department of the Treasury. Biennial. Resume of federal regulations for securing a firearms retail license, complying with federal record keeping requirements, and how to manage the firearm and ammunition sale process while insuring complete and accurate records. List of ATF regional offices.

217. _____. *Forms Catalog.* Washington DC: U.S. Department of the Treasury. Irregular. For the licensed firearms and ammunition dealer. Federal forms required in firearms and ammunition sales with each form identified by federal form number, exact title of the form, government source for the form, government agency supervising the processing of the form, and laws, regulations, and decisions pertaining.

218. _____. *State Laws and Published Ordinances—Firearms.* Washington DC: U.S. Department of the Treasury. Annual. State and local legislation and ordinances regulating the sale of firearms and ammunition to the public. Table of "Common Elements in Laws of the States." Arrangement is alphabetical by state.

219. Wahl, Paul. *Gun Trader's Guide,* 12th ed. South Hackensack NJ: Stoeger, 1986. 464p. $13.95. Identification of modern firearms with current market value. Frequently updated. Similar publications are: Lewis, Jack, *The Gun Digest Book of Modern Gun Values* (Northbrook IL: DBI), which issues every other year; and House of Collectibles, *The Official Price Guide to Collection Guns* (Orlando FL), issued annually.

220. Wishon, Tom W. *Golf Club Identification and Price Guide.* Newark OH: Ralph Maltby, 1985. 300p. $24.95. Golf industry's standard reference to historical golf clubs.

Industry

221. Canada. Statistics Canada. *Sporting Goods and Toy Industries.* Ottawa, Canada. Annual. $21. Statistics on establishments, employees, salaries and wages, production and costs.

222. DiCasoli, Sebastian. *Study of Financial Performance in the Sporting Goods Industry: 1980.* North Palm Beach FL: Sporting Goods Manufacturers Association, 1980. 29p. Membership. Historical trend data on sales and profitability of publicly owned domestic sporting goods manufacturers.

223. Euromonitor. *Sports Equipment.* London, 1982. 42p. $225. Analyzes trends in production and sales in European countries. Assesses overall growth of companies and industry. Data and sales by types of product. Projects 1980s market.

224. ICC Business Ratios. *Sports Goods.* London. Annual. $200. Compares individual and average performance of major companies in the United Kingdom. Provides three-year financial data and ratios.

225. Key Note Publications Ltd. *Sports Goods,* 5th ed. London, 1987. 44p. $100. Analyzes industry structure and trends in the United Kingdom over a five-year span and compares companies in the last three. Financial ratios and future development examined. Market structure and potential for overseas sales reviewed. Bibliography.

226. National Sporting Goods Association. *Cost of Doing Business for Retail Sporting Goods Stores.* Mount Prospect IL. Biennial. $30. Financial statement data and industry ratios by store, sales volume, region, and specialty, full-line, and team business. Productivity ratios are given for sales per employee, profit per employee, sales per square foot, profit per square foot, and inventory turnover.

Market

227. American Fishing Tackle Manufacturers Association. *Outdoor Indexes at a Glance 1977–1985.* Arlington Heights IL. 1986. 29p. Free. Statistical charts on various aspects of fishing, boating, and hunting. Data is national and by United States regions. Number or dollar expenditure for such subjects as fishing licenses, shipment of sporting goods, firearm tax collections. Statistics indexed with 1977 as the base year.

228. Broh, Irwin, and Associates, Inc. *Sporting Goods Market.* Mount Prospect IL: National Sporting Goods Association. Annual. $115. Consumer survey of 80,000 United States families. Estimated retail sales on more than 20 sport categories including equipment, clothing, and footwear. Data on income, education, household size, location, and sports interests.

229. Data Probe, Inc. *Cross Country Skier Magazine's Study of 1985/86 U.S. Retail Sales of Cross-Country Skiing Equipment.* Emmaus PA: Rodale, 1986. 56p. Summary Free to educational institutions. Profile of retail stores, sales, customers, services, and sources of revenue by product.

230. Jesswein, Wayne A., et al.

Profile of the Minnesota Angler. Duluth MN: University of Minnesota, Duluth, Bureau of Business and Economic Research, 1986. 16p. Free. Emphasis on Minnesota and bait, but valuable for the many other facets of fishing the study examines.

231. National Family Opinion Research, Inc. *Hunting Frequency and Participation Study.* Riverside CT: National Shooting Sports Foundation, 1986. 70p. Membership. Survey of hunting activity, hunting attitudes, and firearms ownership.

232. NPD Special Industry Services. *Sports Fishing Participation in (Year).* Arlington Heights IL: American Fishing Tackle Manufacturers Association. Annual. Membership. Survey of fresh and salt water anglers. Statistical charts on numbers for each by sex, frequency, age, income, and region of the country. Identifies new participants. Data on increase in fishing by number and percentage.

233. _____. *Sports Participation in (Year).* Port Washington NY. Annual. $400. Sponsored by the National Sporting Goods Association. Issued in three parts: Series 1 covers 27 sports for individuals; Series 2 covers over 20 team or vehicle sports; and Series 3 is a state-by-state presentation. Survey profiles participants by sex, age, residence, membership in clubs, and sports overlap.

234. U.S. International Trade Administration. *Sporting Goods and Recreational Equipment.* Washington DC: U.S. Department of Commerce. Several countries each year. Analyzes the current and potential market for American production by country. Past, current, and projected sales in general and by type of sporting goods, past, current, and projected imports and market share by major producing country by type of

goods, and grand totals. Data on the local market, marketing practices, and trade regulations.

235. _____. *Summary of Trade and Tariff Information: Small Arms and Parts.* Washington DC. Periodic updates. Report analyzes the United States and foreign market and provides country by country statistics on production of the product.

236. _____. *Summary of Trade and Tariff Information: Sporting Goods.* Washington DC. Periodic updates. Report analyzes the United States and foreign market and provides country by country statistics on production of the product.

237. Williams, Peter W. *Where Do the Trails Lead.* Montreal, Canada: National Ski Industries Association, 1986. 74p. $50. Analyzes the Canadian ski market in cooperation with Tourism Canada, the Canadian Ski Council, and the National Ski Industries Association. Bibliography.

Periodicals

238. *Action Sports Retailer.* South Laguna CA: Pacifica. Monthly. $15. Product-oriented publication for retailers. News, merchandising reports and suggestions, and new equipment, clothing, and supplies information. Special topics each issue and special report, "Buyer's Guide," in each December issue.

239. American Fishing Tackle Manufacturers Association. *Tackle Times.* Arlington Heights IL. Monthly. Membership. Official association publication. News of the association and articles on industry developments. Industry statistics.

240. American Ski Federation. *ASF Washington Letter.* Washington DC. Monthly. Membership. Information on national and state legislation affecting ski areas, ski equipment, and manufacturing and retailing of skiing products.

241. *Archery Business.* Minnetonka MN: Winter Sports Publishing, Inc. 6 issues. Controlled distribution. Articles on all aspects of archery, emphasizing manufacturing and retailing of archery equipment, management, merchandising, and new products. Special report: "Archery Manufacturers Directory" in each December issue. Former title: *Archery Retailer.*

242. Archery Range and Retailers Organization. *ARRO.* Madison WI. Monthly. Membership. Official association publication. Articles on management and operation of retail stores and indoor archery facilities. Association news, new product information, and reports on stores and archery lanes.

243. Athletic Goods Team Distributors. *Team Lineup.* Mount Prospect IL: National Sporting Goods Association. Quarterly. Membership. Official association publication. Information on sports rule changes and their effect on sport store sales to organized athletic teams.

244. *Fishing Tackle Retailer.* Montgomery AL: BASS Communications. 9 issues. Controlled distribution. For the fresh water retailer. Statistics on the industry, number of anglers, sales, buying intentions, and imports and exports. Articles on management and merchandising. Columns on marketing strategies and new products.

245. *Fishing Tackle Trade News.* Vancouver WA: Vickers Communications. 10 issues. $25. Emphasis on retailing. Reports on business methods and problems. Articles on merchandising and information on

new products. Special reports: "Market Analysis/Statistical Reports/Trends and New Products" in each July issue, and "Holiday Buyers Merchandising" in each November/December issue.

246. *Fitness Industry.* North Miami FL: Industry Publishers. 9 issues. Controlled distribution. Features home and institution physical fitness equipment and tanning units. Articles on fitness center operation, new products and supplies, fitness methods, and merchandising.

247. *Golf Industry.* North Miami FL: Industry Publishers. Bimonthly. $12. Golf products, sportswear, and retail operations, including pro-shops and golf course operations. Special reports: "PGA Merchandise Show" in each December/January issue; "Ladies' Golf Products" in each February/March issue; and "Market Report" in each August/September issue.

248. *Golf Shop Operations: A Golf Digest.* Trumbull CT: Golf Digest–Tennis. Bimonthly. $18. Articles on marketing, new products, and store operations. Periodic surveys of sales. Valuable for the pro-shop operator but primarily oriented to the golf sports shop. Former title: *Pro Shop Operations.*

249. International Marketing Institute for Sports. *IMIS Council Newsletter.* North Palm Beach FL: Sporting Goods Manufacturers Association. Quarterly. Membership. The IMIS is the international marketing wing of the Sporting Goods Manufacturers Association. Its function is to monitor the international potential for sporting goods sales. The newsletter reports on the activities of the Council and the international sporting goods scene in general.

250. National Association of Federally Licensed Firearms Dealers.

American Firearms Industry. Fort Lauderdale FL. 11 issues. $20. Official association publication. News of the government, the industry, and new products. Articles on management and procedures. Special issue: *American Firearms Industry* SHOT *Show Directory* (each December, $10).

251. National Shooting Sports Foundation. NSSF *Reports.* Riverside CT. Bimonthly. Membership. News of the foundation, information on legislation, and developments within the shooting sports industry.

252. National Ski Industries Association. *Ski Industry Bulletin.* Montreal, Canada. Quarterly. Membership. Official association publication. News of the association and the industry in Canada.

253. National Sporting Goods Association. *Market Watch Newsletter.* Mount Prospect IL. 6 or more issues. Membership. Intended as a method of periodically informing the industry of fast-breaking trends and events in the industry. Articles on new merchandising practices, successful sales programs, and management tips.

254. _____. *Sports Retailer.* Mount Prospect IL. Monthly. $10. Official association publication. Articles and research reports on the industry and successful retail operations. Columns on retail management, inventory control, and store planning. Special reports: "Industry Overview" in each January issue; "NGSA Fall Market" in each October issue; and "800 Toll Free Directory" in each December issue. Special issue: NSGA *Buying Guide* (each January, $20). Former titles: NSGA *Sports Retailer; Selling Sporting Goods.*

255. NPD Special Industry Services. *Quarterly Sales Trends in the Sporting Goods Market.* North Palm Beach FL: Sporting Goods Manufacturers Association. Quarterly. Membership. Reports on sales geographically and by type of product.

256. *Outdoor Retailer.* South Laguna CA: Pacifica. Monthly. Controlled distribution. For the retailer specializing in equipment for camping, hiking, mountaineering, and other outdoor sports. Articles on products, marketing, and management. Special reports: "Fishing Market" in each July issue and "Buyers Guide" in each December issue.

257. *Outside Business.* Chicago: Mariah. 8 issues. Controlled distribution. Emphasizes outdoor sports equipment. Articles on dealers, marketing, industry trends, management and finance, and new products.

258. Professional Stringers Association. PSA *Newsletter.* Omaha NE. Bimonthly. Membership. Official association publication. News of the association, product updates, and market information.

259. *Racquetball Industry.* North Miami FL: Industry Publishers. Bimonthly. $12. Emphasis is on products and merchandising but contains articles on court operations. Special reports: "Tennis Industry National Buying Show" in each January/February issue; "Annual Court Club Construction" in each March/April issue; "Sporting Goods Manufacturers Show" in each September/October issue; and "Racquet Research" in each November/December issue.

260. *Saltwater Dealer.* Montgomery AL: BASS Communications. 8 issues. Controlled distribution. For the fishing tackle retailer. Statistics on the industry, number of anglers, sales, buying intentions, and imports and exports. Articles on management, marketing, and merchandising.

261. *Shooting Industry.* San Diego CA: Publishers' Development Corp. Monthly. $25. For manufacturers, distributors, retailers, and commercial users of shooting goods and equipment. Articles on the industry, products, and government. Statistics and regulations. Special reports: "National Sporting Goods Association Show" in each January issue, and "Buyer's Guide" in each July issue. Indexed in *Business Index; Trade and Industry Index.*

262. *Shooting Sports Retailer.* Montgomery AL: BASS Communications. 5 issues. Controlled distribution. Statistics on the industry, number of hunters and shooters, sales, buying intentions, and imports and exports. Articles on management, merchandising, marketing strategies, and new products.

263. *Ski Business.* Darien CT: Nick Hock. 11 issues. Controlled distribution. News reports on products, the industry, and the market. Articles on merchandising and new developments in marketing. Special reports: "Annual Ski Show Report" in each March issue and "Market Research Report" in each July issue.

264. *Skiing Trade News.* New York: CBS Magazines. 7 issues. Controlled distribution. Articles on products, merchandising, and management of ski shops. Special report: "Buyers Guide" in each September issue. Indexed in *Business Index; Trade and Industry Index.*

265. *Sporting Goods Business.* New York: Gralla. Monthly. $9. "National news magazine of the sporting goods industry." Emphasis on retailing. News and articles on products, operation, and industry developments. Special report: "National Sporting Goods Association Report" in each January issue. Indexed in *Trade and Industry Index.*

266. *Sporting Goods Dealer.* Saint Louis MO: Sporting News. Monthly. Controlled distribution. "National magazine of the sporting goods trade." Liaison between the manufacturer and the retailer. Information on products. Articles on merchandising, store management, and sales promotion.

267. Sporting Goods Manufacturers Association. *Action Update.* North Palm Beach FL. Bimonthly. Membership. Official association publication. For management level personnel. News and information on the industry and association. Emphasizes product trends.

268. *Sports and Leisure Equipment News.* Droitwich, England: Peterson. Monthly. Emphasizes new products, primarily British. Contains news about the industry and manufacturers.

269. *Sports Business.* Downsview, Canada: Page. 12 issues. $65. Endorsed by the Canadian Sporting Goods Association for the sporting goods retailer. Articles on retail management, store operations, merchandising, marketing, and new products. Special issue: *Sports Business Directory and Buying Guide* (each September/October, $25). Indexed in *Canadian Business Index.* Former titles: *Sporting Goods Trade; Sporting Trade Canada; Sports Trade Canada.*

270. *Sports Merchandiser.* Atlanta GA: W.R.C. Smith. Monthly. $40. Reports on sales and market, articles and special sections on market statistic, and information on merchandising programs and policy. Special reports: "Sales Outlook" in each January issue; "Western Ware—Dealer Sales Survey" in each August issue; and "Racquet Sports—Dealer Sales Survey" in each November issue.

271. *Sports Trader.* Tonbridge, England: Benn. Biweekly. $40. British journal of sports goods and equipment. Articles on equipment, merchandising, and store operations.

272. *Sports Trends.* Atlanta GA: Shore Communication. Monthly. Controlled distribution. For the full-line and mass sporting goods retailers. Emphasizes products. Articles on consumer trends, marketing, and seasonal promotions.

273. *Tack 'N Togs Merchandising.* Minneapolis MN: Miller. Monthly. $18. For the retailer of supplies for the horse and rider. News of products, merchandising, and the industry. Special issue: *Tack 'N Togs Book* (each June, $10).

274. *Tackle and Guns.* Orton Centre, England: EMAP National. Monthly. $15. News of the industry, articles on management and merchandising, and information on new products. Industry and market statistics. Former title: *Fishing Tackle Dealer.*

275. Tackle Representatives Association, International. *Tackle Report.* Arlington Heights IL. Monthly. Membership. Official association publication. News of the association and information for manufacturers' representatives about the industry.

276. *Tennis Buyers Guide.* Trumbull CT: Golf Digest–Tennis. Quarterly. $12. Information on products and producers. Articles on consumer trends and retailing. Reviews industry and market research.

277. *Tennis Industry.* North Miami FL: Industry Publishers. 11 issues. $22. Articles on products, merchandising, shop operations, and business articles. Special reports on court building, racquet survey, racquet research, and court operations.

278. *Tennis/Racquet Trade.* Lyndhurst NJ: Circle. Monthly. $10. For the racquet sports retailer. News and articles on products, marketing, store operation and directory information on manufacturers and products. Former title: *Tennis Trade.*

279. Trophy Dealers and Manufacturers Association. *Trophy Dealer.* Fresno CA. Monthly. Membership. Official association publication. Industry news, information on products and services, and articles on successful operations. Columns on management, product update, and new manufacturers.

280. U.S. Bureau of Alcohol, Tobacco, and Firearms. *Alcohol, Tobacco, and Firearms Quarterly Bulletin.* Washington DC: U.S. Government Printing Office. Quarterly. Free. Federal government's instrument for announcing official rulings and procedures and publishing Treasury decisions affecting firearms dealers.

Databases

281. National Association of Federally Licensed Firearms Dealers. *Firearms Database.* Fort Lauderdale FL. Updated continuously. Membership. Text. Technical data on gun models and ammunition.

Bibliographies/Indexes

282. Lake, Fred, and Wright, Hal. *Bibliography of Archery.* Manchester, England: Simon Archery Foundation, 1974. 501p. Out of print. Books, articles, theses, etc., from the first writing on the subject until 1972. Arrangement is alphabetical by author.

283. Riling, Raymond Lawrence

Joseph. *Guns and Shooting: A Selected Chronological Bibliography.* Philadelphia PA: Riling Arms, 1981. 434p. $75. For arms collectors and dealers, students of firearms, and those interested in the history. Reprint of 1951 Greenwood publication. Probably the most comprehensive list of books and articles published to that date on the subject.

Associations

284. American Fishing Tackle Manufacturers Association. 2625 Clearbrook Dr., Arlington Heights IL 60005. (312) 364-4666. Association of manufacturers and importers. Compiles statistics. Conducts research. Provides management counsel, seminars, trade shows. Publishes handbooks, statistics, directory, periodical. Former name: Associated Fishing Tackle Manufacturers.

285. American Ski Federation. 207 Constitution Ave., N.E., Washington DC 20002. (202) 543-1595. Federation of associations and corporate members from the ski industry. Purpose is to monitor federal and state ski area and product legislation. Conducts research. Publishes periodical.

286. Angling Trade Association. 7 Swallow St., London, England W1R 7HB. (01) 437-7281. Association of manufacturers of fishing products. Affiliated with the British Sports and Allied Industries Federation Ltd. Compiles statistics. Provides seminars, trade fairs.

287. Archery Manufacturers Organization. 200 Castlewood Dr., North Palm Beach FL 33408. (305) 842-4100. Association of manufacturers, distributors, and suppliers. Provides seminars. Publishes standards, handbooks. Former name: Archery Manufacturers and Dealers Association.

288. Archery Range and Retailers Organization. 4609 Femrite Dr., Madison WI 53716. (608) 221-2697. Association of owners of retail shops and/or indoor archery facilities. Provides management counsel. Publishes periodical. Certifies leagues, tournaments. Former name: Archery Lane Operators Association.

289. Association of Importers-Manufacturers for Muzzleloading. 7809 W. 61st Terrace, Overland Park KS 66202. (913) 677-1518. Association of companies and individuals engaged in manufacturing of guns and accessories. Provides management counsel, seminars. Publishes standards, handbooks.

290. Athletic Goods Team Distributors. 1699 Wall St., Mount Prospect IL 60056. (312) 439-4000. A division of the National Sporting Goods Association. Provides information to sporting goods stores acting as agents for sports teams on rule changes that affect equipment sales. Provides seminars. Publishes periodical.

291. British Sports and Allied Industries Federation Ltd. 7 Swallow St., London, England W1R 7HB. (01) 437-7281. Association of manufacturers. Compiles statistics. Provides seminars.

292. Canadian Sporting Goods Association. 1315 De Maisonneuve, W., Suite 702, Montreal, Quebec, Canada H3G 1M4. (514) 845-6113. Association of manufacturers and retailers. Compiles statistics. Conducts research. Provides management counsel, seminars, trade shows.

293. Diving Equipment Manufacturers Association. P.O. Box 217, Tustin CA 92681. (714) 730-0650. Association of companies and organizations promoting sports diving. Compiles statistics. Conducts research. Provides seminars, trade shows. Publishes standards, handbooks.

294. Eastern Ski Representative Association. 4154 W. Lake Rd., Canandaigua NY 14424. (716) 394-3070. Association of sales representatives. Provides seminars, trade shows.

295. Federation of Sports Goods Distributors. 7 Pelham Rd., Lindfield, Sussex, England RH16 2EW. (04) 447-3769. Association of suppliers and retailers. Compiles statistics. Conducts research. Provides management counsel, seminars. Publishes handbooks.

296. Golf Ball Manufacturers Association. 200 Castlewood Dr., North Palm Beach FL 33408, (305) 844-2500. Association of 14 companies. Affiliated with the National Golf Foundation.

297. Golf Ball Manufacturers Conference. 7 Swallow St., London, England W1R 7HB. (01) 437-7281. Association of companies. Affiliated with the British Sports & Allied Industries Federation Ltd. Compiles statistics. Provides seminars.

298. Golf Products and Components Association. 200 Castlewood Dr., North Palm Beach FL 33408. (305) 844-2500. Association of 30 companies. Affiliated with the National Golf Foundation.

299. Midwest Ski Representatives Association. P.O. Box 418, Afton MN 55001. (612) 436-8723. Association of sales representatives. Provides seminars, trade shows.

300. National Association of Federally Licensed Firearms Dealers. 2801 E. Oakland Park Blvd., Fort Lauderdale FL 33306. (305) 561-3505. Association of individuals. Compiles statistics. Conducts research. Provides management counsel, seminars, trade shows. Maintains database. Publishes handbooks, periodicals.

301. National Association of Golf Club Manufacturers. 200 Castlewood Dr., North Palm Beach FL 33408. (305) 844-2500. Association of 20 companies. Affiliated with the National Golf Foundation.

302. National Association of Sporting Goods Wholesalers. P.O. Box 11344, Chicago IL 60611. (312) 565-0233. Association of wholesalers for athletic, boating, camping, firearm, and fishing goods. Compiles statistics. Former name: Sporting Goods Jobbers Association.

303. National Reloading Manufacturers Association. 4905 S.W. Griffith Dr., Suite 101, Beaverton OR 97005, (503) 646-1384. Association of manufacturers and distributors. Conducts research. Publishes handbooks.

304. National Shooting Sports Foundation. P.O. Box 1075, Riverside CT 06878. (203) 637-3618. Foundation sponsored by manufacturers and other firearms organizations. Compiles statistics. Conducts research. Provides management counsel, seminars. Maintains library. Publishes handbooks, statistics, directory, periodical.

305. National Ski Credit Association. 83 Eastern Ave., Saint Johnsbury VT 05819. (802) 748-8080. Association of ski and skiing product companies to maintain a credit report system for members use. Affiliated with the Ski Industries America. Former name: National Ski Clothing and Equipment Association.

306. National Ski Industries Association. 1822A Sherbrooke St., W., Montreal, PQ Canada H3H 1E4. (514) 937-6356. Association of

Canadian manufacturers, distributors, and suppliers. Publishes periodical.

307. National Sporting Goods Association. 1699 Wall St., Mount Prospect IL 60056. (312) 439-4000. Association of manufacturers, importers, wholesalers, and retailers. Compiles statistics. Conducts research. Provides management counsel, seminars, trade shows. Publishes handbooks, statistics, directory, periodicals. Former name: Athletic Goods Manufacturers Association.

308. Professional Golf Club Repairmen's Association. 2035 Harvard Ave., Dunedin FL 33528. (813) 733-4348. Association of repairmen and golf club professionals. Conducts research. Provides seminars. Publishes handbooks, periodicals.

309. Professional Stringers Association. 2209 S. 32nd Ave., Omaha NE 68105. (402) 345-9996. Association of individuals, racquet shop owners, and distributors. Conducts research. Provides seminars. Publishes standards, handbooks, periodical.

310. Ski Industries America. 8377B Greensboro Dr., McLean VA 22102. (703) 556-9020. Association of manufacturers, importers, and distributors. Provides management counsel, seminars, trade shows.

311. Ski Retailers Council. 8377B Greensboro Dr., McLean VA 22102. (212) 874-3030. Association of stores and ski shops. Provides management counsel, seminars.

312. Sporting Arms and Ammunition Manufacturers Institute. P.O. Box 1075, Riverside CT 06878. (203) 637-3618. Association of companies. Conducts research. Provides legal counsel, seminars. Publishes standards.

313. Sporting Goods Agents Association. P.O. Box 998, Morton Grove IL 60053. (312) 296-3670. Association of manufacturers' agents. Conducts research. Provides legal counsel. Former name: Sporting Goods Representatives Association.

314. Sporting Goods Manufacturers Association. 200 Castlewood Dr., North Palm Beach FL 33408. (305) 842-4100. Association of companies. Compiles statistics. Conducts research. Provides seminars. Publishes standards, handbooks, statistics, directory, periodical.

315. Sports Foundation. 1699 Wall St., Mount Prospect IL 60056. (312) 439-4000. Arm of the National Sporting Goods Association. Provides management assistance to the newer and smaller businesses in the industry.

316. Tackle Representatives Association, International. 2625 Clearbrook Dr., Arlington Heights IL 60005. (312) 364-4460. Association of manufacturers' representatives. Publishes directory, periodical.

317. Tennis Manufacturers Association. 200 Castlewood Dr., North Palm Beach FL 33408. (305) 848-1026. Association of companies. Affiliated with the Tennis Foundation of North America. Provides seminars, trade shows.

318. Trophy Dealers and Manufacturers Association. 4644 W. Jennifer, #101, Fresno CA 93711. (209) 275-5100. Association of companies, establishments, and individuals. Compiles statistics. Provides management counsel, seminars, trade shows. Publishes handbooks, directory, periodical.

319. Water Ski Industry Association. 200 Castlewood Dr., North Palm Beach FL 33408. (305) 842-3600. Association of manufacturers and distributors of equipment and supplies. Affiliated with the Sporting

Goods Manufacturers Association. Compiles statistics. Publishes handbooks.

320. Western Winter Sports Representatives Association. 2621 Thorndyke Ave., W., Seattle WA 98199. (206) 284-0751. Association of sales representatives. Provides seminars, trade shows.

321. World Federation of the Sporting Goods Industry. P.O. Box B 1455, Zurich, Switzerland CH-8302. 1-814-1537. Association of national associations with commercial organizations as associate members. Compiles statistics. Conducts research. Provides management counsel, seminars, trade shows. Publishes statistics, directory, periodical.

9. The Recreational Vehicle Industry

SIC Codes: 3716, 3751, 3792, 3799, 5012, 5561, 5571, 5599, 7519, 7699

Enterprises manufacturing, selling, servicing, and/or operating establishments with vehicles for recreation other than water. For enterprises whose primary emphasis is on vehicles for water recreation see Chapter 10, The Boat Industry.

Directories

322. Recreation Vehicle Industry Association. *RVIA Membership Directory and Industry Buyer's Guide.* Reston VA. Annual. $31. Lists member manufacturers, suppliers, representatives, and associate firms giving name, address, phone, and key executives. Arrangement is alphabetical with geographical index. "Buyer's Guide" lists suppliers by 123 product categories with a geographical index.

323. Recreation Vehicle Rental Association. *Who's Who in RV Rental.* Fairfax VA. Annual. $4. Lists over 250 recreational vehicle dealers who rent RVs in both the United States and Canada giving name, address, phone, owner/manager, types and sizes available, costs, and deposit requirements. Arrangement is alphabetical with geographical index. Indicates those dealers that are RVRA members.

324. Society of Motor Manufacturers and Traders. *SMMT Directory of the Motor Industry.* London. Annual. $25. Lists 500 companies producing motor vehicles and vehicle accessories giving name, address, phone, telex, contact, trade names, and products. Arrangement is alphabetical with trade name and product index. Association also publishes a much larger *SMMT List of Members* annually.

Management

325. American Entrepreneurs Association. *Bicycle Sales & Repairs.* Los Angeles, 1984. 111p. $45. Guide to establishing and operating a small business. Legal, management, marketing, operating, and financial procedures. Supplier addresses and a bibliography. Looseleaf format.

326. _____. *Moped Shop.* Los Angeles, 1984. 118p. $39.50. Guide to establishing and operating a small business. Legal, management, marketing, operating, and financial procedures. Supplier addresses and a bibliography. Looseleaf format.

327. Bank of America. *Bicycle Shops.* San Francisco CA, 1980. 20p. $2. Covers procedures for operating a shop. Includes "Sources for Further Information."

328. Harding, B.B. Kip, and Wangberg, David I. *Dealership Business Management.* Midland MI:

Northwood Institute Press, 1984. 211p. $15.95. National Automobile Dealers Association handbook on financial management practice. Much of the practice described is applicable to an RV, motorcycle, or bicycle retail operation.

329. International Snowmobile Industry Association Snowmobile Safety and Certification Committee. *Safety Standards for Snowmobile Product Certification.* Fairfax VA, 1983. 52p. $4. Explanation of the standards program, its components, and procedures for revising the standards.

330. _____. *Safety Standards for Snowmobile Product Certification, Supplement.* Fairfax VA, 1986. 128p. $15. Standards and testing specification and procedures.

331. Recreation Vehicle Industry Association. *Guide to FMVSS (Federal Motor Vehicle Safety Standards).* Reston VA, 1982. 229p. Membership. Rules and regulations pertaining to federal motor vehicle safety standards for the manufacture of recreation vehicles and van conversions. Federal laws and regulations, general advice on problems pertinent to defects and noncompliance, and an index to the RVIA bulletin updates. Illustrated with technical drawings. Looseleaf format.

332. _____. *Handbook for Recreation Vehicle Standards: A Guide to ANSI (American National Standards Institute) A119.2.* Reston VA, 1982. 332p. $70. Information and industry position on the application by the states of standards established by the ANSI. Commentary on each paragraph of A119.2. Illustrated with technical drawings. Looseleaf format.

333. _____. *State Guide for RV Manufacturers.* Reston VA,

1985. 101p. $40. State requirements and regulations for RV manufacturing, standards, licensing, bonding, and certificates required. Lists taxation and regulatory agencies with name, address, phone, and contact.

334. Whitney, Jon, Associates. *Recreation Vehicle Financing.* Reston VA: Recreation Vehicle Industry Association. Annual. $5. Survey of lenders detailing the current and immediate—past situation in direct, indirect, and wholesale financing of the RV industry. Contains 10-year statistical charts on loan, interest, and delinquency rates.

335. Wray, M. Monte. *Merchandising Parts and Service Management of Fixed Operations,* Rev. ed. Midland MI: Northwood Institute Press, 1982. 265p. $15.95. National Automobile Dealers Association handbook on parts sales and inventory management. Much of the practice described is applicable to RV, motorcycle, or bicycle retail operations.

Industry

336. FIND/SVP. *Recreational Vehicle Industry.* Bethesda MD: National Standards Association, 1986. 19p. $250. Analyzes industry trends, provides financial and production data, and profiles leading companies in the industry in the United States.

337. ICC Business Ratios. *Motorcycle Dealers.* London. Annual. $250. Compares individual and average performance of major companies in the United Kingdom. Provides three-year financial data and ratios.

338. Key Note Publications Ltd. *Bicycles,* 5th ed. London, 1987. 36p. $100. Analyzes industry structure and trends over a five-year span and compares companies in the last three. Financial ratios and future development examined. Market structure and potential for overseas sales reviewed. Bibliography.

339. _____. *Motorcycles,* 5th ed. London, 1987. 42p. $100. Analyzes industry structure and trends over a five-year span and compares companies in the last three. Financial ratios and future development examined. Market structure and potential for overseas sales reviewed. Bibliography.

340. Motorcycle Industry Council. *Manufacturers Shipment Reporting System Annual Statistical Report.* Costa Mesa CA. Annual. Membership. Weekly statistics on production, imports, sales by model type, new registrations, and estimated economic value of the motorcycle retail marketplace by state.

341. _____. *Motorcycle Retail Outlet Profile Survey.* Costa Mesa CA. Annual. Membership. Operating characteristics of the "median" retail establishment. Profile of the typical overall store as well as the franchised and non-franchised shop. Average and ratio data on employees, payroll, ownership, expenditures, sales, and brands carried.

342. _____. *Motorcycle Retail Outlet Study.* Costa Mesa CA. Annual. Membership. Number of outlets, employees, and payroll by type of establishment and for each state. Sales volume and type of product or service for franchised and non-franchised shop.

343. _____. *Motorcycle Statistical Annual.* Costa Mesa CA. Annual. $10. Statistics for the current and past year on manufacturers and distributors, the retail market, usage, and motorcycle owner. Motorcycle registration figures and estimated economic value of the

industry by states. Retail sales and imports for the past 15 years are reported along with other motorcycle related data.

344. Recreation Vehicle Industry Association. *RVs: Family Camping Vehicles, Annual Review.* Reston VA. Annual. $5. Historical and current production and shipment statistics. Data on market shares by size and type of vehicle. State and regional deliveries and wholesale and retail volume for the past 10 years.

Market

345. Burke Marketing Research, Inc. *Survey of Motorcycle Ownership and Usage.* Costa Mesa CA: Motorcycle Industry Council. Every five years. Membership. Data on the probability of a motorcycle being in operation, miles traveled on and off-highway by model and season, fuel economy figures, and demographics and occupations of owners and riders.

346. Curtin, Richard T. *Consumer Demand for RVs.* Chantilly VA: Recreation Vehicle Industry Association, 1981. 20p. $10. Survey of 1,500 United States households on vacation preferences, attitude towards camping, and intent to purchase or rent an RV. Demographic analysis of results.

347. _____. *RV Consumer: Current Trends and Future Prospects.* Reston VA: Recreation Vehicle Industry Association, 1985. 28p. $10. Analysis of 2,491 vehicle owning households regarding use. Demographic statistics on intention to buy or rent. Data on percentages of households in the United States owning or intending to buy. Similar study in 1980.

348. Data Probe, Inc. *Bicycling*

Magazine's 1987 Study of U.S. Retail Bicycle Stores. Emmaus PA: Rodale, 1987. 87p. $100. Profile of retail stores, store revenues, products sold, and product sales trends for bicycles, all terrain bicycles, and apparel.

349. International Trade Centre UNCTAD/GATT. *Bicycles and Components: A Pilot Survey of Opportunities for Trade Among Developing Countries*. Geneva, Switzerland, 1985. 160p. $24.95. Market study of bicycle industry and sales potential.

350. Motorcycle Industry Council. *Estimated Motorcycle Population and Usage*. Costa Mesa CA. Annual. Membership. Statistics on number of motorcycles in the United States by model type, engine displacement, and model year for current and past year, estimated number, motorcycle usage, penetration rate by state, and number of motorcycles scrapped.

351. Pannell Kerr Foster, Inc. *Vacation Cost Comparison: Vacations Using Recreation Vehicles vs. Other Types of Vacations*. Reston VA: Recreation Vehicle Industry Association, 1985. 58p. $15. Study for the Recreation Vehicle Industry Association, the Recreation Vehicle Dealers Association, and the National Campground Owners Association. Using a hypothetical family of four, the comparisons determined that an RV vacation was 50 to 75 percent less. Contains detailed statistical analysis for travel to hotels using other forms of transportation.

352. U.S. International Trade Commission. *Summary of Trade and Tariff Information: Motorcycles*. Washington DC. Periodic updates. Analysis of the United States and foreign market and country by country statistics on production of the product.

353. Yankelovich, Skelly and White, Inc. *RV Market: A Social Value-Based Assessment*. Reston VA: Recreation Vehicle Industry Association, 1983. 20p. $5. Survey of consumer attitudes and purchasing potential for RV campers.

Periodicals

354. *American Bicyclist and Motorcyclist*. New York: Cycling Press. Monthly. $24. For retailers and wholesalers of bicycles and mopeds. Information on products, their construction, servicing, and maintenance. Features on merchandising, display, and sales. Reports on trade shows, activities of the National Bicycle Dealers Association, and the industry.

355. *Bicycle Business Journal*. Fort Worth TX: Quinn. Monthly. $12. Articles on the industry, its products, and retail operations for the non-franchised retail and service shops. Former title: *Bicycle Journal*.

356. *Bicycle Dealer Showcase*. Cleveland OH: Harcourt Brace Jovanovich. Monthly. Controlled distribution. For distributors and shop owners. Emphasizes bicycle and moped products and accessories. News and columns on the activities of the Bicycle Manufacturers Association of America and the National Bicycle Dealers Association. Special issue: *Bicycle Dealers Showcase Buyers Guide* (each January, $30).

357. *Bicycle Product News*. Van Nuys CA: Freed Crown Lee. Monthly. $18. News on products and accessories for the bicycle and moped industry and service bulletins.

358. *Bicycle Trade Times*. Dunston, England: Kelthorn. Monthly. $40. British dealer and servicer news magazine. Emphasizes product information and trade and operations news.

359. Bicycle Wholesale Distributors Association. *BWDA Newsletter.* Philadelphia PA. Quarterly. Membership. Official association publication. Product, association, and industry information and other matters affecting distribution activities.

360. *Canadian RV Dealer.* Montreal, Canada: CRV Publications Canada. Bimonthly. $11. Emphasizes Canadian aspects of the industry but includes extensive information on products, news, and operations applicable to all of North America. Former title: *Canadian Camper and RV Dealer.*

361. *DealerNews.* Santa Ana CA: Harcourt Brace Jovanovich. Monthly. Controlled distribution. Retailing and servicing cycles and information on new products. Special issue: *DealerNews Buyers Guide* (each November, $20). Former title: *Motorcycle DealerNews.* Indexed in *Business Index; Trade and Industry Index.*

362. Independent Motorcycle Retailers of America. *IMRA News.* Chicago. Monthly. Membership. Official association publication. News of the association and the industry.

363. International Association of Plumbing and Mechanical Officials. *Directory of the Trailer Research Recommendations.* Los Angeles CA. Monthly. $50. Official association publication. Directory of recreational vehicle and mobile home products with company information. News and information on standards, installation, and regulations.

364. International Snowmobile Industry Association. *ISIA Newsline.* Fairfax VA. Irregular. Membership. Official association publication. News of the association and the industry.

365. *Motor Cycle and Cycle Trader.* Rickmansworth, England: Wheatland Journals. Monthly. $30. For suppliers and retailers of cycles in the United Kingdom. News of products, industry trends, and dealers. Former title: *Cycle Trader.*

366. *Motorcycle Dealer and Trade.* Toronto, Canada: Brave Beaver. Monthly. Controlled circulation. For manufacturers, suppliers, and retailers in Canada. Emphasizes Canadian news but includes information on the United States market.

367. *Motorcycle Industry Business Journal.* Costa Mesa CA: Hancock-Brown. 8 issues. $38. Industry developments, marketing trends, and management and legislative matters for the industry executive.

368. *Motorcycle Industry Magazine.* Thousand Oaks CA: Industry Shopper. Monthly. Controlled distribution. Emphasizes industry and product news, trends, and regulations.

369. *Motorcycle Product News.* Van Nuys CA: Freed Crown Lee. Monthly. $18. Services, parts, supplies, product specifications, photograph of product, and manufacturer's name and address. Special issue: *Motorcycle Product News Trade Directory* (each January, $12).

370. National Bicycle Dealers Association. *Spokesman.* Mission Viejo CA. Quarterly. Membership. Official association publication. News of the association, the industry, and new products.

371. National Motorcycle Retailers Association. *Dealer Trends.* Washington DC. Monthly. Membership. Official association publication. News of the industry, merchandising tips, and the association.

372. Recreation Vehicle Dealers Association of North America.

RVDA News. Fairfax VA. Monthly. $21. Official association publication. News of the association, the industry, and other matters pertaining to products, regulations, and merchandising.

373. Recreation Vehicle Industry Association. *RV Financial Facts.* Reston VA. Quarterly. Membership. Economic, social, and merchandising factors that affect the industry. Evaluation of the consumer, the job market, income, spending habits, and financial management.

374. _____. *RVIA Marketing Report.* Reston VA. Monthly. $150 (includes publication following). RV production and shipments by product type. Compares current and past year monthly data. Unit size and wholesale price information.

375. _____. *RV Roadsigns.* Reston VA. Quarterly. $40. Two-year forecast of manufacturer deliveries to retailers. Statistical analysis.

376. *RV Business.* Agoura CA: TL Enterprises. Monthly. $24. Management and operations, industry developments, and products. Statistics on RV shipments for current month and same month previous year. Special issue: *RV Business Industry Directory* (Each March, $9.95). Former titles: *Recreational Vehicle Business, Recreational Vehicle Dealer, RV Dealer.*

377. *Smart.* Long Beach CA: Cycle News. Monthly. Controlled distribution. News of the all terrain vehicle industry and its products for manufacturers, suppliers, and retailers. Emphasis on product development, industry trends, and sales promotion. Features company and store profiles. Former title: *All Terrain Vehicle Industry.*

378. *Snowmobile Business.* Minnetonka MN: Winter Sports Publishing. 4 issues. $10. News, product information, and accessory and merchandising ideas for retailers and general information for the industry. Special report: "Guide to Suppliers" in each September issue. Former title: *Snow Goer Trade.*

Bibliographies/Indexes

379. Albrecht, Jean, and Knopp, Timothy B., comp. *Off Road Vehicles—Environmental Impact—Management Response: A Bibliography.* Saint Paul MN: University of Minnesota Agricultural Experiment Station, 1985. 50p. Free. Annotated bibliography emphasizing the effects of ORVs on major aspects of the environment. References to management, regulation, and symposia.

380. Luebbers, David J. *Bicycle Resource Guide.* Denver CO, 1981. 136p. $5. Annotated bibliography of 2,078 citations to books, journal and newspaper articles, government and association publications, and catalogs. Some relate to the bicycle industry but most are recreation-oriented. Arrangement by type of publication with author, corporate, geographic, and subject indexes.

381. Mergen, Bernard. *Recreation Vehicles and Travel: A Resource Guide.* Westport CT: Greenwood, 1985. 221p. $29.95. Bibliographic essays on travel, in general, and all types of recreational vehicles, including air and water. Emphasis is on the leisure activity more than on the industry. Each essay is followed by a list of publications mentioned. Author, title, subject and place index provides access to the essays.

382. Schultz, Barbara A., and Schultz, Mark P. *Bicycles and Bicycling: A Guide to Information Sources.* Detroit MI: Gale Research Co., 1979. 300p. $62. Somewhat out of date but still the most comprehensive bibliographic resource on the sport and the industry. Chapters on design, maintenance, legal aspects, and statistics as well as history, technique, competition, and touring. Information on organizations and their activities.

Associations

383. Bicycle Manufacturers Association of America. 1055 Thomas Jefferson St., N.W., Suite 316, Washington DC 20007. (202) 333-4052. Association of companies and associates. Compiles statistics. Conducts research.

384. Bicycle Wholesale Distributors Association. 99 W. Hawthorne Ave., Valley Stream NY 11580. (516) 825-3000. Association of companies with manufacturers as associate members. Publishes periodical. Former name: Cycle Jobbers Association.

385. Canadian Recreational Vehicle Association. 55 York St., Suite 512, Toronto, Ontario, Canada M5J 1S2. (416) 363-8374. Association of manufacturers and distributors of all types of RVs.

386. Cycle Parts and Accessories Association. 122 E. 42nd St., New York NY 10017. (212) 697-6340. Association of companies. Compiles statistics. Conducts research. Publishes handbooks.

387. Independent Motorcycle Retailers of America. 3634 N. Western Ave., Chicago IL 60618. (312) 477-9504. Association of dealers, manufacturers, suppliers, and persons associated with the motorcycle industry. Publishes periodical.

388. International Snowmobile Industry Association. 3975 University Dr., Suite 310, Fairfax VA 22030. (703) 273-9606. Association of manufacturers and distributors. Publishes standards, handbooks, periodical.

389. Light Aircraft Manufacturers Association. 2045 Mars Rd., Livermore CA 94550. (415) 449-5992. Association of manufacturers of light and ultralight aircraft and suppliers to homebuilders of aircraft.

390. Moped Association of America. 130 E. Main St., Malone NY 12953. (518) 483-0106. Association of manufacturers and suppliers. Former name: Motorized Bicycle Association.

391. Motorcycle Industry Council. 3151 Airway Ave., Bldg. P-1, Costa Mesa CA 92626. (714) 241-9251. Association of manufacturers and suppliers. Compiles statistics. Conducts research. Provides management counsel, seminars. Publishes handbooks, statistics. Former name: Motorcycle, Scooter and Allied Trades Association.

392. National Bicycle Dealers Association. P.O. Box 3450, Mission Viejo CA 92690. (714) 951-3451. Association of retail dealers. Provides seminars. Publishes handbooks, periodical.

393. National Independent Bicycle Representatives Association. 1997 Friendship Dr., Suite G, El Cajon CA 92020. (916) 579-6246. Association of individuals. Provides management counsel.

394. National Motorcycle Retailers Association. 1522 K St., N.W., Suite 704, Washington DC 20005. (202) 682-1558. Association of dealers, manufacturers, and suppliers. Provides management counsel, seminars. Maintains library. Formed by merger of Motorcycle Retailers of America and National Motorcycle Dealers Association.

395. Recreation Vehicle Dealers

Association of North America. 3251 Old Lee Hwy., Suite 500, Fairfax VA 22030. (703) 591-7130. Association of year-around retail businesses. Provides management counsel, seminars. Publishes handbooks, directories, periodical.

396. Recreation Vehicle Industry Association. P.O. Box 2999, 1896 Preston White Dr., Reston VA 22090. (703) 620-6003. Association of manufacturers, manufacturers' representatives, and suppliers. Compiles statistics. Conducts research. Provides management counsel, seminars, trade shows. Publishes handbooks, statistics, directories, periodicals.

397. Recreation Vehicle Rental Association. 3251 Old Lee Hwy., Suite 500, Fairfax VA 22030. (703) 591-7130. Association of rental dealers. Compiles statistics. Provides seminars. Publishes directory. Affiliated with the Recreation Vehicle Dealers Association of North America.

398. Society of Motor Manufacturers and Traders. Forbes House, Halkin St., London, England SW1X 7DS. (01) 235-7000. Association of manufacturers, importers, suppliers, and dealers of all types of automotive equipment including recreational vehicles. Compiles statistics. Conducts research. Provides management counsel, seminars, trade shows. Publishes handbooks, statistics, directories.

10. The Boat Industry

SIC Codes: 3732, 4493, 5091, 5551, 7999.

Enterprises manufacturing, selling, servicing, and/or operating establishments with vehicles for water recreation. For enterprises whose primary emphasis is vehicles for other than water recreation see Chapter 9, The Recreational Vehicle Industry.

Directories

399. American Boardsailing Industries Association. *ABIA Membership List.* Addison IL. Irregular. Membership. Lists member manufacturers, importers, and suppliers giving name of company, address, phone, and key executives.

400. *Boating Almanac.* Severna Park MD: Boating Almanac. Annual (6v). $8.50 per volume. Lists marinas and boating facilities for pleasure boats from Maine to Florida giving name, location, phone, and facilities available. Arrangement is geographical.

401. National Marine Representatives Association. *N.M.R.A. Directory.* Glen Ellyn IL. Annual. $10. Lists 300 independent suppliers of boats, motors, and accessories giving name, address, phone, manufacturers represented, territory, and clientele. Arrangement is geographical.

402. *Pacific Boating Almanac.* Ventura CA: Western Marine Enterprises. Annual (2v). $15 per volume.

Lists marinas and boating facilities for pleasure boats in the West Coast states, British Columbia, and Mexico giving name, location, phone, and facilities available. Arrangement is geographical.

Management

403. Adie, Donald W. *Marinas, Working Guide to Their Development and Design,* 3d ed. London: Architectural Press; New York: Nichols, 1984. 367p. $85. Guide to planning, designing, and constructing a marina. British influence but applicable to American situations. Extensive and detailed diagrams with bibliography and index.

404. American Entrepreneurs Association. *Sailboat Time-Share Leasing.* Los Angeles, 1984. 119p. $39.50. Guide to establishing and operating a small business. Legal, management, marketing, operations, and financial procedures. Supplier addresses and a bibliography. Looseleaf format.

405. Chamberlain, W. Clinton. *Marinas: Recommendations for Design, Construction and Management,* 3d ed. Chicago: National Marine Manufacturers Association, 1983. 287p. Guide to planning, organizing, and operating a marina. Examples, diagrams, and planning forms. Actual situations as well as models. Updated edition of a 1961 work by Chaney, Charles A.

406. McGinnis, John. *Boat Mar-*

ket Analysis: Using Industry Statistics to Improve Your Market Effectiveness. Chicago: National Marine Manufacturers Association, 1982. 23p. Membership. Manual for conducting a simple local market analysis. Proposes methodology and describes information sources. Steps outlined and illustrated.

407. National Marine Bankers Association. *Lender's Boating Handbook: Including How to Perfect Recreational Marine Loans.* Chicago: National Marine Manufacturers Association, 1984. 28p. Membership. Guide for the retailer in making, processing, and securing underwriting of consumer loans. Includes forms and outlines procedures.

408. National Marine Manufacturers Association. *NMMA Certification Handbook.* Chicago. Annual. Association engineering manual of recommended practices for the manufacturing of boats, motors, and other marine products for pleasure boats. Former title: *B.I.A. Certification Handbook.*

409. _____. *Recommended Practices: Marine Service,* 6th ed. Chicago, 1979. 80p. Membership. Handbook for the marine service dealer. Contains standards for shop organization, modifications and outfitting, and repair and maintenance.

410. Norvell, Douglas G. *Financial Profiles of Five Marinas.* Chicago: National Marine Manufacturers Association, 1984. 59p. Membership. Comparative study for the financial community as well as owners.

411. _____, Maulding, William R., and Otto, William R. *Marine Floorplanning: How to Serve the Inventory Finance Needs of the Recreational Boating Community.* Chicago: National Marine Manufacturers Association, 1986. 31p. Mem-

bership. Study of current inventory financial practices with recommendations for future policy. For bank lenders and boat industry.

412. Robert Snow Means Company, Inc. *Boat Cost Guide.* Kingston MA. Annual. $29.95. Manual for determining the cost of repairs, maintenance, equipment, and improvements for boats, motorboats, and sailboats.

Industry

413. ICC Business Ratios. *Boat Builders.* London. Annual. $200. Compares individuals and average performance of major companies in the United Kingdom. Provides three-year financial data and ratios.

414. International Council of Marine Industry Association. *Boating Industry Reports and Statistics.* Weybridge, England. Annual. $80. Industry data for Western European countries, Australia, Canada, South Africa, and the United States. Reports design trends, market trends, legislation. Statistics include establishments, employees, boat and engine production, sales, imports and exports.

415. National Marine Bankers Association. *NMBA Summary Annual Report.* Chicago. Annual. Free. Statistics on terms, turnover, charge-offs, and delinquencies in loans to boat dealers in the United States.

Market

416. American Fishing Tackle Manufacturers Association. *Outdoor Indexes at a Glance 1977–1985.* Arlington Heights IL, 1986. 29p. Free. Statistical charts on number and average length and cost of a boat, number and average cost of a boat trailer, and number, average horsepower and cost, and price indexes of motors annually from 1977 through 1985.

417. National Marine Manufacturers Association Marketing Services Department. *Boating.* Chicago. Annual. Membership. Statistics on boating usage by type of boat and by state.

418. National Marine Manufacturers Association. *Boating Registration Statistics.* Chicago. Annual. $20. Data by state, by length, and type of craft. More detailed than Coast Guard statistics (see **419**).

419. U.S. Coast Guard. *Boating Statistics.* Washington DC. Annual. Free. Primarily a report on boating accidents but contains statistics on registered boats, length, propulsion categories, and hull materials. Data on number of boats per 1000 population and per square mile by state.

420. U.S. International Trade Commission. *Summary of Trade and Tariff Information: Pleasure Boats.* Washington DC. Periodic updates. Report analyzes the United States and foreign market and provides country by country statistics on production of the product. Data on motorboat engines.

Periodicals

421. American Boat and Yacht Council. *ABYC News.* Amityville NY. Irregular. Free. Articles on boat and equipment standards, information on design and construction, and news of the council.

422. *Boat and Motor Dealer.* Skokie IL: Van Zevern. Monthly. $20. Emphasis on marketing. Articles and news on the consumer market, products, and merchandising. Features on dealerships and

sales promotions. Calendar of boat shows and industry events. Special report: "Market Manual" in each January issue.

423. *Boating Business.* London: Ravenshead Marine. Monthly. $15. Provides coverage of the British boat industry. Articles on the market, products, and the industry. Indexed in *Predicast F&S Index: United States.*

424. *Boating Industry.* New York: Whitney Communications. Monthly. $20 (includes *Boating Product News*). Articles and data on consumer trends and market, information on the industry and news of firms and individuals. Special issue: *Boating Industry Marine Buyers' Guide* (each December, $25). Indexed in *Business Periodicals Index; Trade and Industry Index.*

425. *Boating Product News.* New York: Whitney Communications. 11 issues. $20 (includes *Boating Industry*). Supplements *Boating Industry* by providing data and information on new products and producers.

426. *International Boat Industry.* Sutton, England: Business Press. Bimonthly. $45.50. Articles on the international boating scene with emphasis on business developments and trends plus information on markets and countries.

427. *Marine and Recreation News.* Saint Clair Shores MI: Marina News. Weekly. $5. Tabloid linking members of the Michigan Marine Dealers Association, but also contains news of the industry and marinas in the Great Lakes region. Former title: *Marina News.*

428. Marine Retailers Association of America. *MRAA Newsletter.* Chicago. Monthly. Membership. Official association publication. News of the association and the industry.

429. *Marine Trades.* Mississauga, Canada: Arthurs Publications. Quarterly. $15. Magazine of the boat industry of Canada. Articles and news on the industry, its products, and its businesses.

430. National Marina Manufacturers Consortium. *NMMC Newsletter.* Macomb IL. Monthly. Membership. Official association publication. News of the association and the industry.

431. National Marine Bankers Association. *Business of Pleasure Boats.* Chicago. Quarterly. Membership. Official association publication. Information on the state of marine financing, industry lending statistics, and manufacturer and dealer financing.

432. National Marine Manufacturers Association. *Inter-Port.* Chicago. Weekly. $100. Official association publication. News, statistics, trends, products, and trade show data. Former titles: *Boating News, Monday Morning Report.*

433. National Marine Representatives Association. *NMRA Newsletter.* Glen Ellyn IL. Monthly. Membership. Official association publication. News of the association and the industry.

434. *Sailboard News: The International Trade Journal of Boardsailing.* Fair Haven VT: Sports Ink Magazines. Monthly. $20. News of the industry and boardsailing. Features on products, manufacturers, and sailing locations.

Bibliography

435. American Boat and Yacht Council. *Boating Information: A Bibliography and Source List.* Amityville NY 1986. Controlled distribution. Reference to boats, boating

organizations, safety, and seamanship.

Associations

436. American Boardsailing Industries Association. 223 Interstate Rd., Addison IL 60101. (312) 628-8273. Association of companies. Compiles statistics. Publishes directory.

437. American Boat and Yacht Council. P.O. Box 806, Amityville NY 11701. (516) 598-0550. Association of professionals. Purpose is to develop standards and practices for the industry. Conducts research. Provides seminars. Publishes standards, handbooks, periodical.

438. American Boat Builders and Repairers Association. 715 Boylston St., Boston MA 02116. (617) 266-6800. Association of companies. Provides seminars. Former name: Atlantic Coast Boat Builders and Repairers Association.

439. American Canoe Manufacturers Union. 439 E. 51st St., New York NY 10022. (212) 421-5220. Association of companies. Conducts seminars.

440. American Sailing Council. 401 N. Michigan Ave., Chicago IL 60611. (312) 836-4747. Association of members of the National Marine Manufacturers Association involved in sailing. Purpose is to expand the market for sailboats and sailing. Affiliated with the National Marine Manufacturers Association.

441. Association of Marine Engine Manufacturers. 401 N. Michigan Ave., Chicago IL 60611. (312) 836-4747. Association of companies producing marine engines for recreational use. Affiliated with the National Marine Manufacturers Association. Former names: Marine

Engine Manufacturers Association, Outboard Motor Manufacturers Association.

442. International Council of Marine Industry Associations. Boating Industry House, Vale Rd., Weybridge, Surrey, England KT13 9NS. Weybridge 54511. Federation of boat industry associations. Compiles statistics. Publishes standards, handbooks, statistics.

443. Marine Retailers Association of America. 444 N. Michigan Ave., Suite 3664, Chicago IL 60611. (312) 822-0444. Association of companies involved in the recreational boating industry. Provides management counsel, seminars. Publishes handbooks, periodical.

444. National Association of Boat Manufacturers. 401 N. Michigan Ave., Chicago IL 60611. (312) 836-4747. Association of companies that build pleasure boats. Affiliated with the National Marine Manufacturers Association.

445. National Association of Marine Products and Services. 401 N. Michigan Ave., Chicago IL 60611. (312) 836-4747. Association of companies that manufacture recreational marine equipment. Compiles statistics. Conducts research. Provides seminars. Affiliated with the National Marine Manufacturers Association. Former name: Marine Accessories and Services Association.

446. National Marina Manufacturers Consortium. P.O. Box 6040, Macomb IL 61455. (309) 833-1117. Association of companies and individuals involved in building floating docks. Purpose is to promote and aid in the development of marinas. Publishes periodical.

447. National Marine Bankers Association. 401 N. Michigan Ave., Suite 2950, Chicago IL 60611. (312) 836-4747. Association of banks, savings institutions, and credit unions which extend credit to consumers, retailers, and manufacturers of recreational boating equipment. Compiles statistics. Conducts research. Provides seminars. Publishes statistics, handbooks, periodical.

448. National Marine Manufacturers Association. 401 N. Michigan Ave., Chicago IL 60611. (312) 836-4747. Association of members of four affiliated organizations: American Sailing Council, Association of Marine Engine Manufacturers, National Association of Boat Manufacturers, National Association of Marine Products and Services. Compiles statistics. Conducts research. Provides management counsel, seminars, trade shows. Publishes handbooks, statistics, periodical.

449. National Marine Representatives Association. 16-2 Saint Thomas Colony, Glen Ellyn IL 60020. (312) 587-1253. Association of individuals. Provides trade shows. Publishes directory, periodical.

450. Ship and Boat Builders National Federation. Boating Industry House, Vale Rd., Weybridge, Surrey, England KT13 9NS. Weybridge 54511. Umbrella organization for the small craft industry. Members are companies. Affiliates: Association of British Sailmakers, Association of Brokers and Yacht Agents, Marine Engine and Equipment Manufacturers Association, Marine Trades Association. Compiles statistics. Conducts research. Provides seminars, trade shows. Publishes statistics, handbooks.

451. Society of Small Craft Designers. V195 Fontenoy E., Boyne City MI 49712. (616) 582-2924. Association of professionals and companies. Conducts research. Provides management counsel, seminars, trade shows. Publishes handbooks.

452. Yacht Architects and Brokers Association. Seven Riverside Dr., Pembroke MA 02359. (617) 826-9940. Association of professionals and companies. Provides management counsel.

11. The Home Amusements Industry

SIC Codes: 3942, 3944, 5092, 5945.

Enterprises manufacturing, selling, and/or servicing toys and products for hobby or play indoors.

Directories

453. American Stamp Dealers Association. *ASDA Membership Directory*. Lake Success NY. Annual. Free. Gives name, address, phone, type of business or activity in which engaged, specialties, and year became member. Arrangement is alphabetical with specialty and geographical index.

454. Association of Crafts and Creative Industries. *ACCI Directory*. Zanesville OH. Annual. $10. Lists over 1500 company members giving name, address, phone, and type of business or activity involvement. Arrangement is alphabetical.

455. British Toy and Hobby Manufacturers Association. *BTHMA Directory*. London, England. Annual. $4.50. Lists members giving name, address, and company. Arrangement is alphabetical.

456. Canadian Toy Manufacturers Association. *Toy and Decorative Fair Directory*. Kleinburg, Canada. Annual. $10. Lists exhibitors at the annual Canadian trade show of the association giving name, address, and phone. Arrangement is alphabetical. Former title: *Canadian Toy Fair Directory*.

457. International Federation of Stamp Dealers' Association. *IFSDA Directory*. London. Annual. Lists name, address, phone, and staff of national affiliates, federation staff and committees.

458. Model Railroad Industry Association. *MRIA Membership Roster*. Cedarburg WI. Annual. Membership. Lists members giving company name, address, phone, key executives, and products. Alphabetical.

459. *Official Toy Trade*. New York: Edgell. Annual. $10. Lists manufacturers, manufacturer's reps, wholesalers, character licensing organization, and trade associations giving name, address, phone, key personnel, and product information. Arrangement is classified by type of activity then alphabetical for manufacturers, geographical for reps, and by product or service for others. Product and trade name indexes. Former title: *Toys, Hobbies, and Crafts Directory*.

460. *Suppliers of Craft Materials*. Toronto, Canada: Ontario Crafts Council. Biennial. $2. Lists Canadian manufacturers, importers, wholesalers, and retailers giving name, address, phone, type of business, products, and availability of catalog. Arrangement is geographical and by type of business.

461. Toy Manufacturers of America. *American International Toy Fair Directory*. New York. Annual. $5. Lists exhibitors at the annual association trade show giving name, address, and phone. Arrangement is by fair site location with company and product index.

Management

462. American Entrepreneurs Association. *Hobby Shop*. Los Angeles, 1984. 116p. $45. Guide to establishing and operating a small business. Legal, management, marketing, operations, and financial procedures. Supplier addresses and a bibliography. Looseleaf format.

463. _____. *Shell Shop*. Los Angeles, 1984. 119p. $39.50. Guide to establishing and operating a small business. Legal, management, marketing, operations, and financial procedures. Supplier addresses and a bibliography. Looseleaf format.

464. _____. *Stuffed Toy Animals Vending*. Los Angeles, 1984. 100p. $24.50. Guide to establishing and operating a small business. Legal, management, marketing, operations, and financial procedures. Supplier addresses and a bibliography. Looseleaf format.

465. Hobby Industries of America. *Retailer's Guide to Sales and Profits*. Elmwood Park NJ, 1981. 44p. $20. How to operate a hobby store. Bibliography of trade publications.

Industry

466. Canada. Statistics Canada. *Sporting Goods and Toy Industries*. Ottawa, Canada. Annual. $21. Statistics on establishments, employees, salaries and wages, production, and costs.

467. FIND/SVP. *Toy and Game Industry*. Bethesda MD: National Standards Association, 1980. 107p. $550. Analyzes industry trends, provides financial and production data, and profiles leading companies in the industry in the United States.

468. Hobby Industries of America. *Annual Size of Industries Report*. Elmwood NJ. Annual. Membership. Charts indicating sales performance currently and for the previous five years of various types of models, e.g. miniatures, trains, planes; crafts, e.g. needlecrafts, decoupage, stained glass, and other categories. Overall analysis of industry sales.

469. ICC Business Ratios. *Toy Industry*. London. Annual. $300. Compares individual and average performance of major companies in the United Kingdom. Provides three-year financial data and ratios.

470. Key Note Publications Ltd. *Toys and Games,* 7th ed. London, 1987. 34p. $100. Analyzes industry structure and trends over a five-year span and compares companies in the last three. Financial ratios and future development examined. Market structure and potential for overseas sales reviewed. Bibliography.

471. Toy Manufacturers of America. *Toy Industry Factbook*. New York. Annual. Membership. Statistics on production, imports, sales, and finances.

Market

472. Euromonitor. *Toys and Games Report*. London. 1982. 77p. $225. Examination of the United Kingdom market, its growth and development in the past decade, and its prospects for the 1980s. Data on consumer demand, market share, and retail distribution. Market analysis by product. Over 50 British firms analyzed.

473. NPD Special Industry Services. *Toy Market Index.* Port Washington NY. Annual. The most detailed, current, and comprehensive analysis of the United States market. Consumer survey of sales, brand preferences, purchasing patterns, and other market factors for United States households.

474. U.S. International Trade Commission. *Summary of Trade and Tariff Information: Dolls and Stuffed Toy Animals.* Washington DC. Periodic updates. Analyzes the United States and foreign market and provides country by country statistics on production.

475. _____. *Summary of Trade and Tariff Information: Toys, Games, and Wheel Goods.* Washington DC. Periodic updates. Analyzes the United States and foreign market and provides country by country statistics on production.

Periodicals

476. American Independent Designers Association. *AIDA Newsletter.* Huntsville AL. Semiannual. Membership. Official association publication. News of the association and the industry.

477. American Stamp Dealers Association. *ASDA Newsletter.* Lake Success NY. Monthly. Membership. Official association publication. News of the association and the industry.

478. Association of Crafts and Creative Industries. *ACCI News.* Zanesville OH. Monthly. Membership. Official association publica-

tion. News of the association and the industry.

479. *Craft and Hobby Dealer.* Cheltenham, England: Marom. Bimonthly. $7. British source of news and information on craft and hobby products and retail operations. Special report: "Trade Directory" in each July issue.

480. *Craft and Needlework Age.* Englishtown NY: Hobby Publications. Monthly. $15. For chain, department, and variety store buyers. Emphasis on product information. Articles on merchandising, displays, sales tips, and industry trends. Typical issues contains new product displays in separate sections on crafts, needlework, yarns, quilts, homesewing, and art materials. Special issue: *Hobby Publications Trade Directory* (each June, $25).

481. *Craft Trends.* Norcross GA: Archibald. Monthly. Controlled distribution. Information of craft, needlework, and art materials. Data on consumer trends, merchandising, and new product techniques and applications.

482. *Creative Products News.* Lake Forest IL: Cottage Communications. Monthly. $30. New products for crafts, needlework, art supplies, and miniatures. Special report: "Buyer's Guide" in each October issue.

483. Hobby Industries of America. *Horizons.* Elmwood Park NJ. Monthly. Membership. Official association publication. News and articles of the association, the industry and activities, and hobby shop management and merchandising.

484. *Hobby Merchandiser.* Englishtown NY: Hobby Publications. Monthly. $12. For wholesalers and retailers including chain, department, and variety stores. Articles on products, markets, and merchandising techniques.

485. International Federation of Stamp Dealers' Association. *IFSDA Report*. London. Quarterly. Membership. Official association publication. News of international market, efforts to reduce stamp exchange problems, and local associations.

486. *Miniatures Dealer*. Clifton VA: Boynton. Monthly. $20. Wholesaling and retailing. Store operations, new products, and plans for making miniatures.

487. Miniatures Industry Association of America. *MIAA News*. Elmwood Park NJ. Monthly. Membership. Official association publication. News of the association and the industry.

488. Model Railroad Industry Association. *MRIA Reporter*. Cedarburg WI. Bimonthly. Membership. Official association publication. News of the association and the industry.

489. *Model Retailer*. Clifton VA: Boynton. Monthly. $20. For store owners and wholesalers who market model boats, cars, trains, etc. Store operations, merchandising, and new products. Special reports: "Hobby Industries of America Trade Show" in each January issue; "WRAMS Show" in each April issue; "Toledo Show" in each June issue; "Tools and Supplies Directory" in each August issue; "Distributor Directory" in each September issue; and "Holiday Buying" in each October issue.

490. National Association of Toy Retailers. *Toys International and the Retailer*. London: Batiste. Monthly. $40. Official association publication. News of the British market, merchandising, and products.

491. National Plastercraft Association. *Plastercrafter*. Jeffersonville IN. Bimonthly. Membership. Official association publication. News

and articles on the association, the industry in the United States, products, merchandising. Instructional programs offered.

492. *Playthings*. New York: Geyer-McAllister. Monthly. $18. Principal industry information magazine for the merchandiser of toys, hobbies, and crafts. Sales and promotional techniques, sales and earnings of toy companies, and new products. Special reports: "Hobby Show" in each January issue; "Toy Fair" in each February issue; "Who's Who in Importing" in each November issue. Special issue: *Playthings Directory* (each May, $18). Indexed in *Business Periodicals Index, Predicast F&S Index: United States, Trade and Industry Index*.

493. *Profitable Craft Merchandising*. Peoria IL: PJS. Monthly. $18. Emphasizes new products. Sales promotion, marketing techniques, and store set-ups and operations. Special report: "Craft Supply Directory" in each June issue.

494. Society of Craft Designers. *SCD Newsletter*. Bimonthly. Membership. Official association publication. News of the association and the industry.

495. *Stamp Wholesaler*. Albany OR: Van Dahl. 28 issues. $16.95. Gives market price for individual stamps, news of the trade, and business operations. Information on stamps as an investment.

496. *Toy and Hobby World*. New York: International Thompson Retail. Monthly. $60. Industry news tabloid. Products, merchandising projects, and other industry-related facts and data.

497. *Toys and Games*. Downsview, Canada: Page. Bimonthly. $40. Contains new products, industry trends and developments, and trade shows and events in Canada and the United States. Articles on marketing, retailing, and sales promotion. Features on stores and future toys.

498. *Toys and Games Trader.* Rickmansworth, England: Wheatland. Monthly. $10. Information on home amusements marketing in the United Kingdom. Emphasis on new products. Articles on merchandising, sale promotion, and display. Special issue: *Toys and Games Trader Yearbook* (each July, $5). Incorporating: *Games and Toys.*

Database

499. Association of Crafts and Creative Industries. *Craft Information Database.* Zanesville OH. Updated irregularly. Membership. News. Online service enhancing the interchange of information on individuals and products within the industry in the United States.

Bibliographies/Indexes

500. Craven, Robert R., comp. *Billiards, Bowling, Table Tennis, Pinball, and Video Games: A Bibliographic Guide.* Westport CT: Greenwood, 1983. 163p. $29.95. Bibliography for persons interested in playing, studying, and researching these games. Each chapter introduced by an essay placing game in historical perspective. Business and industry aspects not emphasized, but, for an in-depth examination of the games, this bibliography is the place to start. Author-name index and guide to associations.

501. Mergen, Bernard. *Play and Playthings: A Reference Guide.* Westport CT: Greenwood, 1982. 281p. $35. Bibliographical essays on play, in general, and all types of playthings. Emphasis is on leisure aspects more than on industry. List of publications mentioned follows essays. Author, title, subject index.

Associations

502. American Independent Designers Association. 605 Davis Circle, Huntsville AL 35801. (205) 536-2532. Association of companies that design and market cross stitch needle art products. Provides management counsel, seminars. Publishes standards, periodical.

503. American Stamp Dealers Association. Five Dakota Dr., Suite 102, Lake Success NY 11042. (516) 775-3600; (800) 645-3826. Association of individuals. Provides seminars, trade shows. Publishes directory, periodical.

504. Association of Crafts and Creative Industries. 1100-H Brandywine Blvd., Zanesville OH 43701. (614) 452-4541. Association of professionals and companies in the craft supply industry. Provides seminars, trade shows. Maintains database. Publishes directory, periodical. Former name: Mid-America Hobby-Craft Association.

505. British Toy and Hobby Manufacturers Association. 80 Camberwell Rd., London, England SK10 4TJ. (01) 701-7271. Association of individuals. Compiles statistics. Provides management counsel, seminars, trade shows. Publishes directory.

506. Canadian Toy Manufacturers Association. P.O. Box 294, Kleinberg, Ontario, Canada L0J 1C0. (416) 851-1118. Association of companies. Publishes directory.

507. Ceramic Arts Federation International. P.O. Box 6334, 2503 E.

Westport Dr., Anaheim CA 92806. (714) 533-3820. Association of companies and individuals manufacturing, marketing, and instructing in the producing of ceramic products. Provides management counsel, seminars, trade shows.

508. Craft Hobby and Industry Association. 89 Saint Nicholas Market, Bristol, England BS1 1JG. (207) 229-0405. Association of companies. Compiles statistics. Provides management counsel, seminars. Affiliated with the Hobby Industries of America.

509. Game Manufacturers Association. 3304 Carter Ln., Piano TX 75023. (214) 242-1516. Association of companies that produce manual and electronic adventure games.

510. Greater Toy Center. 200 Fifth Ave., New York NY 10010. (212) 675-4633. A showroom operation for toy manufacturers and sales representatives.

511. Hobby Industries of America. 319 E. 54th St., Elmwood Park NJ 07407. (201) 794-1133. Association of individuals and companies manufacturing, wholesaling, retailing, and publishing in the hobby field. Compiles statistics. Provides management counsel, seminars, trades shows. Publishes handbooks, directory, periodical.

512. International Federation of Stamp Dealers' Association. 27 John Adams St., London, England WC2N 6HZ. (01) 930-8333. Federation of 27 national associations. Maintains library. Publishes handbooks, directory, periodical.

513. Miniatures Industry Association of America. 319 E. 54th St., Elmwood Park NJ. (201) 794-1133. Association of companies manufacturing one inch to one foot furniture, dolls, and home reproductions. Provides management counsel, semi-

nars, trade shows. Publishes periodical.

514. Model Railroad Industry Association. P.O. Box 72, Cedarburg WI 53012. (414) 377-3078. Association of companies. Provides management counsel, seminars, trade shows. Publishes directory, periodical.

515. National Association of Doll and Stuffed Toy Manufacturers. 605 Third Ave., 18th Floor, New York NY 10158. (212) 916-9200. Association of companies organized for the purpose of collective bargaining with employees. Provides management counsel.

516. National Association of Toy Retailers. 20 Knave Wood Rd., Kemsing, Sevenoaks, Kent, England TN15 6RH. (09) 592-2628. Association of companies. Provides seminars. Publishes periodical.

517. National Plastercraft Association. 1435 Youngstown Center, Jeffersonville IN 47130. (812) 283-8112. Association of manufacturers, wholesalers, and retailers of plaster products for the hobby industry in the United States. Provides management counsel, seminars, trade shows. Publishes handbooks, directory, periodical. Former name: Plastercraft Association.

518. Non-Powder Gun Products Association. 200 Castlewood Dr., North Palm Beach FL 33408. (305) 842-4100. Association of companies producing air guns and ammunition. Provides trade shows.

519. Society of Craft Designers. P.O. Box 7744, Columbus GA 31908. (404) 327-1522. Association of designers of hobby products and other individuals related to hobby product design. Conducts research. Provides management counsel, seminars. Publishes periodical.

520. Toy Manufacturers of Amer-

ica. 200 Fifth Ave., New York NY 10010. (212) 675-1141. Association of companies. Compiles and publishes statistics. Provides trade shows. Publishes directory.

521. Toy Wholesalers Association

of America. 66 E. Main St., Morristown NJ 08057. (609) 234-9155. Association of companies. Former name: National Toy Wholesalers Association.

12. The Gift Industry

SIC Codes: 2679, 2771, 3199, 3229, 3231, 3499, 3961, 5199, 5947, 5961, 7359.

Enterprises manufacturing and selling products or operating services for individual and/or group celebrations or commemorations.

Directories

522. *Canadian Jewelry and Giftware Directory*. Toronto, Canada: Lloyd. Annual. $37.50. Lists manufacturers, distributors, importers and exporters, and manufacturers' agents throughout Canada giving business name, address, branch offices, phones, telex, and products. Arrangement is alphabetical with product and trade name index.

523. Chicago Giftware Association. *Chicago Market*. Minneapolis MN: Bolger. Semiannual. Free. Lists manufacturers' agent members of association plus product and other news giving name, location in Chicago Merchandise Mart, phone, and tradenames and products handled. Arrangement is alphabetical with product index.

524. Howard, Melanie S., ed. *Greeting Card Industry Directory,* 2nd ed. Washington DC: Greeting Card Association, 1986. 100p. $25. Lists member companies of Greeting Card Association giving name, address, phone, executives, and guide to products and services. Arrangement is alphabetical with product index.

525. *Rep Directory*. New York: Lin Berla Enterprises. Annual. $125. Lists manufacturers' representatives in gift, stationery, tabletop, and housewares trade giving company name, address, phone, contact, territory, number of employees, products handled, and business history data. Arrangement is alphabetical with product, territory, and trade show participation indexes.

526. *Salesman's Guide Nationwide Directory of Gift, Housewares, and Stationery Buyers*. New York: Salesman's Guide. Annual with 2 supplements. $95. Lists over 6,000 large stores or chains giving name, headquarters address, buying office, type of store, number of stores, business volume, executives, and contacts. Arrangement is geographical with alphabetical index.

Management

527. American Entrepreneurs Association. *Balloon Delivery Service*. Los Angeles, 1984. 159p. $29.50. Guide to establishing and operating a small business. Legal, management, marketing, operations, and financial procedures. Supplier addresses and a bibliography. Looseleaf format.

528. _____. *Balloon Vending*. Los Angeles, 1984. 87p. $34.50.

Guide to establishing and operating a small business. Legal, management, marketing, operations, and financial procedures. Supplier addresses and a bibliography. Looseleaf format.

529. _____. *Gift Shop.* Los Angeles, 1984. 115p. $34.50. Guide to establishing and operating a small business. Legal, management, marketing, operations, and financial procedures. Supplier addresses and a bibliography. Looseleaf format.

530. _____. *Hearts, Rainbows and Unicorns Store.* Los Angeles, 1984. 116p. $34.50. Guide to establishing and operating a small business. Legal, management, marketing, operations, and financial procedures. Supplier addresses and a bibliography. Looseleaf format.

531. _____. *Party Goods, Gift Store.* Los Angeles, 1986. 129p. $55. Guide to establishing and operating a small business. Legal, management, marketing, operations, and financial procedures. Supplier addresses and a bibliography. Looseleaf format.

532. Bank of America. *Gift Stores.* San Francisco CA, 1980. 20p. Free. Covers procedures for opening and operating. Includes "Sources for Further Information."

Industry

533. ICC Business Ratios. *Giftware.* London. Annual. $250. Compares individual and average performance of major companies in the United Kingdom. Provides three-year financial data and ratios.

534. Key Note Publications Ltd. *Giftware.* London, 1987. 32p. $100. Analyzes industry structure and trends over a five-year span and compares companies in the last three. Financial ratios and futue development examined. Market structure and potential for overseas sales reviewed. Bibliography.

535. _____. *Greeting Cards,* 5th ed. London, 1987. 34p. $100. Analyzes industry structure and trends over a five-year span and compares companies in the last three. Financial ratios and future development examined. Market structure and potential for overseas sales reviewed. Bibliography.

Market

536. Fairchild Publications. *Tabletop and Giftwares.* New York, 1986. 50p. $15. Analysis of the market for giftware and tabletop accessories.

Periodicals

537. *Gift and Stationery Business.* New York: Gralla. Monthly. $10. For the high-volume retailer. Primarily a news and product information magazine. Articles on store management and operation techniques and people who have been successful. Special report: "Directory of Suppliers" in each September issue. Former title: *Giftware Business.*

538. *Gift Digest.* Dallas TX: Market Place. 5 issues. $15. Industry news and trends, product information, merchandising and sales suggestions. Gift show coverage and trends in wholesale market.

539. *Gift Reporter.* New York: George Little Management. Monthly. Controlled distribution. News reports of gift, tableware, and stationery products and the industry. Emphasis on successful retailing procedures and practices.

540. *Gifts and Decorative Acces-*

ories. New York: Geyer-McAllister. Monthly. $28. For retail store buyers. National and international industry news, market data, and product information. Profiles of retailers and their merchandising methods. Display and promotion tips. Special issue: *Gifts and Decorative Accessories Buyers Directory* (each September, free with subscription). Indexed in *Trade and Industry Index.*

541. *Gifts and Tablewares.* Don Mills, Canada: Southam Communications. 7 issues. $30. Articles on all segments of the Canadian gift, tableware, and accessories trade from manufacturer to retail seller. Emphasizes product news. Domestic and foreign information.

542. *Giftware News.* New York: Talcott Communications. Monthly. $24. News of products for department, gift, stationery, tabletop, and accessory stores. Sales and operation techniques. Each issue contains a special section covering such gift topics as seasonal, tabletop, wedding, etc. Specil report: "Directory" of manufacturers and suppliers in each March issue.

543. Greeting Card Association. *Card News.* Washington DC. Monthly. Membership. News of association, its members, and new products. Some marketing tips.

544. *Greetings Magazine.* New York: Mackay. Monthly. $10. For the greeting card retailer. News of products and styles, merchandising techniques, industry events. Special report: "Buyers Guide," issued irregularly.

545. *Hospital Gift Shop Management.* Van Nuys CA: Creative Age. Monthly. $35. Management, buying, merchandising, financial planning, and shop operations. Examples of hospital-shop interaction and interrelationship.

546. *Party and Paper Retailer.* Stamford CT: 4 Ward. Monthly. Controlled distribution. For the retailer of paper and plastic party goods, balloons, candles, favors, and decorations. Primarily a product and industry news magazine.

547. *Selling Christmas Decorations.* Chatham NJ: Edgell. Annual. Controlled distribution. For retail buyers and merchandising managers of natural and artificial Christmas trees, ornaments, and accessories. Product information, promotional tips, and analysis of consumer trends.

548. *Souvenir.* New York: Talcott Communications. Quarterly. Controlled distribution. Began publication October 1987 to all facets of the souvenir industry. Trends, management, marketing, industry profiles, successful operating techniques, and new product data. Covers trade shows.

549. *Souvenirs and Novelties.* Philadelphia PA: Kane Communications. 7 issues. $15. Industry, products, and store operations. Trends, purchasing, and merchandising. Trade show coverage. Special report: "Buyer's Guide" in each August issue.

550. *Special Events.* Los Angeles: Miramar. 9 issues. $25. For professional who provide products and services for parties and "gala events" of all sizes, private or public. Emphasis is on use of products, preparations, the happening, and its management. Features on "successful parties."

551. *Trim-A-Tree Merchandising.* New York: International Thompson Retail. Annual. Controlled distribution. For retailers of artificial Christmas trees, ornaments, and accessories for Christmas. Products, safety standards, government regulations, and merchandising.

Associations

552. Canadian Gift and Tableware Association. 224 Merton St., Toronto, Ontario, Canada M4S 1A1. (416) 497-5771. Association of manufacturers, importers, wholesalers, and retailers.

553. Gift Association of America. 1511 K St., N.W., Suite 716, Washington DC 20005. (202) 638-6080. Association of retailers and wholesalers. Provides seminars. Former name: Gift and Decorative Accessories Association of America.

554. Giftware Association. Saint Dunstan's House, 2-4 Carey Lane, London, England EC2V 8AA. (01) 606-0871. Association of companies and individuals. Affiliated with the British Jewelry and Giftware Federation which compiles statistics and publishes periodicals and reports.

555. Greeting Card Association. 1350 New York Ave., N.W., Suite 615, Washington DC 20005. (202) 393-1778. Association of companies. Publishes directory, periodical. Former name: National Association of Greeting Card Publishers.

556. National Tabletop Association. 41 Madison Ave., Suite 7D, New York NY 10010. (212) 481-3830. Association of manufacturers and distributors of decorative table gift accessories. Provides seminars.

557. Souvenir and Novelty Trade Association. 401 N. Broad St., Suite 226, Philadelphia PA 19108. (215) 925-9744. Association of companies and individuals. Compiles statistics. Conducts research. Provides management counsel, seminars, trade shows.

13. The Amateur Photography Industry

SIC Codes: 3861, 5043, 5946, 7384, 7699.

Enterprises manufacturing, selling, and/or servicing products for personal photography.

Management

558. American Entrepreneurs Association. *One Hour Photo Processing Lab.* Los Angeles, 1987. 188p. $55. Guide to establishing and operating a small business. Legal, management, marketing, operations, and financial procedures. Supplier addresses and a bibliography. Looseleaf format.

559. Bank of America. *Independent Camera Shops.* San Francisco CA, 1974. 16p. $2. Covers procedures for opening and operating. Includes "Sources for Further Information."

Industry

560. ICC Business Ratios. *Photographic Industry.* London. Annual. $250. Compares individual and average performance of major companies in the United Kingdom. Provides three-year financial data and ratios.

561. Key Note Publications Ltd. *Photography.* London, 1986. 36p.

$100. Analyzes industry structure and trends over a five-year span and compares companies in the last three. Financial ratios and future development examined. Market structure and potential for overseas sales reviewed. Bibliography.

562. Photo Marketing Association International. *Cost of Doing Business Survey.* Jackson MI. Annual. $60. Survey of photo retailers and photo finishers. Provides statistics and operating ratio data.

563. _____. *PMA Industry Trends Report.* Jackson MI. Annual. $60. Analysis of the worldwide photographic equipment and supply industry. Production and distribution statistics.

564. *PTN Photographic Industry Market Review.* Woodbury NY: PTN. Annual. $300. Analysis of size, structure, and growth rate of industry. Survey of economic indicators, distribution patterns, consumer trends, and impact of new products.

Market

565. Euromonitor. *Photography Report.* London. 1982. 68p. $295. Examination of the United Kingdom market, its growth and development in the past decade, and its prospects for the 1980s. Data on consumer demand, market share, and retail distribution. Video, dry film, and other new technologies analyzed. Market analysis by product.

566. FIND/SVP. *Worldwide Amateur Photography Market.* Bethesda MD: National Standards Association, 1981. 63p. $400. Forecasts outlook for cameras and photoproducts to consumers in all regions of the world. Assesses new technologies and impact of home video and dry film techniques. Estimates shipments, exports, and laboratory needs.

567. Photo Marketing Association International. *Consumer Photographic Survey.* Jackson MI. Annual. Membership. Survey of consumer attitudes, habits, and intentions on photography purchasing. Statistics on sales and consumer spending. Graphic format.

568. U.S. International Trade Commission. *Summary of Trade and Tariff Information: Photographic Equipment, Supplies, and Recording Media.* Washington DC. Periodic updates. Analyzes the United States and foreign market and provides statistics on production of the product.

Periodicals

569. *Photo Business.* New York: Billboard. Monthly. $40. For the retail photo and video store market. Articles on products, industry trends, and merchandising.

570. *Photo Lab Management.* Santa Monica CA: PLM. Monthly. $8. News and articles on products and processes. Management tips.

571. Photo Marketing Association International. *Photo Marketing.* Jackson MI. Monthly. $12. Official association publication. Studies and reports on marketing trends. Management information for finishers and retailers. Merchandis-

ing tips. Indexed in *Predicasts F&S Index: United States.*

572. *Photo Trader.* London: Henry Greenwood. 26 issues. $40. British photography and camera store magazine. News of products, processes, the industry, and store operations.

573. *Photographic Processing.* Woodbury NY: PTN. Monthly. Controlled distribution. For firms engaged in photofinishing. Emphasizes products and processes. Articles on management, marketing, and industry trends.

574. *Photographic Trade News.* Woodbury NY: PTN. Semimonthly. $6. For retailers and finishers serving the amateur photographer. News of the industry, products, and firms. Tips and examples on management and merchandising. Special reports: "Forecast" in each January issue and "State of the Industry" in each September issue. Special issue: *Photographic Trade News Master Buying Guide and Directory* (each February, $10).

575. *Photovideo.* Toronto, Canada: Maclean Hunter. 9 issues. $41. For photo retailers and processors, video distributors and retailers, professional photographers, and commercial and industry video producers. News of industry developments, new technology, and products. Features on photography and video merchandising, professional techniques, and foreign products and competition. Statistics on production, sales, and trends. Special issue: *Photovideo Directory* (each May, $20).

Associations

576. British Photographic Industry Limited. 273-287 Regent St., London, England W1V 5DG. (01)

629-8543. Association of companies manufacturing audio and video tapes and discs. Compiles statistics.

577. International Minilab Association. 222 S. Elm St., Greensboro NC 27401. (919) 273-5897. Association of photofinishing companies. Compiles statistics. Conducts research. Provides management counsel, seminars, trade shows.

578. National ·Association of Photo Equipment Technicians. 3000 Picture Place, Jackson MI 49201. (517) 788-8100. Association of individuals involved in camera equipment repair. Division of the Photo Marketing Association International.

579. National Association of Photographic Manufacturers. 600 Mamaroneck St., Harrison NY 10528. (914) 698-7603. Association of companies manufacturing photographic film image equipment, and supplies. Compiles statistics. Provides seminars.

580. Photo Marketing Association International. 3000 Picture Place, Jackson MI 49201. (517) 788-8100. Association of individuals, retail stores, and companies. Compiles statistics. Conducts research. Provides management counsel, seminars, trade shows. Maintains library. Publishes handbooks, statistics, directory, periodicals. Former name: Master Photo Dealers' and Finishers' Association.

581. Photographic Manufacturers and Distributors Association. 866 United National Plaza, Suite 436, New York NY 10017. (212) 688-3520. Association of companies manufacturing cameras and photographic equipment. Provides seminars. Former name: Photographic Merchandising and Distributing Association.

14. The Musical Instrument Industry

SIC Codes: 3931, 5099, 5199, 5736, 7699.

Enterprises manufacturing, selling, and servicing equipment and accessories for the playing of music.

Directories

582. *Canadian Music Directory.* West Hill, Canada: Lloyd. Annual. $30. Canadian manufacturers, importers, exporters, agents, wholesalers, and servicers of musical instruments and home audiovideo products giving name, branch offices, phone and telex number, and products. Arrangement is alphabetical.

Management

583. Erlandson, Ray S. *Starting and Managing a Small Retail Music Store.* Washington DC: U.S. Government Printing Office, 1970. 81p. Out of Print. Small Business Administration pamphlet. Dated but still valuable as a basic outline for planning, organizing, managing, operating, and marketing.

548. William, Raymond M. *Business of Education for Retail Music Stores.* Chicago: National Association of Music Merchants, 1983. 1v. Membership. For new music store entrepreneurs. Gives information on

the music business, locating, planning, management, and merchandising.

Industry

585. National Association of Music Merchants. *Retail Music Products Industry Report.* Chicago. Annual. Membership. Product and sales statistics for current year.

Market

586. American Music Conference. *Music USA.* Chicago. Annual. $25. Survey of amateur music participation and statistics on sales of music and musical instruments.

Periodicals

587. *Canadian Music Trade.* Toronto, Canada: Norris Publications. Bimonthly. $8. For music retailers. News of instruments, sheet music, recordings, accessories, trends, and successful operations. Emphasizes store merchandising and management.

588. *Music and Sound Retailer.* Port Washington NY: Retailer. Monthly. $18. For the retailer of electronic musical instruments and sound reinforcing equipment. Emphasizes retail management techniques. News, surveys, dealer profiles, and merchandising tips.

589. *Music Trades Magazine.* Englewood NJ: Music Trades. Monthly. $12. For retailers of musical instruments. Articles on products, merchandising, and store operations. Data on industry trends and production. Special issue: *Music Trades Magazine Purchaser's Guide to the Music Industry* (each October, included in subscription). Indexed in *Music Index, Predicasts F&S Index: United States.*

590. *Musical Merchandise Review.* Chestnut Hill MA: Larkin-Pluznick-Larkin. Monthly. $24. Primarily a musical instrument product promotion magazine. Articles on merchandising and product promotion. Data on industry activities and trends.

591. National Association of Music Merchants. *NAMM Music Retailer News.* Carlsbad CA. 6 issues. Membership. Association and industry news, retailing suggestions, and new product information. Data on trends and purchasing patterns.

Associations

592. Association of Music Industries. 62 Park View, Hatch End, Pinner, Middlesex, England HA5 4LN. (01) 428-4700. Association of companies manufacturing, wholesaling, and importing musical instruments, accessories, and amplification equipment. Provides seminars. Former name: Association of Musical Instrument Industries.

593. Guitar and Accessories Music Marketing Association. 135 W. 29th St., New York NY 10001. (212) 564-0251. Association of com-

panies manufacturing stringed musical instruments other than piano and band instruments. Former names: National Association of Musical Merchandise Manufacturers; Guitar and Accessories Manufacturers of America.

594. Music Distributors Association. 135 W. 29th St., New York NY 10001. (212) 564-0251. Association of suppliers and distributors of musical instruments, sheet music, and accessories. Former name: National Association of Musical Merchandise Wholesalers.

595. Music Industries Association of Canada. 415 Yonge St., Tenth Fl., Toronto, Ontario, Canada M5B 2E7. (416) 598-7737. Association of manufacturers, distributors, and retailers of music, musical instruments, and sound recordings.

596. Music Trades Association. P.O. Box 249, London, England W4 5EX. (01) 994-7592. Association of companies in the musical instrument, sheet music, and audio and video hardware and software industries. Provides seminars, trade shows.

597. National Association of Band Instrument Manufacturers. 7019 30th Ave., Kenosha WI 53141. (414) 658-1644. Association of companies.

598. National Association of Electronic Keyboard Manufacturers. 1600 Royal St., Jasper IN 47540. (812) 482-1600. Association of companies. Former name: National Association of Electronic Organ Manufacturers.

599. National Association of Music Merchants. 5140 Avenide Encinas, Carlsbad CA 92008. (619) 438-8001. Association of retailers, suppliers, and manufacturers of musical instruments and sheet music. Provides seminars, trade shows. Publishes statistics, periodical.

600. National Association of School Music Dealers. 317 E. Walnut, Springfield MO 65806. (417) 866-1986. Association of retail stores and companies selling instruments and sheet music to and servicing the education market.

601. National Council of Music Importers and Exporters. 135 W. 29th St., New York NY 10001. (212) 564-0251. Association of companies importing and/or exporting musical instruments and sheet music. Provides management counsel. Former name: National Association of Music Importers.

602. Piano Manufacturers Association International. 15080 Beltwood Parkway, E., Suite 108, Dallas TX·75244. (214) 241-8957. Association of companies. Compiles statistics. Former name: National Piano Manufacturers Association.

15. The Recreation/Entertainment School Industry

SIC Codes: 7911, 7999.

Enterprises providing instruction and/or training for amateurs interested in developing skills for participating in recreation and entertainment activities.

Directories

603. American Sail Training Association. *Sail Training Ships and Programs Directory*. Newport RI. Biennial. $8. Each listing gives name of vessel, statistics, homeport, waters sailed, season, contact, and cost. Sections for fulltime and part-time service. Arrangement is alphabetical in each. "Fleet in Review" chart gives number of trainees, primary use, length, and rig for each ship.

604. Council on Hotel, Restaurant, and Institutional Education. *U.S. and International Directory of Schools*. University Park PA, 1985. 64p. $5. Lists both private and public secondary and post-secondary schools giving names and address. For Council members lists areas of study, certificates or degrees offered, and name of contact. Arrangement is geographical.

605. Incorporated Society of Musicians. *Professional Register of Private Teachers of Music*. London. Annual. $20. Membership directory giving name, address, phone, and specialization. Arrangement is alphabetical.

606. International Association of Cooking Professionals. *IACP Directory of Institutional Members*. Washington DC. Annual. Free. Directory of cooking schools worldwide giving name, address, phone, staff, and specialization. Arrangement is alphabetical with geographical index.

607. International Dance-Exercise Association. *Industry Directory*. San Diego CA. Annual. Membership. Lists individual and business members giving name, address, and phone. Arrangement is alphabetical with geographical index.

608. *International Directory of Modeling and Talent Agencies and Schools*. New York: Peter Glenn Publications. Annual. $25. Worldwide listing by name, address, phone, name of owner or manager, and whether school, agencies, or both. Arrangement is geographical.

609. National Association of Sailing Instructors and Sailing Schools. *Directory of American Sailing Schools*. Middletown NJ. Biennial. Free. Each listing gives name, address, phone, and types of courses and boats. Arrangement is geographical.

610. Smith, Karen J., ed. *Informed Performer's Directory of Instruction for the Performing Arts*. New York: Avon Books, 1985. 184p. $9.95. New

York oriented handbook about instruction offered in 450 selected institutions outside of higher education. Lists programs for acting, comedy, dancing, musical, sports, etc. Details on location, programs, facilities, class size, fees, sex composition, staff, and scholarships. Arrangement by field with institution index.

611. United States Professional Tennis Association. *USPTA Directory.* Wesley Chapel FL. Annual. Membership. Members giving name, address, and phone. Arrangement is alphabetical with division membership listing. Includes association by-laws, list of sanctioned tournaments, and calendar of events.

612. Wasserman, Steven R., ed. *Lively Arts Information Directory,* 2nd ed. Detroit MI: Gale Research, 1985. 1040p. $165. Compendium of addresses of agencies, schools, programs, publications, and awards in the performing arts giving name, address, date, and specialty. Lists non-degree dance, music, and theater schools in the United States and Canada. Arrangement is geographical with alphabetical name index.

Management

613. American Entrepreneurs Association. *Windsurfing School.* Los Angeles, 1984. 113p. $34.50. Establishing and operating a small business. Legal, management, marketing, operations, and financial procedures. Supplier addresses and a bibliography. Looseleaf format.

614. Farrell, Charles. *How to Operate a Successful Dance Studio.* New York, Gordon, 1986. 55p. $79.95. Procedures, forms, and management tips.

615. National Association of Sail-

ing Instructors and Sailing Schools. *NASISS/School Accreditation & Student Certification.* Middletown NJ, 1987. 14p. Membership. Procedures and forms.

616. _____. *NASISS/School Administrator's Manual.* Middletown NJ, 1987. 1v. Membership. History of the association, accreditation, standards, programs, procedures, and reports. Looseleaf format.

617. Zima, Marie. *Dance Studio: Business Managing for Aerobics, Dance, and Gymnastic Teachers.* Jefferson NC: McFarland, 1987. 140p. $13.95. How-I-did-it handbook on locating, rental, promotion, marketing, scheduling, teaching, finances, and pitfalls. Index.

Industry

618. Goeldner, Charles R. and Manire, Jim. *Ski School Survey.* Boulder CO: University of Colorado Bureau of Business Research, 1985. 57p. Controlled distribution. For the National Ski Areas Association. Survey of members with analysis and statistics.

Periodicals

619. Accordian Teachers' Guild. *ATG Bulletin.* Valparaiso IN. Monthly. Membership. Official association publication. News of compositions, performance, people, and the association.

620. Aerobics and Fitness Association of America. *Aerobics and Fitness.* Sherman Oaks CA. 9 issues. Membership. Official association publication. News of the association, people, the industry, and certification.

621. American Aerobics Association. *AAA Newsletter*. Durango CO. Quarterly. Membership. Official association publication. News of the association, people, the industry, and certification.

622. American Bridge Teachers' Association. *ABTA Quarterly Magazine*. Tulsa OK. Quarterly. Membership. Official association publication. News of tournaments, rules, playing techniques, and the association.

623. American Culinary Federation. *Culinary Review*. Saint Augustine FL. Monthly. Membership. Official association publication. News of the industry, events, awards, and people. Articles on apprenticeship programs.

624. American Professional Racquetball Organization. *Teacher's Court*. Scottsdale AZ. Quarterly. Membership. Official professional publication. News of the association, its members, instructional materials, equipment, and events.

625. American Sail Training Association. *Day's Run*. Newport RI. Quarterly. Membership. Articles on vessels, training programs, and events.

626. _____. *Running Free*. Newport RI. Quarterly. Membership. Official association publication. News of the association, its members and vessels, and activities.

627. American Sailing Association. *Affiliated News*. Marina Del Ray CA. Monthly. Membership. Official association publication. News of the association, members, schools, and activities.

628. _____. *Professional Sailing Instructor*. Marina Del Ray CA. Bimonthly. Membership. Articles on developments and trends pertaining to sailing instruction. News of programs and clinics.

629. Association of British Riding

Schools. *Horse World/Pony Express*. Huntingdon, England. Monthly. Membership. Official association publication.

630. Camp Horsemanship Association. *CHA Newsletter*. Lawrence MI. Semiannual. Membership. Official association publication. Articles on instruction, safety, and dealing with youth.

631. Dance Masters of America. *DMA Bulletin*. Wauchula FL. 5 issues. Membership. News of competitions, research, and awards. Articles on techniques and instruction.

632. _____. *DMA Magazine*. Wauchula FL. Bimonthly. Membership. Official association publication. News of the association, people, and studios.

633. Horsemanship Safety Association. *HSA Newsletter*. Lake Placid FL. Quarterly. Membership. Official association publication. News of the association, programs, people, and the industry.

634. Imperial Society of Teachers of Dancing. *Dance*. London. Bimonthly. $10. Official association publication. Articles on all forms of dance, competitions, technique, and the dance world. Indexed in *Magazine Index*.

635. Imperial Society of Teachers of Dancing United States Ballroom Branch. *Imperial Dance Letter*. Warminster PA. Bimonthly. Membership. Official association publication. News of instruction, technique, competitions, courses, and the association.

636. International Association of Cooking Professionals. *Commentary*. Washington DC. Monthly. Membership. Official association publication. News of the industry, events, and people. Articles on certification and apprenticeship programs.

637. International Dance-Exercise Association. *Dance Exercise Today.* San Diego CA. 9 issues. Membership. Official association publication. News of programs, techniques, fitness, products, industry, and members.

638. International Dance Teachers' Association. *Dance Teacher.* Brighton, England. Monthly. $35. Official association publication.

639. National Association of Sailing Instructors and Sailing Schools. *NASISS Newsletter.* Middletown NJ. Quarterly. Membership. Official association publications. News of the association, courses, certification, programs, and events.

640. Professional Association of Diving Instructors. *Dive Industry News.* Santa Ana CA. Quarterly. Membership. Official association publication. News and articles on training, safety, equipment, instruction, and certification. Lists course offerings and calendar of events.

641. Professional Karate Association. *Contact.* Beverly Hills CA. Quarterly. Membership. Official association publication. Reports on developments in the sport and techniques. News of contact karate schools and sporting events. Calendar of events.

642. Professional Skaters Guild of America. *Professional Skater.* Rochester MN. Bimonthly. $12. Official association publication. News of competitions, techniques, training, professionals, and the industry.

643. Roundalab. *Roundalab Journal.* Cresskill NJ. Quarterly. Membership. Official association publication. News of events, dance variations, teaching, teachers, and the association.

644. Society of Roller Skating Teachers of America. *SRSTA Newsletter.* Lincoln NE. Biweekly. Membership. Official association publication. News of the association, the industry, teaching, competitions, and employment.

645. Speed Coaches Association. *Speed Newsletter.* Lincoln NE. Monthly. Membership. Official association publication. News of training programs, rules, competitions, training, and seminars.

646. United States Fencing Coaches Association. *Swordmaster.* New York. Quarterly. Membership. Official association publication. News and articles on instruction, technique, events, and international fencing activities.

647. United States Professional Tennis Association. *Advantage Magazine.* Wesley Chapel FL. Bimonthly. Membership. Emphasis on tennis instruction. Profiles of professionals and instructors. News of new equipment, clinics, and competitions.

648. _____. *USPTA Newsletter.* Wesley Chapel FL. Bimonthly. Membership. Official association publication. News of the association, the industry, and events.

649. United States Professional Tennis Registry. *Tennispro.* Hilton Head Island SC. Bimonthly. Membership. Official association publication. Focus on programs and techniques for teaching tennis. Profiles of teaching pros. News and features about rule changes, new equipment, and job opportunities. Calendar of clinics, testing, and competitions.

650. United States Ski Coaches Association. *American Ski Coach.* Park City UT. Bimonthly. Membership. Official Association publication. News of programs, certification, rules, technique, events, competitive skiing, health, and safety.

651. _____. *USSCA Journal.*

Park City UT. Quarterly. Membership. Official association publication. Articles on coaching, skiing techniques, training, and school organization.

652. Wilderness Education Association. *Graduate Newsletter.* Macomb IL. Semiannually. Membership. Official association publication. News of graduates of the Leadership Training Program, courses and programs, and instruction.

Associations

653. Accordian Teachers' Guild. 148 Shorewood Dr., Valparaiso IN 46383. (219) 465-1236. Association of teachers. Conducts research. Publishes periodical.

654. Aerobics and Fitness Association of America. 15250 Ventura Blvd., #310, Sherman Oaks CA 91403. (818) 905-0040. Association of teachers, professionals, and enthusiasts. Compiles statistics. Conducts research. Provides seminars. Publishes handbooks, periodical. Certifies instructors.

655. American Academy of Teachers of Singing. 75 Bank St., New York NY 10014. (212) 242-5744. Association of teachers. 30 to 40 members.

656. American Aerobics Association. 6317 Florida Rd., Durango CO 81301. (303) 247-4109. Association of certified teachers. Conducts research. Publishes periodical. Certifies instructors.

658. American Culinary Federation. P.O. Box 3466, Saint Augustine FL 32084. (904) 824-4468. Association of chefs. Provides seminars. Publishes periodical. Certifies apprenticeship programs.

659. American Professional Racquetball Organization. 5089 N. Granite Reef Rd., Scottsdale AZ 85253. (602) 945-0143. Association of teachers and others who derive their income from racquet sports. Provides seminars. Publishes handbooks, periodical. Certifies instructors.

660. American Sail Training Association. Newport Harbor Center, 365 Thomas St., Newport RI 02840. (401) 846-1775. Association of operators of deepwater schools. Compiles statistics. Provides seminars. Publishes handbooks, directory, periodicals.

661. American Sailing Association. 13922 Marquesas Way, Marina Del Ray CA 90292. (213) 822-7171. Association of schools, instructors, and students. Provides management counsel, seminars. Publishes standards, handbooks, periodicals. Certifies instructors, programs.

662. American Ski Teachers of Natur Tecknik. P.O. Box 34, Marshall Creek PA 18335. (717) 223-0730. Association of certified ski instructors. Provides seminars. Certifies instructors.

663. Association of British Riding Schools. 7 Deer Park Rd., Sautry, Huntingdon, Cambs, England PE17 5TT. (048) 783-0443. Provides placement service. Publishes handbooks. Publishes periodical. Certifies programs.

664. Callerlab. P.O. Box 679. Pocono Pines PA 18350. (717) 646-8411. Association of square dance callers in the United States. Provides seminars. Publishes standards, handbooks. Certifies instructors, programs.

665. Camp Horsemanship Association. P.O. Box 188, Lawrence MI 49064. (616) 674-8074. Association of stables, camps, and colleges in the United States and Canada offering riding programs and certified riding instructors. Compiles statistics. Provides seminars. Publishes standards, handbooks, periodical. Certifies programs.

666. Dance Educators of America. P.O. Box 509, Oceanside NY 11572. (516) 766-6615. Association of certified teachers most of whom are associated with American musical theatre. Provides seminars. Certifies instructors.

667. Dance Masters of America. P.O. Box 1117, Wauchula FL 33873. (813) 773-2417. Association of teachers and studio owners. Provides management counsel, seminars. Publishes periodicals. Former name: American National Association, Masters of Dancing.

668. Horsemanship Safety Association. 20 Lakefront Ln., N.W., Lake Placid FL 33852. (813) 465-1365. Association of schools. Conducts research. Publishes handbooks, periodical.

669. Imperial Society of Teachers of Dancing. Euston Hall, Birkenhead St., London, England WC1H 8BE. (01) 837-9967. Association of certified teachers. Provides seminars. Publishes periodical. Certifies instructors.

670. Imperial Society of Teachers of Dancing United States. Ballroom Branch, 68 Centennial Rd., Warminster PA 18974. (215) 674-0340. Association of certified teachers. Provides seminars. Publishes periodical. Certifies instructors.

671. Incorporated Society of Musicians. 10 Stratford Place, London, England W1N 9AE. (01) 629-4413. Association solo performers and private teachers. Provides seminars. Publishes directory.

672. International Academy of Twirling Teachers. 300 S. Wright Rd., Janesville WI 53547. (608) 754-2239. Association of teachers and others affiliated with baton twirling. Provides seminars. Certifies instructors. Former name: National Academy of Accredited Twirling Teachers.

673. International Association of Cooking Professionals. 1001 Connecticut Ave., N.W., Suite 800, Washington DC 20036. (202) 293-7716. Association of school owners, teachers, and professional chefs. Compiles statistics. Conducts research. Provides seminars. Publishes handbooks, directory, periodical. Certifies instructors, programs. Former names: Association of Cooking Schools; International Association of Cooking Schools.

674. International Dance-Exercise Association. 24437 Morena Blvd., 2nd Floor, San Diego CA 92101. (619) 275-2450. Association of certified teachers largely in the United States and Canada. Conducts seminars. Publishes standards, handbooks, directory, periodical. Certifies instructors.

675. International Dance Teachers' Association. 76 Bennett Rd., Bridgton, England BN2 5JL. (027) 368-5652. Association on teachers primarily in the United Kingdom. Compiles statistics. Provides seminars. Publishes periodical.

676. League of Professional Theatre Training Programs. 721 Broadway, Rm. 714, New York NY 10003. (212) 598-4573. Association of non-collegiate schools in the United States.

677. National Association of Sailing Instructors and Sailing Schools. 15 Renier Ct., Middletown NJ 07748. (201) 671-6190. Association of schools in the United States. Provides management counsel, seminars. Publishes standards, handbooks, periodical. Certifies instructors, programs.

678. National Association of Scuba Diving Schools. 641 Willow St., Long Beach CA 90806. (213) 595-5361. Association of schools and stores in the United States. Purpose is cooperative purchasing of equipment and supplies for retailing. Former name: National Association of Skin Diving Schools.

679. National Association of Underwater Instructors. P.O. Box 14650, Montclair CA 91763. (714) 621-5801. Association of certified teachers in the United States. Provides seminars. Maintains library. Certifies instructors.

680. Organization of Professional Acting Coaches and Teachers. 3968 Eureka Dr., Studio City CA 91604. (212) 877-4988. Association of non-academic teachers. Certifies instructors.

681. Patience T'ai Chi Association. 2620 E. 18th St., Brooklyn NY 11235. (212) 332-3477. Association of certified teachers. Provides seminars. Certifies instructors.

682. Professional Association of Diving Instructors. 1243 E. Warner Ave., Santa Ana CA 92705. (714) 540-7234. Association of certified teachers. Provides seminars. Publishes standards, handbooks, periodical. Certifies instructors, programs.

683. Professional Karate Association. 2930 Hutton Dr., Beverly Hills CA 90210. (213) 550-8831. Association of professionals and amateurs. Provides seminars. Publishes standards, handbooks, periodical. Certifies programs.

684. Professional Skaters Guild of America. P.O. Box 5904, Rochester MN 55930. (507) 281-5122. Association of coaches. Provides seminars. Publishes standards, periodical. Certifies instructors.

685. Professional Ski Instructors of America. 5541 Central Ave., Boulder CO 80301. (303) 477-0842. Association certified teachers. Provides management counsel, seminars. Maintains library. Publishes standards. Certifies instructors.

686. Roundalab. 3 Churchill Rd., Cresskill NJ 07626. (201) 568-5857. Association of round dancing teachers. Provides seminars. Publishes standards, handbooks, periodical. Certifies instructors.

687. Society of Roller Skating Teachers of America. 7700 A St., Lincoln NE 68510. (402) 489-8811. Association of certified and apprentice teachers. Provides seminars. Publishes periodical. Certifies instructors through the Roller Skating Rink Operators Association.

688. Speed Coaches Association. P.O. Box 81846, Lincoln NE 68501. (402) 489-8811. Association of certified and apprentice coaches. Provides seminars. Publishes periodical. Certifies coaches through the Roller Skating Rink Operators Association.

689. United States Fencing Coaches Association. P.O. Box 274, New York NY 10159. (212) 532-2557. Association of certified fencing teachers and associates. Provides seminars. Publishes standards, handbooks, periodical. Certifies instructors.

690. United States Professional Tennis Association. P.O. Box 7077, Wesley Chapel FL 34249. (813) 973-3777. Association of professional tennis teachers and college coaches. Provides seminars. Publishes directory, periodicals. Certifies competitions.

691. United States Professional Tennis Registry. P.O. Box 5902, Hilton Head Island SC 29938. (800) 421-6289. Association of certified teachers. Compiles statistics. Provides seminars. Publishes standards, handbooks, periodical. Certifies instructors. Former name: Professional Tennis Registry.

692. United States Ski Coaches Association. P.O. Box 1747, Park City UT 84060. (801) 649-9090. Association of certified coaches. Provides seminars. Publishes handbooks, periodicals. Certifies instructors.

693. Wilderness Education Association. Dept. of Recreation and Park Administration, Western Illinois University, Macomb IL 61455. (309) 298-2209. Service organization preparing wilderness leadership instructors and others in survival skills. Provides seminars. Publishes handbooks, periodical. Certifies instructors.

16. The Entertainment Agency Industry

SIC Codes: 7829, 7922, 7941.

Enterprises managing and booking entertainers and entertainment.

Directories

694. *Artists and Their Agents.* Eastbourne, England: John Offord. Annual. $19.95. Lists theatrical agents, managers, and promoters in Great Britain giving name, address, phone, and clients. Arrangement is alphabetical with client index.

695. Association of Representatives of Professional Athletes. *ARPA Directory.* Century City CA. Annual. Membership. Each listing gives name, address, phone, profession, and names of individuals represented. Arrangement is alphabetical.

696. *Billboard's International Talent and Touring Directory.* New York: Billboard. Annual. $22. Lists talent management and booking agencies and tour-related services worldwide giving name, address, phone, key executives, and services. Arrangement is geographical.

697. *Booking Contacts.* New York: American Music Database. Annual. $40. Lists booking agents, promoters, artist representatives, and organizations contracting regularly for musical performances giving name, address, phone, and spe-

cialization. Arrangement is classified by type of activity.

698. *International Directory of Modeling and Talent Agencies and Schools.* New York: Peter Glenn. Annual. $25. Worldwide listing by name, address, phone, name of owner or manager, and whether school, agency or both. Arrangement is geographical.

699. *Music and Booking Source Directory.* Santa Monica CA: Music & Booking. Annual. $65. Lists locations where live music is booked, agents, promoters plus artists, recording companies, and record and equipment manufacturers giving name, address, and contact and brief data for agencies and companies. Arrangement is classified by activity or product with alphabetical name and geographical indexes.

Management

700. Elliott, Tom. *Clowns, Clients, and Chaos.* Boston MA: Tom Elliott, 1983. 150p. $17.95. Sourcebook to "everything you need to know to start your own talent agency." Personnel advise and experiences of the author. Procedures and forms. Bibliography.

701. Frascogna, Xavier M., and Hetherington, H. Lee. *Successful Artist Management.* New York: Billboard, 1978. 256p. $17.50. Step-by-step examination of the responsibilities of the performing artist manager. Lists and analyzes junctures on the manager's journey to success. Summarizes each major activity and outlines procedures. Index.

702. Fishof, David, and Shapiro, Eugene D. *Putting It on the Line.* New York: Morrow, 1983. 221p. $14.95. "Negotiating secrets, tactics, and techniques of a top sports and entertainment agent." More reminiscences than management information but outlines the functions of the agent in the entertainment industry in today's high-priced entertainer world.

703. Hurst, Walter E. *Managers', Entertainers', and Agents' Book,* 2nd ed. Hollywood CA: Seven Arts, 1980. 92p. $15. Manual of procedures and forms for a prospective or beginning entertainment agent. References and index.

Periodicals

704. Association of Representatives of Professional Athletes. *ARPA-Gram.* Century City CA. 10 issues. Membership. Official association publication. News of negotiations, contracts, legal and financial matters, and the professional sports industry.

705. Association of Talent Agents. *ATA Newsletter.* Los Angeles. Monthly. Membership. Official association publication. News of film and TV negotiations, contracts, legal cases, rulings, and interpretations.

706. International Group of Agents and Bureaus. *GAB Confidential.* Glendora CA. Monthly. Membership. Official association publication. News of the association, events, and public relations.

707. International Theatrical Agents Association. *Bull Sheet.* Dallas TX. Monthly. Membership. Official association publication. News of the association, entertainers, booking, and contracts.

708. National Association of Performing Arts Managers and Agents. *NAPAMA Newsletter.* Philadelphia PA. Quarterly. Membership. Official association publication. News of the industry, contracts, performers, and the association and its members.

Associations

709. Association of Representatives of Professional Athletes. 10000 Santa Monica Blvd., Suite 312, Century City CA 90067. (213) 553-5607. Association of lawyers, CPAS, and professional agents. Compiles statistics. Provides management counsel, seminars. Publishes standards, directory, periodical.

710. Association of Talent Agents. 9255 Sunset Blvd., Suite 318, Los Angeles CA 90069. (213) 274-0628. Association of agents for actors largely on the West Coast. Compiles statistics. Provides seminars. Publishes periodical. Former name: Artist Managers Guild.

711. Entertainment Agents' Association. 18 Charing Cross Rd., London, England WC2H OHR. (01) 240-1724. Association of British agencies and agents.

712. International Group of Agents and Bureaus. 18825 Hilcrest Rd., Glendora CA 91740. (818) 335-5127. Association of speakers bureau in business for more than two years. Computerized directory. Publishes periodical.

713. International Theatrical Agents Association. P.O. Box 25505, Dallas TX 75225. (214) 349-

3025. Association of agencies booking entertainers into hotels, motels, and lounges. Provides seminars. Computerized directory. Publishes periodical.

714. National Association of Performing Arts Managers and Agents. P.O. Box 27539, Philadelphia PA 19118. (215) 233-1161. East Coast emphasis. Provides management counsel, seminars. Publishes periodical.

715. Personal Managers Association. 35 Brompton Rd., London, England SW3 1DE. (01) 581-0084. Association of managers of British entertainers.

17. Show Business

SIC Codes: 7922, 7929, 7999.

Enterprises providing live, professional entertainment in a temporary location for a limited timespan.

Directories

716. American Council for the Arts. *Guide to Corporate Giving,* 4th ed. New York, 1987. 600p. $60. Each listing gives name of corporation, address, foundation name, contact, phone, amount and types of contributions, and criteria and selection process for arts giving. Arrangement is alphabetical with geographical and kind of arts organization/activity supported. Index.

717. *Angels.* New York: Leo Shull. Annual. $150. Investors in show business and motion picture productions. Separate volumes for theatre and film. Each listing gives name, address, amount invested, and names of productions backed. Latest edition 1985.

718. *British Alternative Theatre Directory.* Eastbourne, England: John Offord. Annual. $20. Lists non-tradition, youth, puppet companies, pageants, local arts festivals giving name, address, purpose, contact, and dates. Arrangement is classified by activity with name index.

719. *British Theatre Directory.* Eastbourne, England: John Offord. Annual. $40. Lists performing arts centers and companies, festivals, schools, agents, suppliers, and much more giving name of company, address, phone, and contact. Arrangement is classified by activity/product/service.

720. *Cavalcade of Acts and Attractions.* Nashville TN: Billboard. Annual. $40. Lists touring companies, performing groups, and individual entertainers giving name, address, phone, manager, agent, places played, and nature of the act or show. Arrangement is classified by type of show with cross indexing.

721. Central Opera Service. *Directory of Opera/Musical Theatre Companies and Workshops in the U.S. and Canada.* New York. Annual. $9.25. Each listing gives name, address, phone, artistic director or administrator, auditorium where company or workshop performs with facility statistics, and code system indicating budget classification and type of company or workshop. Arrangement is geographical.

722. *Dance Magazine Performing Arts Directory.* New York: Danad. Annual. $35. Lists dance companies, dancers, mime, schools, agents, and suppliers giving name, address, phone, key personnel, and, for companies, organizational data. Arrangement is by three main categories: dance, music, resources then classified by activity.

723. Epstein, Lawrence S., ed. *Guide to Theatre in America.* London: Macmillan; New York: Collier

Macmillan, 1985. 443p. $60. Not as "comprehensive" as the author states, but a broad list of theatre companies, theaters, suppliers, support agencies, and people. Each listing gives name and address and, for organizations, contact and description. Arrangement is classified by type of organization or activity and then geographically. Name index but no organization access.

724. *Handel's National Directory for Performing Arts Organizations,* 4th ed. Dallas TX: INFOMART, 1987. 1070p. $225. Lists groups, theaters, and other facilities in the United States giving name, address, phone, contact name, and organizational information. Arrangement is geographical by state with index by type of organization or facility.

725. Institute of Outdoor Drama. *Outdoor Drama List.* Chapel Hill NC. Annual. Free. Theatrical companies divided into four sections: paid cast, partially paid, unpaid, and regional. Each listing gives name, executives, address, phone, and season. Arrangement is geographical.

726. _____. *Outdoor Drama Theatre.* Chapel Hill NC. Irregular. Free. Series of single-sheet bulletins with photo, amphitheatre description and diagram, play summary, history, address, and phone for permanent dramatic pageants in the United States. Looseleaf format.

727. *International Music and Opera Guide.* London: Tantivy; New York: Zoetrope. Annual. $12.95. Lists classical music and opera professional companies, festivals, schools, stores, periodicals, and organizations giving name, address, contact, and, for many, organizational and activity information. Arrangement is classified then geographical.

728. Kullman, Colby H., and Young, William C. *Theatre Companies of the World.* Westport CT: Greenwood, 1986. 2v. $95. Lists permanent groups of performers worldwide giving name, address, and descriptive history of the company and its productions. Arrangement is alphabetical under country with countries arranged by continents. Bibliography of readings and company and personal name index.

729. *Motion Picture, TV and Theatre Directory.* Tarrytown NY: Motion Picture Enterprises. Semiannual. $10. Lists companies providing services to the motion picture, television, and theater production industry. Paid listing giving name, address, and phone. Arrangement is classified by type of service, then geographical.

730. *New York on Stage.* New York: Theatre Development Fund. Annual. $3. New York theatre production companies and theaters give name, address, phone, and, for companies, description. Divided into company and theater sections. Arrangement is alphabetical under each.

731. Opera America. *Profile: Opera America and the Professional Opera Companies.* Washington DC. Annual. $11. Lists American companies giving name, address, phone, budget, attendance, program and audition policy, ticket information, and key executives.

732. *Regional Theatre Directory: A National Guide to Employment in Regional Theatres.* Dorset VT: Dorset Theatre Festival and Colony House/Theatre Directories. Annual. $10. Lists theatre companies in the United States. For professionals and students seeking employment. Each listing gives name, address, union, type of contract and employment, history, type of productions, season, and facilities.

733. *Summer Theatre Directory.* New York: Leo Shull. Publications. Annual. $10. Lists theatre companies in the United States and Canada giving name, address, contact, casting policy, production data, and employment opportunities. Arrangement is geographical.

734. *Summer Theatre Directory: A National Guide to Summer Employment for Professionals and Students.* Dorset VT: Dorset Theatre Festival and Colony House/Theatre Directories. Annual. $10. Lists theatre companies in the United States giving name, address, union, type of contract and employment, history, type of productions, and facilities.

735. *Theatre Profiles: The Illustrated Guide to America's Nonprofit Professional Theatres.* New York: Theatre Communications Group. Biennial. $18.95. Each listing gives name, address, phone, staff, productions for the previous two years, and key production staff. Arrangement is alphabetical with personnel name index. Articles on current theatre topics.

Management

736. Blims, Michael, and Sproat, Ron. *More Dialing, More Dollars: 12 Steps to Successful Telemarketing.* New York: American Council for the Arts, 1986. 94p. $7.95. Procedures and forms for organizing and conducting an in-house campaign for contributors, members, and/or subscribers.

737. Brownrigg, W. Grant. *Effective Corporate Fundraising.* New York: American Council for the Arts, 1982. 162p. $12.95. Strategies for conducting campaigns. Procedures and forms.

738. Elder, Eldon. *Will It Make a Theatre.* New York: Off Off Broadway Alliance, 1979. 208p. $12.95. Guide to finding, renovating, financing, and bringing up to code a nontraditional performing space. Diagrams, charts, regulations, and an index.

739. Ennis, Philip H., and Bonin, John. *Understanding the Employment of Actors.* Washington DC: National Endowment for the Arts, 1977. 31p. Free. Condensation of a more detailed report. Concentrates on Actors' Equity Association, its role, and its contract negotiations and requirements. Recommends research on employment, unemployment, and earnings in the theatre.

740. Farber, Donald C. *Producing Theatre: A Comprehensive Legal and Business Guide.* New York: Limelight, 1987. 382p. $19.95. Legal aspects of obtaining a property, production, the producing company, financing, contracts, movie rights, and road tours. One-third devoted to sample legal forms. Bibliographic references and index.

741. Foundation for the Extension and Development of the American Professional Theatre. *Challenge of Change.* New York, 1987. 170p. $14.95. Papers presented at the 15th Annual National Conference of FEDAPT. Theme was centered on the developing of management strategies in the performing arts at a time of crisis. The whole spectrum of change is examined, but financial change is featured. Particularly appropriate for the current crisis.

742. _____. *FEDAPT Box Office Guidelines,* 2nd ed. New York, 1980. 66p. $2. Procedures and forms for organization, ticket sales, accounting, and management.

743. _____. *FEDAPT Subscription Guidelines,* 2nd ed. New York, 1977. 66p. $3. Definition, audience, and procedures and forms used by the Actors Theatre of Louisville, Kentucky.

744. _____. *In Art We Trust: The Board of Trustees in the Performing Arts.* New York, 1981. 72p. $5. Proposals and comments at FEDAPT workshops on functions and responsibilities of trustees. Sample by-laws appendixed.

745. _____. *Investigation Guidelines for Developing and Operating a Commercial Dinner Theatre.* New York, 1980. 25p. $3. Compilation of comments by consultants, managers of dinner theaters, and other professionals presented at a FEDAPT workshop. More investigation than guidelines.

746. Golden, Joseph. *Help!: A Guide to Seeking, Selecting and Surviving an Arts Consultant.* Syracuse NY: Cultural Arts Council of Syracuse and Onandaga County, 1983. 46p. $6.50. What consultants can do, should do, how to do it, and what they should accomplish for the arts organization and its management.

747. Golden, Joseph, ed. *In Good Form: Paperwork That Works.* Madison WI: Association of College, University and Community Arts Administrators, 1985. 179p. For nonprofit theatre companies. Procedures as well as forms.

748. _____. *On the Dotted Line: The Anatomy of a Contract.* Syracuse NY: Cultural Arts Council of Syracuse and Onandaga County, 1979. 77p. $9.95. Step-by-step explanation of what is a contract, how to negotiate, and what to expect. 22 point checklist and six standard contracts.

749. Goldovsky, Boris, and Wolf, Thomas. *Touring Opera: A Manual for Small Companies.* Norfolk VA: National Opera Association, 1975. 112p. $7.50. One of the few manuals describing how to successfully get an opera tour going and completed. What to produce, equipment, transportation, cast, booking, and promotion discussed. Procedures and forms.

750. Green, Joann. *Small Theatre Handbook: A Guide to Management and Production.* Harvard MA: Harvard Common, 1981. 163p. $8.95. Handbook for the beginner on creating, administrating, selecting, staging, producing, publicizing, and breaking even for less than $100,000. Selected bibliography, directory, and index.

751. Ham, Roderick. *Theatre Planning.* Cambridge, England: Balding & Mansell; Toronto, Canada: University of Toronto Press, 1972. 292p. Out of print. Covers designing, seating, stage and production area planning, and economics and administration. Diagrams, comparative statistics, glossary, and index.

752. Horwitz, Tem. *Arts Administration: How to Set Up and Run Successful Nonprofit Arts Organizations.* Chicago: Lawyers for the Creative Arts, 1978. 256p. $15. For the nonprofessional in the arts. Information on nonprofit, incorporation, by laws, trustees, tax exemption, and contracts. Procedures and forms.

753. _____, ed. *Law and the Arts—Art and the Law.* Chicago: Lawyers for the Creative Arts, 1979. 228p. $6.95. Nine unrelated essays covering a variety of the arts. Interesting reading but not much detail.

754. Institute of Outdoor Drama. *IOD Bulletin.* Chapel Hill NC. Irregular. $1 per issue. Brief guides to establishing, financing, operating, producing, and publicizing outdoor theatre. Looseleaf format.

755. Kemen, Lynne M. *Financial Record-Keeping System: Why and How.* New York: Off Off Broadway Alliance, 1980. 40p. $5. Procedures and forms for financial and accounting records for a nonprofit professional theatrical company.

756. Langley, Stephen. *Theatre Management in America: Principles and Practice,* Rev. ed. New York: Drama, 1980. 490p. $19.95. Textbook for theatre management class. Production for commercial, stock, resident, college, and community theatre. Fundamentals, business management, audience promotion detailed. Management forms in appendix. Bibliography and index. Good beginning performing arts management resource.

757. McArthur, Nancy. *How to Do Theatre Publicity.* Berea OH: Good Ideas, 1978. 247p. $19.50. Theatre market discussed. Defines goals, organization, and responsibilities. Major emphasis on dealing with media and how to work with management, stars, and unions. Provides examples of press manual and releases.

758. Melillo, Joseph V., ed. *Market the Arts!* New York: Foundation for the Extension and Development of the American Professional Theatre, 1983. 287p. $19.95. Essays by company and theater managers on the process, principles, applications, problems, and alternatives of marketing the performing arts. Brief and practical.

759. Moore, Lou, and Kassak, Nancy, eds. *Computers and the Performing Arts.* New York: Theatre Communications Group, 1980. 113p. $7.95. Report on the National Computer Project for the Performing

Arts. Recommendations, applications, and case studies.

760. Morison, Bradley G., and Dalgleish, Julie Gordon. *Waiting in the Wings: A Larger Audience for the Arts and How to Develop It.* New York: American Council for the Arts, 1987. 250p. $21.95. Selling the community on the performing arts as a prerequisite to a successful subscription campaign is the message of this guide which uses the "steps to success" of the Tucson Symphony Orchestra as the case study.

761. National Endowment for the Arts Research Division. *Audience Development: An Examination of Selected Analysis and Prediction Techniques Applied to Symphony and Theatre Attendance in Four Southern Cities.* Washington DC, 1981. 47p. Free. Attitudinal study of past and future attendance. Extensive charting of data. Activity/interest/opinion—lifestyle matrix and telephone survey questionnaire appendixed.

762. Newman, Danny. *Subscribe Now!: Building Arts Audiences Through Dynamic Subscription Promotion.* New York: Theatre Communications Group, 1983. 276p. $10.95. Examines all facets of subscription as a performing arts financial support process from leadership through promotion to media usage and follow-ups. Essential reading for theatre owners and managers.

763. Ortiz, Melba. *Budgeting.* Madison WI: Association of College, University and Community Arts Administrators, 1984. 18p. Budgeting and budget control procedures for a small, non-profit theatre company outlined with sample forms.

764. Raymond, Thomas C.; Greyser, Stephen A.; and Schwalbe, Douglas S. *Cases in Arts Adminis-*

tration. Cambridge MA: Arts Administration Research Institute, 1974. 404p. $29. Readings for management program in arts administration. Institutional case studies for performing arts centers, theatre groups, orchestras, dance groups, and fine arts centers. Topical sections for goal setting, organizational issues, community relations, administration, finance, marketing, and facilities.

765. Reiss, Alvin H. *Arts Management Reader.* New York: Audience Arts, 1979. 686p. $32.50. Articles by Reiss and other authors, many of which appeared in his magazine, *Art Management.* How-to emphasis. Chronology and checklist of key management studies and surveys prior to 1979. Index.

766. _____. *Cash In!: Funding and Promoting the Arts.* New York: Theatre Communications Group, 1986. 224p. $12.95. Light-hearted guide to ways to meet fundraising goals for non-profit performing arts organizations. Campaigns, special events, benefits, etc., examined and outlined.

767. Shagan, Rena. *Road Show.* New York: American Council for the Arts, 1985. 288p. $14.95. Nuts and bolts of planning, booking, travel, contacts, promotion, management, and technical details. Appendix of forms, resources, and technical questionnaire.

768. Skal, David J., ed. *Graphic Communications for the Performing Arts.* New York: Theatre Communications Group, 1981. 152p. $12.95. Examples of theater posters, billboards, and promotional materials. Brief explanatory text, but heavy emphasis on materials.

769. Taubman, Joseph. *Performing Arts Management and Law.* New York: Law-Arts Publishers, 1972– .

Periodic supplements. Legal definitions, commentary, and cases on performing arts management with emphasis on copyright as applied to theatrical productions. Excellent for definitions. Subject index.

770. Theatre Communications Group. *Performing Arts Ideabooks.* New York. Irregular. $12 per year. Manuals, each proposing ideas and procedures for solving a current management problem. Volume 1, number 1 (Arnold, Mark/*Dialing for Dollars*) was concerned with telephone subscription sales.

771. Turk, Frederick J., and Gallo, Robert P. *Financial Management Strategies for Arts Organizations.* New York: American Council for the Arts, 1986. 200p. $12.95. Strategic planning, budgeting, organization, information systems, fund accounting, ratio analysis, and grants management are covered in this guidebook prepared by these non-profit accountants with Peat, Marwick, Mitchell & Co.

772. Visser, David. *Hitting the Road: Marketing Tours.* New York: Theatre Communications Group, 1982. 28p. $5. Planning, financing, promoting procedures for the small, non-profit company outlined.

773. Voegeli, Thomas J. *Handbook for Tour Management.* Madison WI: Center for Arts Administration, Graduate School of Business, University of Wisconsin— Madison, 1975. 55p. Organization model for performing arts tour. Procedures, diagrams, and forms.

774. Vogel, Frederic B., ed. *No Quick Fix: Planning.* New York: Foundation for the Extension and Development of the American Professional Theatre, 1985. 96p. $9.95. Theatrical management planning step-by-step process, procedure, and forms.

775. Wehle, Mary M. *Financial Management for Arts Organizations.* Cambridge MA: Arts Administration Research Institute, 1975. 163p. Manual for beginners with definitions, procedures, and sample forms.

776. _____. *Financial Practice for Performing Arts Companies.* Cambridge MA: Arts Administration Research Institute, 1977. 163p. Accounting manual for beginners with procedures and forms.

777. Wolf, Thomas. *Presenting Performances: A Handbook for Sponsors,* 5th ed. New York: American Council for the Arts, 1983. 164p. $12.95. Written as a rulebook to assist performing arts volunteers in setting realistic, organized, achievable goals, this work, presented in the form of management rules, offers a succinct menu for administrative decisionmaking. Appendixes provide forms for nonprofit corporation bylaws, contacts, press releases, and fundraising.

Industry

778. Canada. Statistics Canada. *Culture Statistics/Performing Arts.* Ottawa, Canada. Annual. $21. Statistical overview of the performing arts productions and attendance. Data on establishments, performances, attendance, employees, salaries and wages, and costs.

779. Central Opera Service. *Opera Annual U.S. Survey Statistics.* New York. Annual. Free. Statistics on performing groups, performances, types of opera performed, and budget balance sheet data. Current and previous years. Published separately and in *Opera News.*

780. National Endowment for the Arts Research Division. *Conditions and Needs of the Professional American Theatre.* Washington DC, 1981. 131p. Study and statistics on attendance, audience, finances, employment, and contribution of profit and nonprofit theatre in the United States. Recommendations on federal funding.

781. Theatre Communications Group. *TCG Survey.* New York. Annual. Membership. Statistical and fiscal data on nonprofit professional theatre companies. Overview of 125 theatres with detailed analysis of income, expenses, employment, and audience for a core group of approximately 50. Has been collected but not published in recent years.

Market

782. Mitchell, Arnold. *Professional Performing Arts: Attendance Patterns, Preferences, and Motives.* Madison WI: Association of College, University and Community Arts Administrators, 1985. 2v. $40. Sampling of American current patterns and potential for attendance at professional arts presentations. Survey looks at age, education, income, lifestyle, and psychological factors. Extensive statistical charts.

783. National Research Center for the Arts. *Americans and the Arts.* New York: Louis Harris, 1984. 122p. $5. Nationwide survey of public opinion in the United States towards arts patronage. Conducted for Philip Morris, Inc. Definitely a marketing "best buy."

Periodicals

784. Alliance of Resident Theatres. *Theatre Times.* New York. 6 issues. $15. Trade as well as official association periodical. News of the industry, nonprofit professional theatres in New York, management and financial tips, government legislation and relations, and grants and awards. Former title: *Off Off Broadway Alliance. OOBA Newsletter*.

785. American Council for the Arts. *Update*. New York. Monthly. Membership. Official association publication. News of community and state councils, arts activities and management, and legislative and national developments, and the arts industry.

786. American Dinner Theatre Institute. *ADTI Newsletter*. Sarasota FL. Monthly. Membership. Official association publication. News of members, operations, management, and food service developments, and the theatrical industry.

787. American Music Festival Association. *American Music Fest*. Anaheim CA. Annual. Membership. Articles on music festivals in America, the performers and their works, and activities of the association.

788. *Arts Management*. New York: Radius Group. 5 issues. $15. Articles and news on community and nonprofit arts organizations and companies. Management, financial, promotional, funding, and audience information.

789. Association of College, University and Community Arts Administrators. *ACUCAA Bulletin*. Washington DC. 10 issues. Membership. Official association publication. News of members, tours, and professional activities. Calendar of events, seminars, and workshops. Announcement of research and publications.

790. *Back Stage*. New York: Back Stage. Weekly. $45. Service news magazine for the communications and entertainment industry especially film, television and stage. Film and television news dominate. *Business Screen* section provides management and statistical data. Information on industry, government involvement, productions, labor, and equipment and services. Special issue: *Television, Film, Tape, and Production Directory* (each March). Indexed in *Predicasts F&S Index: United States, Trade and Industry Index*.

791. British Theatre Association. *Drama: The Quarterly Theatre Review*. London. Quarterly. $15. Primary emphasis is drama but contains articles on theatre, stage, and production management and theater operations. Indexed in *British Humanities Index, Humanities Index*.

792. Central Opera Service. *COS Bulletin*. New York. Quarterly. Membership. Official association publication. News of the United States and Canadian opera community, information on legislation and fund raising, survey statistics, management tips, calendar of workshops, and profiles of companies, conductors, and composers.

793. *Daily Variety*. Hollywood CA: Daily Variety. Daily. $85. Entertainment industry's news daily covering film, television, theatre, and night clubs. Productions, events, and artistic accomplishments. Financial, governmental, and regulatory information.

794. *Entertainment and Arts Management*. Eastbourne, England: John Offord. Monthly. $50. News and articles on all aspects of entertainment management with emphasis on community and nonprofit professional theatre.

795. Institute of Outdoor Drama. *IOD Newsletter*. Chapel Hill NC. Quarterly. $4. Official publication.

News of the Institute, outdoor dramas across the United States, program planning and changes, personnel, and new materials.

796. International Society of Performing Arts Administrators. *Performing Arts Forum*. Austin TX. 7 issues. $15. Official association publication. News of the association, musical events and festivals, and members.

797. *Journal of Arts Management and Law*. Washington DC: Helref. Quarterly. $55. Articles and decisions on management, contract, corporate, labor, and legal aspects of the performing arts. Indexed in *Index to Legal Periodicals, Music Index*.

798. National Association for Regional Ballet. *Dance/America*. New York. Quarterly. $25. Official association publication. Community-oriented newsletter about local dance companies and their activities and the work of regional associations for ballet.

799. National Mime Association. *Mime News*. Claremont CA. 5 issues. Membership. News of the mime movement, mime theatre productions, and the association.

800. Opera America. *Intercompany Announcements*. Washington DC. Monthly. $37.50. Official association publication. For members, funding organizations, and the media. Articles on opera companies throughout the Americas. News of research, statistics, performance management, funding, grants, and legislation. Reviews and calendar of events and performances.

801. *Playboard: Professional Stage Magazine*. Burnaby, Canada: Arch-Way. Monthly. $12. News and articles on productions, auditions, tours, management, and statistics. Western Canada orientation.

802. *Show Business*. New York: Leo Shull. Weekly. $35. News of theatrical productions, auditions, casts, financing, production companies, and the industry. Tabloid format.

803. Theatre Communications Group. *American Theatre*. New York. Monthly. $27. News of theatre trends, productions, government involvement in the arts, companies, people, events, and book reviews. One of the best monthly theatre news forums.

804. *Theatre Crafts*. New York: Theatre Crafts. 10 issues. $24. Emphasis on production and equipment for theatre and television. Features on set design, costuming, and technical theatre. Profiles of theatre productions. News of scenery, lighting, and sound equipment. Special issue: *Theatre Crafts Directory of Manufacturers, Distributors, and Suppliers of Products for the Performing Arts* (each June/July, $10). Indexed in *Education Index, Magazine Index, Reader's Guide*.

805. Theatre Development Fund. *TDF Sightlines*. New York. Quarterly. Membership. Official association publication. News of industry, productions, and theaters.

806. *Theatrical Index*. New York: Price Berkely. Weekly. $10. Theatrical productions seeking backers. Data on name of production, agent or contact, address, phone, and description of production.

807. *Variety*. New York: Variety. Weekly. $75. The entertainment world's official newspaper. News articles are supplemented with extensive management, industry, and market statistics. Special reports: "Anniversary," "Show Business" in January issue, "NAPTE Convention," in February issue, "American Film Market" in March issue, "International Television" in April issue, "International Film (Cannes)" in May issue, "Auditorium-Arena" in July issue, "Home Video" in September issue, "MIFED (Milan)" in October issue, and "Canadian" in November issue. Indexed in *Film Literature Index, Music Index, Predicasts F&S Index: United States, Trade and Industry Index.*

Databases

808. Association of College, University and Community Arts Administrators. *Nonprofit Arts Organizations.* Washington DC. Updated continuously. Membership. Directory. Activity and statistical information on performing arts organizations in the United States. Not online.

Bibliography

809. Whalon, Marion K. *Performing Arts Research: A Guide to Information Sources.* Detroit MI: Gale Research, 1976. 280p. $62. Sounds important, but is performance-oriented and devoid of all but a few directory references to business sources.

810. Wilmeth, Don B. *American and English Popular Entertainment: A Guide to Information Sources.* Detroit MI: Gale Research, 1980. 465p. $62. Good historical, but very limited business sources. Three parts: general European, English, and American popular, entertainment, entertainment by form, e.g., circus, outdoor amusements, variety shows, and popular theatre in the United States and Great Britain. Brief annotated citations to books and articles. Serials lists, museums, and "concerned" organizations plus author, title, and subject indexes.

811. _____. *Variety Entertainment and Outdoor Amusements: A Reference Guide.* Westport CT: Greenwood, 1982. 242p. $35. Narrative bibliography to history and sources for 11 show business entertainment forms. Limited business and outdoor amusement references. United States emphasis but some British resources. Final chapter is bibliography of most important sources. Selective index.

Associations

812. Alliance of Resident Theatres. 325 Spring St., Rm. 315, New York NY 10013. (212) 989-5257. Association of nonprofit professional theatre companies in New York City. Compiles statistics. Conducts research. Provides management counsel, seminars. Publishes handbooks, periodical. Former name: Off Off Broadway Alliance.

813. American Council for the Arts. 1285 Avenue of the Americas, New York NY 10019. (212) 245-4510. Association of community and state arts councils and arts related organizations in the United States. Compiles statistics. Conducts research. Provides management counsel, seminars. Maintains library. Publishes handbooks, directory, periodical. Absorbed: Advocates for the Arts; Arts, Education and Americans. Former names: Arts Councils of America; Associated Councils of the Arts; Community Arts Councils.

814. American Dinner Theatre Institute. P.O. Box 2537, Sarasota FL 33578. (813) 365-1754. Association of owner/operators of professional theatres. Publishes periodical.

815. American Music Festival Association. 2323 W. Lincoln Ave., Suite 225, Anaheim CA 92801. (714)

535-7591. Federation of state and regional associations. Compiles statistics. Conducts research. Provides seminars. Publishes periodical.

816. Arts and Business Council. 130 E. 40th St., New York NY 10016. (212) 683-5555. Service organization performing liaison between nonprofit arts groups and the business community. Purpose is to assist in securing corporate gifts in support of arts projects. Provides management counsel.

817. Association of College, University and Community Arts Administrators. 1112 16th St., N.W., Suite 620, Washington DC 20036. (202) 833-2787. Association of nonprofit arts organizations involved in the presentation of professional performances. Compiles statistics. Provides management counsel, seminars. Maintains database. Publishes handbooks, periodical. Former name: Association of College and University Concert Managers.

818. British Theatre Association. 9 Fitzroy Sq., London, England W1P 6AE. (01) 387-2666. Association of companies and professional. Purpose is to advance the development of professional theatre. Provides seminars. Publishes periodical.

819. Central Opera Service. Metropolitan Opera, Lincoln Center, New York NY 10023. (212) 957-9871. Association of professional opera and musical theatre companies, opera workshops, and individuals associated. Compiles statistics. Conducts research. Provides management counsel, seminars. Maintains library. Publishes statistics, handbooks, periodical.

820. Council of Resident Summer Theatres. 405 E. 54th St., New York NY 10022. (212) 759-7977. Association of managers of professional playhouses. Compiles statistics. Pro-

vides management counsel. Former name: Stock Manager's Association.

821. Foundation for Extension and Development of the American Professional Theatre. 165 W. 46th St., Suite 310, New York NY 10036. (212) 869-9690. Service organization providing consultation and guidance to professional theatre and dance companies in the United States. Compiles statistics. Conducts research. Provides management counsel, seminars. Publishes handbooks.

822. Gay Theatre Alliance. P.O. Box 294, Village Station, New York NY 10014. (212) 467-4713. Association of theatre companies and professionals. Compiles statistics. Conducts research. Provides management counsel, seminars.

823. Institute of Outdoor Drama. 202 Graham Memorial, University of North Carolina, Chapel Hill NC 27514. (919) 933-1328. Research and advisory agency of the University. Compiles statistics. Conducts research. Provides management counsel, seminars. Maintains library. Provides standards, handbooks, directory, statistics, periodical.

824. International Brotherhood of Magicians. 28 N. Main St., Kenton OH 43326. (419) 675-7150. Association of professionals, assistants, amateurs, agents, and suppliers.

825. International Dance Alliance. 755 Seventh Ave., New York NY 10011. (212) 691-6500. Service organization seeking to facilitate dance performances internationally. Affiliated with the Institut Internationale du Theatre, Paris.

826. International Society of Performing Arts Administrators. P.O. Box 200238, Austin TX 78720. (512) 346-1328. Association of local concert managers and promoters. Publishes periodical. Former name:

International Association of Concert and Festival Managers.

827. International Theatre Institute (Institut Internationale du Theatre). 1 Rue Miollis, Paris, France F-75732 Cedex 15, 1 45682650. Federation of national theatre centers and performing arts associations. Purpose is to facilitate worldwide exchange of performing arts presentations.

828. International Theatre Institute of the United States. 220 W. 42nd St., Suite 1710, New York NY 10036. (212) 944-1490. Service organization. United States center for the Institut Internationale du Theatre, Paris. Provides management counsel. Maintains library.

829. League of American Theatres and Producers. 226 W. 47th St., New York NY 10036. (212) 764-1122. Association of theatrical producers and owners of legitimate theatres. Purpose is labor negotations and lobbying. Compiles statistics. Conduct research. Provides management counsel.

830. League of Off-Broadway Theatres and Producers. 130 W. 42nd St., Suite 1300, New York NY 10036. (212) 730-7130. Association of smaller legitimate theatre owners and producers.

831. League of Resident Theatres. 929 N. Water St., Milwaukee WI 53202. (414) 273-7121. Association of regional theatres. Purpose is labor negotiations and management cooperation. Provides management counsel.

832. National Association for Regional Ballet. 1123 Broadway, New York NY 10010. (212) 645-0042. Association of dance companies affiliated with one of the five regional dance associations in the United States. Compiles statistics. Conducts research. Provides management

counsel, seminars. Publishes handbooks, periodical.

833. National Endowment for the Arts. 1100 Pennsylvania Ave., N.W., Washington DC 20506. (202) 682-5400. United States government created independent agency for bestowing grants, providing support, and conducting research into all aspects of the arts. Has supported many performing arts projects and unwritten research into arts organization and management for nonprofit companies.

834. National Mime Association. Pamona College, Holmes Hall, Rm. 7, Claremont CA 91711. (714) 621-8186. Association for the promotion of mime theatre. Founded 1984. Publishes periodical.

835. Opera America. 633 E St., N.W., Washington DC 20004. (212) 347-9262. Association of professional performing companies in the United States, Canada, and Latin America. Compiles statistics. Conducts research. Provides management counsel, seminars. Publishes handbooks, directory, periodical.

836. Theatre Communications Group. 355 Lexington Ave., New York NY 10017. (212) 697-5230. Service organization for nonprofit professional theatre companies. Compiles statistics. Conducts research. Provides seminars. Publishes handbooks, directory, periodical.

837. Theatre Development Fund. 1501 Broadway, New York NY 10036. (212) 221-0885. Nonprofit corporation to support commercial theatre productions. Provides management counsel, theatre ticket services. Publishes handbooks, directory, periodical.

838. Theatrical Management Association. Bedford Chambers, Coventry Garden, London, England WC2E 8HQ. (01) 836-0971. Association of owners, proprietors, and managers of commercial and non-profit live entertainment and places where it is performed. Compiles statistics. Conducts research. Provides seminars. Maintains library.

18. The Motion Picture Industry

SIC Codes: 5735, 7812, 7819, 7822, 7829, 7832, 7833, 7841.

Enterprises producing, distributing, showing in theaters, selling, and/or renting film and/or videotape motion pictures.

Directories

839. *American Film Festival Program.* New York: Educational Film Library Association. Annual. Free. Lists distributors showing at festival giving name, address, and contributions. Valuable for its currency.

840. *Angels.* New York: Leo Shull. Annual. $150. Investors in show business and motion picture productions. Separate volumes for theatre and film. Each listing gives name, address, amount invested, and names of productions backed. Latest edition 1985.

841. Association of Independent Video and Filmmakers. *AIVF Guide to Film and Video Distributors.* New York. Biennial. $8.95. Each listing gives name, address, phone, contact, and areas of interest or service. Arrangement is geographical.

842. *AVMP/Audio Video Market Place, a Multimedia Guide.* New York: Bowker. Annual. $49.95. Lists 4,500 producers, distributors, and servicers of the audio, motion picture, and video industries in the United States giving name, address,

key executives, and list of products or services. Arrangement is geographical by state with classified products and services and names and numbers indexes. Should be among the first motion picture/music directories purchased.

843. Bension, Shmuel, ed. *Producer's Masterguide.* New York: New York Production Manual. Annual. $69.95. Lists 50,000 production companies and service organizations in film and video in the United States, Canada, and Great Britain giving name, address, phone, and services. Arrangement is classified by activity then geographical. No name index.

844. British Film Institute. *BFI Film and Television Yearbook.* London: BFI. Annual. $25. Overview of industry plus production companies for film and video, studios and labs, distributors, finance sources, societies, and government agencies giving name, address, and phone. Arrangement is classified by activity with name index.

845. *Directory of International Film and Video Festivals.* London: British Film Institute and the British Council. Biennial. $20. Competitive, non-competitive, and marketing events. Each listing gives name, location, dates, categories, awards, and entry requirements. Arrangement is geographical with date, category, and venues indexes.

846. *Film Canada Yearbook.* Toronto, Canada: Cine-Communications. Annual. $20. Production, distribution, and exhibition companies, service, union, and government agencies, and networks and festivals giving name, address, phone, activity, and key personnel. Arrangement is classified by activity with name index. Former title: *Canadian Film Digest Yearbook*.

847. *Home Viewer's Official Video Software Directory*. Philadelphia PA: Home Viewer. Annual. $41.95. Over 750 companies manufacturing and/or supplying blank and pre-recorded tapes, VCRs, and accessories giving name, address, phone, contact, branch offices, and products and services. Industry statistics, market data, and special reports on the industry and products.

848. *International Film Guide*. London: Tantivy, New York: Zoetrope. Annual. $12.95. Lists production companies, distributors, services, festivals, schools, and private and public motion picture agencies in 65 nations giving name, address, and, for some, additional information. Arrangement is by country.

849. *International Motion Picture Almanac*. New York: Quigley. Annual. $55. Classified yearbook-directory of the motion picture business. Short on details but excellent for the business user seeking companies and agencies. Contains motion picture "Who's Who." United States, Canada, Great Britain, and some worldwide data. Most directory listings give name, address, and phone. Many statistical and award charts.

850. International Tape/Disc Association. *ITA Source Directory*. New York. Annual. Membership. Lists member manufacturers and suppliers of audio, computer, and video products giving name, address, contact, and products. Arrangement is classified by type of product.

851. *International Television and Video Almanac*. $55. Classified yearbook-directory similar to "International Motion Picture Almanac" above. Includes same "Who's Who" sections.

852. *Kemps International Film and Television Yearbook*. London: Kemps Group. Annual. $50. Similar in approach to other annuals above. Lists production companies, supplier, professionals, and agents in Great Britain and worldwide giving name and address. British emphasis. Arrangement is geographical, then classified by subject under each country.

853. *Motion Picture, TV and Theatre Directory*. Tarrytown NY: Motion Picture Enterprises. Semiannual. $10. Companies providing services to the motion picture, television, and theater production industry. Paid listing giving name, address, and phone. Arrangement is classified by type of service, then geographical.

854. National Association of Theater Owners. *Encyclopedia of Exhibition*. New York. Annual. Membership. Directory of motion pictures and theaters. For theaters gives name, address, phone, and contact. Arrangement is geographical.

855. National Association of Video Distributors. *NAVD Membership Roster*. Washington DC. Annual. Free. Each listing gives name, address, phone, area served, and products handled. Arrangement is alphabetical.

856. *On Location: The National Film and Videotape Production Directory*. Los Angeles: On Location. Annual. $80. Lists 100,000 public and private facilities, organizations, and services in the United States, Canada, Mexico, and the Virgin

Islands available to production companies filming "on location," giving name, address, phone, and type of facility or service. Arrangement is geographical.

857. Professional Audiovideo Retailers Association. *PARA Membership Directory.* Kansas City MO. Annual. Membership. Lists retail stores giving name, address, phone, and executives. Arrangement is geographical.

858. *Screen International Film and TV Yearbook.* London: King; Philadelphia PA: Taylor & Francis. Annual. $58. Lists production companies, studios, distributors, agents, trade organizations, and prominent motion picture and TV personalities worldwide giving name, address, phone, and key executives for companies. Arrangement is geographical.

859. *Studio Blu-Book Directory.* Hollywood CA: Hollywood Reporter. Annual. $45. Hollywood's most comprehensive directory to companies, services, and people in the industry or related to it, e.g. hotels, restaurants, clubs. Serves as almanac, telephone directory, and index. Arrangement is classified by activity then alphabetically by name.

860. *Variety International Motion Picture Market Place.* New York and London: Garland. Annual. $50. Worldwide motion picture companies and agencies. Each listing gives name, address, telephone/cable/telex numbers, key executive, and activities. Arrangement is geographical with classified activity and name and number indexes.

Management

861. American Entrepreneurs Association. *Financing and Selling Movie and Television Productions.* Los Angeles, 1985. 203p. $55. Guide to establishing and operating a small business. Legal, management, marketing, operating, and financial procedures. Supplier addresses and a bibliography. Looseleaf format.

862. _____. *Video Production Company.* Los Angeles, 1984. 154p. $49.95. Guide to establishing and operating a small business. Legal, management, marketing, operating, and financial procedures. Supplier addresses and a bibliography. Looseleaf format.

863. _____. *Videocassette Rental Store.* Los Angeles, 1986. 144p. $49.50. Guide to establishing and operating a small business. Legal, management, marketing, operations, and financial procedures. Supplier addresses and a bibliography. Looseleaf format.

864. American Institute of Certified Public Accountants Committee on the Entertainment Industries. *Accounting for Motion Picture Films,* 2nd ed. New York: American Institute of Certified Public Accountants, 1979. 25p. $5. Rules, procedures, and examples.

865. Association of Independent Producers. *Independent Production Handbook.* London, 1983. 1v. $50. British approach to motion picture and TV production. Management techniques, procedures, and forms. Looseleaf format.

866. Baumgarten, Paul A., and Farber, Donald C. *Producing, Financing, and Distributing Film,* Rev. ed. New York: Limelight, 1987. 250p. $25. Emphasis on agreements and contracts for property, talent, facilities, distribution, and exhibition. Its narrative format with no index makes reference consultation difficult. The information provided negates these limitations.

867. *Brooks' Standard Rate Book.* Los Angeles: S.J. Brooks. Annual. $25. Union rates for all guilds and unions in the film and television industry.

868. Chamness, Danford. *Hollywood Guide to Film Budgeting and Script Breakdown,* Rev. ed. Los Angeles: S.J. Brooks, 1986. 223p. $22.95. Demonstrates breaking down a script for the production finance board in preparation for estimating the costs of a feature film. Provides budgeting procedure guidelines.

869. Goodell, Gregory. *Independent Feature Film Production: A Complete Guide from Concept Through Distribution.* New York: St. Martin's, 1982. 323p. $17.95. Probably the best current filmmaking business book. Examines concept, business and legal structure, financial and production processes, marketing, and distribution. Sample budgets in appendix. Index.

870. Gregory, Mollie. *Making Films your Business.* New York: Schocken, 1979. 256p. $6.95. Beginner's text for starting out, producing, and, one hopes, succeeding in the motion picture business.

871. J. Lahm Consultants, Inc. *Video Movie Manual.* White Plains NY: Knowledge Industry, 1986. 1v. $395. Guide to planning, organizing, staffing, managing, promoting, and marketing a video software store. Products, equipment, and accessories. Examples of successful businesses. Looseleaf format.

872. Jacobs, Bob. *How to Be an Independent Video Producer.* White Plains NY: Knowledge Industry, 1986. 197p. $34.95. Covers setting up shop, financing, managing, producing, and marketing detailed with quotes from luminaries in the field.

873. Lazer, Ellen A., ed. *Guide to Home Video Marketing.* White Plains NY: Knowledge Industry, 1986. 160p. $175. Managing the marketing strategy, advertising, publicity, and direct marketing techniques. Examples of successful strategies.

874. Loh, Stan. *Start and Run a Profitable Video Store.* Blue Ridge Summit PA: TAB, 1984. 168p. $10.95. Step-by-step manual and business plan for opening and operating a small video retail store. Procedures and forms.

875. Mayer, Michael F. *Film Industries: Practical Business/Legal Problems in Production, Distribution and Exhibition,* Rev. ed. New York: Hastings, 1978. 230p. $12.50. Study and commentary. Required background reading for any motion picture industry novice.

876. Reichert, Julia. *Doing It Yourself: A Handbook on Independent Film Distribution.* New York: Association of Independent Video and Filmmakers, 1977. 76p. $7.95. Management tips, promotion techniques, procedures, and forms.

877. Robertson, Joseph F. *Motion Picture Distribution Handbook.* Blue Ridge Summit PA: Tab, 1981. 252p. $19.95. Background, producers, sources, policies, and procedures outlined.

878. Singleton, Ralph S. *Filmmaker's Library Series.* Beverly Hills CA: Lone Eagle, 1984–86. 4v. $61.80. Series of workbooks containing procedures and forms for motion picture producing. The series includes the following titles: *Film Scheduling—Film Budgeting Workbook; Film Scheduling: Or How Long Will It Take to Shoot Your Movie; Filmmaker's Dictionary;* and *Movie Production and Budget Forms . . . Instantly!*

879. Squire, Jason E., ed. *Movie Business Book.* Englewood Cliffs

NJ: Prentice Hall, 1983. 414p. $24.95. Articles by authorities and major film luminaries on properties, financing, production, management, promotion, distribution, and technology. Contract forms.

880. U.S. Senate Committee on the Judiciary. *Home Video Recording: Headings September 23, 1986.* Washington DC: U.S. Government Printing Office, 1987. 109p. Statements and documents on videotape copyright infringement versus "fair use" of the same types of media presented by industry, academic and other professional users, and consumer groups.

881. Wasco, Janet. *Movies and Money: Financing the American Film Industry.* Norwood NJ: Ablex, 1982. 247p. $37.50. Historical analysis of the role of the American banking industry in financially underwriting the American motion picture industry from the 1890s to 1970s era of conglomeration, diversification and internationalization. Excellent for understanding business aspects of the industry.

882. Weise, Michael. *Film and Video Budgets.* Westport CT: Michael Weise Film Productions, 1984. 345p. $14.95. Written to supplement his *Independent Film and Videomakers Guide* (see **883**). Basic concepts, procedures, and forms. Numerous balance sheet and financial examples. Sample contracts.

883. _____. *Independent Film and Videomakers Guide.* Westport CT: Michael Weise Film Productions, 1984. 386p. $14.95. Procedures for financing, securing backing, market research, producing, budgeting, promotion, distribution, and music video. Appendix includes forms and list of non-theatrical, foreign television, and pay cable buyers.

884. Wiegand, Ingrid. *Professional Video Production.* White Plains NY: Knowledge Industry, 1985. 215p. $39.95. Emphasis on video production regardless of its ultimate purpose. Script preparation, studio and equipment, production, graphics and animation, and editing examined in relationship to time and cost. Essential reading for independent entrepreneurs and managers.

Industry

885. *Art Murray's Box Office Register.* Hollywood CA. Annual. $70. Compilation of financial data from film distributors on box office activities. For each motion picture listed gives distribution information, box office income, and screen week total. Arrangement is alphabetical by title and by order of gross income and weekly totals. Based upon similar data published weekly in *Variety.*

886. Auty, Martyn, and Roddick, Nick, eds. *British Cinema Now.* London: BFI, 1985. 168p. $22.50. Essays on the industry, the producers, the films, and the audience from the business prospective. Excellent brief introduction to the state of the British film industry.

887. Balio, Tino, ed. *American Film Industry.* Madison WI: University of Wisconsin Press, 1985. 664p. $32.50. Essays by scholars and prominent film leaders on the major aspects of industry business growth and development. Selected bibliography and indexes to specific motion pictures and general subjects.

888. Canada. Statistics Canada. *Motion Picture Production.* Ottawa, Canada. Annual. $21. Statistical overview of establishments, employees, salaries and wages, revenues, and types of films produced.

889. _____. *Motion Picture Theaters and Film Distribution.* Ottawa, Canada. Annual. $21. Statistical overview of establishments, prices, revenues, and types of features shown.

890. *Current Research in Film.* Norwood NJ: Ablex. 1985– . Series of collections of articles on the business and economic aspects of the motion picture industry. Researched articles on current and historical projects and preferences which influence the financial and legal stability of the industry. Author and subject indexes to each volume.

891. Euromonitor. *UK Cinema.* London: Euromonitor, 1980. 113p. $115. Analysis trends in production and sales. Assesses overall growth of companies and industry. Projects 1980s market.

892. *Home Video and Cable Yearbook 1982–83.* White Plains NY: Knowledge Industry, 1982. 263p. $85. Planned as an annual publication, this almanac of the industry has been published only twice. Provides a wealth of information available elsewhere but not in collected form. Of particular importance is information and financial data on video-related companies and industry statistics.

893. Hope Reports, Inc. *Hope Reports Video II.* Rochester NY, 1987. 88p. $75. Statistics on home video industry operations.

894. James, Theodore E. *Motion Picture Industry Data.* San Francisco CA: Montgomery Securities Institutional Research, 1980. 49p. Background data and statistical analysis of the industry based upon company production and financial records. Includes statistics on television and cable purchases.

895. Key Note Publications Ltd. *Cinemas and Theatres,* 4th ed. London, 1986. 42p. $100. Analyzes industry structure and trends in the United Kingdom over a five-year span and compares companies in the last three. Financial ratios and future development examined. Market structure and potential for overseas tourists reviewed. Bibliography.

896. Kindem, Gorham, ed. *American Movie Industry: The Business of Motion Pictures.* Carbondale IL: Southern Illinois University Press, 1982. 474p. $18.95. Case studies of producers and productions.

897. Slide, Anthony. *American Film Industry: A Historical Dictionary.* Westport CT: Greenwood, 1986. 441p. $49.95. Film business definitions and brief histories of over 100 motion picture companies. Name index.

898. Steinberg, Cobbett. *Film Facts.* New York: Facts on File, 1980. 476p. $19.95. Statistics, market data, awards, directories, and history. Interesting to consult for general industry information but little depth. Mostly trivia.

899. _____. *TV Facts.* New York: Facts on File, 1984. 478p. $19.95. Statistics, market data, awards, directories, and history. Interesting to consult for general industry information but little depth. Mostly trivia. 249647

Market

900. Edgerton, Gary R. *American Film Exhibition and an Analysis of the American Motion Picture's Market Structure, 1963–1980.* New York: Garland, 1983. 224p. $36. Study of the fragmentation, stabilization, and restructuring that took place in the American film industry after the Paramount distribution decision. Discusses the effect of growing control of distribution and exhibition of major motion pictures by a small group of companies, the effect of foreign films, and the future of domestic distribution and exhibition.

901. Euromonitor. *Aspects of Video.* London, 1981. 59p. $275. Report on the market for video recorders in the United Kingdom. Analysis trends in sales, assess overall growth and type of demand. Projects 1980s market.

902. Hope Reports, Inc. *Hope Reports 1986 Market Trends: A Special Report and General Forecast on AV Media Potential.* Rochester NY, 1986. 19p. $55. Charting audio-video production, growth, and sales potential. Based upon the *Hope Reports Industry Quarterly* market letter.

903. Video Marketing, Inc. *Camcorders and the Video Photography Market.* Hollywood CA, 1987. 1v. $275. Analysis and forecast of videocamera market. Data on leading consumers and target markets, company profiles of major producers.

904. _____. *Direct Marketing Prerecorded Videocassettes.* Hollywood CA, 1986. 98p. $195. Analysis and case studies of mail order, video club, and catalog operations. Profiles of major clubs. Tips on pricing, margins, and marketing techniques.

905. _____. *Home Video Marketplace,* 2d ed. Hollywood CA, 1986. 1v. $495. Contains 25 chapters and over 100 statistical charts, tables, and graphs. Analyzes market for hardware, software, and blank tapes. Detailed picture of sales, ownership, and consumer expenditure. Not to be confused with a video production directory with a similar title published by Knowledge Industry Publications, Inc.

906. _____. *Sponsored Home Video.* Hollywood CA, 1987. 108p. $695. Introduction, case studies, and market analysis of this emerging form of product advertising directly to the consumer via videocassette. Discusses how and why it works.

907. _____. *Video Marketing Consumer Survey.* Hollywood CA, 1982. 50p. $145. Profile of the video-cassette customer.

908. _____. *Video Marketing Retail Survey.* Hollywood CA. Annual. $99. Sales data compiled from 400 video stores throughout the United States.

Periodicals

909. Adult Film Association of America. *AFAA Bulletin.* New York. Monthly. Membership. Official association publication. News of legislation, laws, and legal decisions. Case studies. Management and legal tips. Information on new productions.

910. American Film Institute. *American Film: The Magazine of the Film and Television Arts.* Washington DC. 10 issues. $20. Articles on the current film and video scene. Limited industry-management-marketing news. Value to the film or video producer is its news of the Institute's involvement in funding. Indexed in *Film Literature Index.*

911. Association of Independent Video and Filmmakers. *Independent.* New York. Monthly. Membership. Official association publication. Information on business and legal questions, fundraising, distribution. News of productions, festivals, grants, equipment, and services. Indexed in *Film Literature Index.*

912. *Back Stage.* New York: Back Stage. Weekly. $45. Service news magazine for the communications and entertainment industry especially film, television and stage. Film and television news dominate. *Business Screen* section provides management and statistical data. Information on industry, government involvement, productions, labor, and equipment and services. Special issue: *Back Stage Television, Film, Tape, and Production Directory* (each March, $20). Indexed in *Predicasts F&S Index: United States, Trade and Industry Index.*

913. *Box Office: The National Film Monthly.* Chicago: RLD Communication. Monthly. $35. World, national, and local industry news, management and operations features, production and distribution statistics and trends. Special section each month on theater facilities and operations. Special reports: "Snack Bar" in each July issue; "Automation and Computerization" in each August issue; "Buyer's Guide" in each September issue; "Merchandising and Concessions" in each November issue; and "Trade Shows" in each December issue. Indexed in *Film Literature Index, Predicasts F&S Index: United States.*

914. *Canadian Video Retailer.* Downsview, Canada: RL Publishing. 10 issues. $15. Primarily a reviewing medium for new videotapes and discs but does contain statistics and merchandising tips.

915. *Daily Variety.* Hollywood CA: Daily Variety. Daily. $85. Entertainment industry's news daily covering film, television, theatre, and night clubs. Productions, events, and artistic accomplishments. Financial, governmental, and regulatory information.

916. *Entertainment Merchandis-*

ing. Cleveland OH: Harcourt Brace Jovanovich. Monthly. $24. Primarily a new audio, video, and compact disc product listing medium. Limited number of news and merchandising articles.

917. *Hollywood Reporter.* Hollywood CA: Hollywood Reporter. Daily. $89. West Coast emphasis. Trade, production, and celebrity news. Box office, film, and TV statistics. Special report: "Cannes Festival" in each May issue.

918. *Home Video Publisher.* White Plains NY: Knowledge Industry. Weekly. $275. Market report and analysis of the home video publishing opportunities. Industry statistics, trends, and marketing channels. Attempts to project consumer interest and demand. Monthly market indicators. Video cassette "best seller" list.

919. Hope Reports, Inc. *Hope Reports Industry Quarterly.* Rochester NY. Quarterly. $250. Statistics on manufacturing expenditures, costs, profits, production, and distribution of home audio and video recordings. Dollar and unit sales for over 150 products. Market information and forecasts.

920. *Independent Film Journal: Trade Paper for Exhibitors of Motion Pictures.* New York: Pubsun. Monthly. $25. Buying and booking data, production news, articles on theater facilities and operations, information on film ratings and censorship issues. Special reports: "Adult Film" in each March issue; "Distribution Guide" in each August issue; and "Equipment, Concessions and Services Buyer's Guide" in each September issue. Former name: *Film Journal.* Indexed in *Film Literature Index.*

921. International Association of Independent Producers. *Communi-*

cation Arts International. Washington DC. Quarterly. $6. Official association publication. News on performing arts production and recording. Text in English with summaries in Chinese, French, German, and Spanish. Production techniques, management, law, patents, industry and marketing statistics.

922. International Documentary Association. *International Documentary.* Los Angeles. Quarterly. Membership. Official association publication. News of the industry, producers, productions, management, marketing, events, and reviews.

923. International Tape/Disc Association. ITA *News Digest.* New York. Bimonthly. Membership. Official association publication. Contains news of the association and the industry.

924. *Leisure Time Electronics.* New York: CBS Magazines. Monthly. $24. For the high volume audiovideo retailer. Articles on new product marketing programs, consumer buying patterns, and retailer sales projections. Case histories of successful sales programs.

925. *Motion Picture Investor.* Carmel CA: Paul Kagan. Monthly. $395. Investment newsletter on motion picture productions and public stock of film companies.

926. *Music Video Retailer.* Chestnut Hill MA: Larkin-Pluznick-Larkin. Monthly. $20. Articles on merchandising records and tapes. Product news. Special reports: "Directory of (over 10,000) Record and Tape Stores" in each May issue; "Music and Video Suppliers Directory" in each October issue; "Top 100 Retail Chains" in each December issue. Former title: *Music Retailer.*

927. National Association of Theatre Owners. NATO *News and*

Views. New York. 22 issues. $36. Marketing statistics, management tips, legislation, legal rulings, and film reviews.

928. *On Location Magazine.* Los Angeles: On Location. Monthly. $44. "The film and videotape production magazine." Articles on preproduction, postproduction, special effects, animation, and commercials. Features on shooting locations and layouts. News of films in production, companies, and management. Heavily illustrated. Indexed in *Film Literature Index.*

929. *Photovideo.* Toronto, Canada: Maclean Hunter. 9 issues. $41. For photo retailers and processors, video distributors and retailers, professional photographers, and commercial and industry video producers. News of industry developments, new technology, and products. Features on photography and video merchandising, professional techniques, and foreign products and competition. Statistics on production, sales, and trends. Special issue: *Photovideo Directory* (each May, $20).

930. *Variety.* New York: Variety. Weekly. $75. The entertainment world's official newspaper. News articles are supplemented with management, industry, and market statistics. Special reports: "Anniversary," "Show Business" in January issue, "NAPTE Convention," in February, "American Film Market" in March, "International Television" in April, "International Film (Cannes)" in May issue, "Auditorium-Arena" in July, "Home Video" in September issue, "MIFED (Milan)" in October, and "Canadian" in November issue. Indexed in *Film Literature Index, Music Index, Predicasts F&S Index: United States, Trade and Industry Index.*

931. *Video Business.* New York: International Thompson Retail. Monthly. $48. The news, marketing, and merchandising magazine of the video industry. Articles on new product development, market and industry analysis. Special issue: *Buyer's Guide* (each June).

932. Video Marketing, Inc. *Video Marketing Newsletter.* Hollywood CA. Bimonthly. $347. For the executive. News service monitoring the home video market. Industry news, statistics, and calendar of events. Indexed in *Predicasts F&S Index: United States.*

933. _____. *Video Marketing Surveys and Forecasts.* Hollywood CA. Monthly. $4500. Surveys, charts, and market analysis for the home video industry. Sales and product statistics. Glossary and index. Looseleaf format. Note expense, but cost is worth it for entrepreneurs.

934. Video Software Dealers Association. *VSDA Reports.* Marlton NJ. Monthly. Membership. Official association publication. News of the association and the industry.

935. *Video Software Dealer.* Los Angeles: VSD. Monthly. $24. Information and reviews on new software releases. Some hardware data. News and articles on industry developments, dealers, and markets.

936. *Video Store Magazine.* Cleveland OH: Harcourt Brace Jovanovich. Monthly. $24. Management and merchandising techniques for the retail video software and hardware outlet. Extensive product information. Industry statistics. Special report: "Home Video Buyer's Guide" in each September issue.

937. *Video Store Report.* Cleveland OH: Harcourt Brace Jovanovich. Every two weeks. $199. Statistical supplement to the "Video Store Magazine." Contains market indica-

tors tracking the performance of video stores.

Bibliographies/Indexes

938. American Film Institute. *Factfile.* Washington DC, 1979. 1v. Series of brief bibliographies and directories on the motion picture industry. Of special note to the business person are: *Film/Video Festivals and Awards; Independent Film and Video; Third World Cinema;* and *Film/Television: A Research Guide.*

939. Armour, Robert A. *Film: A Reference Guide.* Westport CT: Greenwood, 1980. 251p. $35. Bibliographical essays on major aspects of the motion picture including one on "Film Production." Light on business sources but excellent list of "Reference Works and Periodicals." Bibliography of resources cited at the end of each essay. Motion picture chronology and subject index.

940. Austin, Bruce A. *Film Audience: An International Bibliography of Research with Annotations and an Essay.* Metuchen NJ, and London: Scarecrow, 1983. 179p. $17.50. Articles and books on "a neglected aspect of film research." Author's focus is on psychology, habits, and attendance statistics of motion picture "goers." Bibliography preceded by excellent essay justifying its existence. Valuable for market study, though not directed specifically towards marketing needs.

941. *Film Literature Index.* Albany NY: Film and Television Documentation Center. Quarterly with annual cumulation. $225. Citations to articles in over 225 international film and television periodicals. Alphabetical author/subject arrangement. Emphasis on film and television programming, but covers all aspects of motion picture industry, companies, production, management, and marketing.

942. Fisher, Kim N. *On the Screen: A Film, Television, and Video Research Guide.* Littleton CO: Libraries Unlimited, 1986. 209p. $35. Lists 700 selected and annotated English language sources. Not the most detailed or comprehensive bibliography but one of the few that provides any references to research materials of value to motion picture industry study.

943. MacCann, Richard Dyer, and Perry, Edward S. *New Film Index: A Bibliography of Magazine Articles in English, 1930–1970.* New York: Dutton, 1975. 522p. Out of print. Section on "Motion Picture Industry."

944. Writer's Program, New York. *Film Index: A Bibliography— Volume 2: Film as Industry.* White Plains NY: Kraus International, 1985. 587p. $95. Reprint of a 1941 WPA Writer's Program bibliography considered a classic in historical bibliography. Arrangement of citations is by subject category then alphabetical by author or main entry. Primary for historical industry study.

Associations

945. Adult Film Association of America. 30 E. 30th St., New York NY 10016. (212) 247-1899. Association of producers, distributors, and exhibitors. Main purpose is to combat censorship. Compiles statistics. Provides seminars. Publishes periodical.

946. Alliance of Motion Picture and Television Producers. 14144 Ventura Blvd., Third Fl., Sherman Oaks CA 91423. (818) 995-3600. Association of major producing companies.

947. American Film Institute. John F. Kennedy Center for the Performing Arts, Washington DC 20566. (202) 828-400. Nonprofit corporation providing encouragement and financial support to independent filmmakers. Compiles statistics. Conducts research. Provides seminars, trade shows. Publishes handbooks, periodical.

948. American Film Marketing Association. 1000 Washington Blvd., Culver City CA 90232. (213) 275-3400. Association of distributors and producers of independent English language films. Provides management counsel, seminars.

949. Association of Independent Cinemas. 93 Wardour St., London, England W1V 4JB. (01) 734-0919. Association of theater owners and managers.

950. Association of Independent Producers. 17 Great Pulteney St., London, England W1R 3DG. (01) 437-3549. Associations of film companies and filmmakers. Purpose is to broaden the financial base for independent filmmaking. Compiles statistics. Conducts research. Provides management counsel, seminars. Maintains library.

951. Association of Independent Video and Filmmakers. 625 Broadway, Ninth Fl., New York NY 10012. (212) 473-3400. Association of companies and individuals involved in independent video or film creation. Compiles statistics. Conducts research. Provides management counsel, seminars. Publishes periodical.

952. Association of Video Dealers. P.O. Box 25, Godalming, Surrey, England GU7 1PL. (048) 682-3429. Association of companies. Provides seminars, trade shows.

953. Black Filmmaker Foundation. 80 Eighth St., Suite 1704, New York NY 10011. (212) 924-1198. Association of producers, would-be producers, and supporters. Purpose is to support and distribute black productions. Provides seminars. Maintains library.

954. British Film and Television Producers Association. 162 Wardour St., London, England W1V 4AB. (01) 437-7700. Association of companies. Provides management counsel, seminars.

955. Independent Feature Project. 21 W. 86th St., New York NY 10024. (212) 496-0909. Association of independent film producers. Compiles statistics. Conducts research. Provides management counsel, seminars. Publishes audio and video tapes on production, financing, management, marketing, and distribution.

956. Independent Film Distributors Association. 55 Greek St., London, England W1V 6DB. (01) 437-9392. Association of companies. Compiles statistics. Provides seminars.

957. Independent Film Makers Association. 77 Wardour St., London, England W1V 3PH. (01) 439-0460. Association of companies. Purpose is to promote the independent producer and products. Conducts research. Provides management counsel, seminars.

958. International Association of Independent Producers. P.O. Box 2801, Washington DC 20013. (202) 638-5595. Association of companies and individuals worldwide involved in production of film, video, and recordings. Compiles statistics. Provides management counsel, seminars. Publishes periodical.

959. International Documentary Association. 8480 Beverly Blvd., Los Angeles CA 90048. (213) 655-7089. Association of companies and individuals producing nonfiction film and video. Compiles statistics. Conducts research. Provides management counsel, seminars. Publishes periodical.

960. International Federation of Phonogram and Videogram Producers. 123 Pall Mall, London, England SW1Y 5EA. (01) 930-1752. Federation of national associations. Purpose is primarily international copyright protection.

961. International Tape/Disc Association. Ten Columbus Circle, New York NY 10019. (212) 956-7110. Association of companies manufacturing audio and video tapes, home computers, software and optical/laser media. Compiles statistics. Provides seminars. Publishes standards, directory, periodical.

962. Motion Picture Association of America. 522 Fifth Ave., New York NY 10036. (212) 840-6161. Association of the nine principle producers and distributors of motion pictures in the United States. Purpose is primarily political action. Compiles statistics. Conducts research. Publishes standards, handbooks, statistics.

963. National Association of Theatre Owners. 1560 Broadway, Suite 714, New York NY 10036. (212) 730-7420. Association of motion picture theater owners. Publishes directory, periodical. Former name: Theatre Owners of America.

964. National Association of Video Distributors. 1255 23rd St., N.W., Washington DC 20037. (202) 452-8100. Association of individuals who wholesale home video software. Publishes directory.

965. Professional Travelogue Sponsors. P.O. Box 13905, Atlanta GA 30324. (404) 872-2697. Association of producers of travel documentaries. Purpose is to increase the quality of films and travel lectures. Former name: Professional Travel Film Directors Association.

966. Society of Film Distributors. 72 Dean St., London, England W1V 5HS. (01) 437-4383. Association of British companies.

967. Video Software Dealers Association. 3 Eves Dr., Suite 307, Marlton NJ 08053. (609) 424-7117. Association of companies. Compiles statistics. Publishes periodical.

19. The Music Industry

SIC Codes: 3652, 5099, 5735, 7929.

Enterprises producing, performing, and distributing music or recordings of music. For enterprises whose primary emphasis is instruments and materials for playing music see Chapter 14, The Musical Instrument Industry.

Directories

968. Association of Canadian Orchestras. *Directory of Canadian Orchestras and Youth Orchestras.* Toronto, Canada. Annual. $3. Each listing gives name, address, phone, conductor, and season. Arrangement is geographical.

969. Association of Professional Recording Studios. *Guide to APRS Member Studios.* Rickmansworth, England. Annual. Membership. Each listing gives name, address, phone, key executives, and description of facilities. Arrangement is geographical.

970. *AVMP/Audio Video Market Place, A Multimedia Guide.* New York: Bowker. Annual. $49.95. Lists 4,500 producers, distributors, and servicers of the audio, motion picture, and video industries in the United States giving name, address, key executives, and list of products or services. Arrangement is geographical by state with classified products and services and names and

numbers indexes. Should be among the first motion picture/music directories purchased.

971. *Billboard's Country Music Sourcebook.* New York: Billboard. Annual. $22. Lists organizations, recording companies, and talent and promotion agencies giving name, address, phone, and key executives or contact. Arrangement is classified and geographical.

972. *Billboard's International Buyer's Guide.* New York: Billboard. Annual. $53. Record companies, music publishers, record and tape wholesalers, services, supplies, and accessories for the United States and worldwide. Each listing gives name, address, phone, key executives, products or services, and branch offices. United States record companies and music publishers are arranged alphabetically. Other organizations are arranged geographically by state. Foreign companies, agencies, and organizations are arranged by business category under each country. Current and retrospective music and home entertainment industry and consumer statistics.

973. *Billboard's International Manufacturing and Packaging Directory.* New York: Billboard. Annual. $22. Lists tape manufacturers and wholesalers, production facilities and servicers, and music production companies worldwide giving name, address, phone, key executives, and services worldwide. Arrangement is classified geographically. Product or service index. Former titles: *Billboard's Audio/ Video/Tape Source Book; Billboard's International Tape Directory*.

974. *Billboard's International Recording Equipment and Studio Directory*. New York: Billboard. Annual. $22. Lists recording studios, record producers and manufacturers, and music industry suppliers giving name, address, phone, key executives, and services worldwide. Arrangement is classified except recording studios in the United States and Canada which are arranged geographically. Product or service index.

975. *British Music Yearbook*. London: Reingold. Annual. $20. Lists over 10,000 professional companies, manufacturers, organizations, agents, and musical artists in England, Scotland, Wales, and Northern Ireland giving name, address, and phone and, for some, statistics, services, product lines, etc. Arrangement is classified by activity with subject index. Industry statistics and information found in the introductory chapters. Inadequate subject index and no name index.

976. Byrczek, Jan A., ed. *European Jazz Directory*. New York: Jazz World Society, 1983. 1v. $95. For producers, performers, and booking agents doing business in Europe. Clubs, festivals, radio and television stations, magazines, professional services, record producers, distributors, educators, and "very important people." Arrangement varies by type of activity. Does not totally meet the needs of the groups to whom it is addressed, but it is the only English language sourcebook with as broad a scope.

977. _____, ed. *Jazz World Directory*. New York: Jazz World Society. Annual. $95. Artists, bands, booking agencies, clubs that feature jazz, festivals, record producers, etc. Computer-based. Arrangement varies by type of activity.

978. *Canadian Music Directory*. West Hill, Canada: Lloyd. Annual. $30. Lists Canadian producers, manufacturers, importers, exporters, agents, wholesalers, and servicers of records and musical instruments giving name, branch offices, phone, telex, and products or services. Arrangement is classified.

979. *Cash Box International Directory*. New York: Cash Box. Annual. $20. Record producing companies, importers, exporters, distributors, music publishers, agents, studios, and coin machine manufacturers in the United States and worldwide. Each listing includes, at minimum, name, address, and phone. Some entries contain names of key executives, product or service, and operating data. Arrangement is classified with separate United States and international sections.

980. Chamber Music America. *CMA Membership Directory*. New York. Annual. $15. Lists ensembles giving name, address, phone, year established, and activities. Also included are associate individual and support organizational members. Arrangement of ensembles is geographical then alphabetical with alphabetical index.

981. Craven, Robert R. *Symphony Orchestra of the United States: Selected Profiles*. Westport CT: Greenwood, Inc., 1986. 521p. $55. Essays on 126 orchestras giving name, address, background, organization, plus performance information. Includes at least one orchestra from every state. Arrangement is geographical. Chronology and selected bibliography.

982. _____. *Symphony Orchestras of the World: Selected Profiles.* Westport CT: Greenwood, 1987. 2v. $56. Essays on 118 leading orchestras in 42 countries giving name, address, background, and organization. Arrangement is geographical. Chronology and selected bibliography.

983. Gospel Music Association. *GMA Official Resource Directory.* Nashville TN. Irregular. $5. Professionals, companies, agencies, radio and television stations, and book stores featuring gospel music. Each listing gives name, address, and phone. Arrangement is alphabetical except for stations.

984. Incorporated Society of Musicians. *ISM Yearbook.* London. Annual. $20. Membership directory giving name, address, phone, and specialization. Alphabetical.

985. *International Music and Opera Guide.* London: Tantivy; New York: Zoetrope. Annual. $12.95. Lists classical music and opera professional companies, festivals, schools, stores, periodicals, and organizations giving name, address, contact, and, for many, organizational and activity information. Arrangement is classified then geographical.

986. International Tape/Disc Association. *ITA Source Directory.* New York. Annual. Membership. Lists member manufacturers and suppliers of audio, computer, and video products giving name, address, contact, and products. Arrangement is classified by type of product.

987. *Kemps International Music and Recording Industry Year Book.* London: Kemps Group; New York: Bowker. Annual. $30. Lists servicers of the music industry in Great Britain and worldwide giving name, address, and phone. Arrangement is geographical then classified by activity.

988. *Music and Booking Source Directory.* Santa Monica CA: Music & Booking. Annual. $65. Lists locations where live music is booked, agents, promoters plus artists, recording companies, and record and equipment manufacturers giving name, address, and contact and brief data for agencies and companies. Arrangement is classified by activity or product with alphabetical name and geographical indexes.

989. *Music Directory Canada.* Toronto, Canada: Norris-Whitney Communications. Annual. $20.95. Over 4000 Canadian companies and organizations involved in the music business giving name, address, phone, and products or services. Arrangement is classified.

990. *Music Industry Directory,* 7th ed. Chicago: Marquis Who's Who, 1983. 678p. $67.50. United States and Canadian associations, agencies, unions, professional companies, competitions, festivals, schools, publications, and industry firms giving name, address, phone, key executives, and, for many, description of activities. The most massive assemblage of music industry referrals published.

991. *Musical America International Directory of the Performing Arts.* New York: ABC Leisure Magazines. Annual. $55. Lists musical organizations and musicians giving name, address, contact, and, for some, other organizational and service data. Arrangement is classified with alphabetical name index.

992. Professional Audiovideo Retailers Association. *PARA Membership Directory.* Kansas City MO. Annual. Membership. Each listing gives name, address, phone, and executives.

993. Rabin, Carol Price. *Music Festivals in America,* Rev. ed. Stockbridge MA: Berkshire Traveller, 1983. 286p. $10.95. Travel guide list of 170 festivals in the United States and Canada (only 9) giving name, address, description, type of music performed, artists who have performed, ticket and reservation information, and phone.

994. _____. *Music Festivals in Europe and Britain.* Stockbridge MA: Berkshire Traveller, 1984. 190p. $10.95. Travel guide list including Israel, Russia, Turkey, and Japan giving name, address, description, type of music performed, artists who have performed, ticket and reservation information, and phone.

Management

995. American Entrepreneurs Association. *Recycled-record Store.* Los Angeles, 1985. 145p. $39.50. Guide to establishing and operating a small business. Legal, management, marketing, operations, and financial procedures. Supplier addresses and a bibliography. Looseleaf format.

996. Audits and Surveys, Inc. *Home Taping in America, 1983.* New York, 1983. 32p. Controlled distribution. Survey and analysis of the extent of unauthorized taping of copyrighted audiotapes in the United States. Prepared for and distributed by the Recording Industry Association of America.

997. Baskerville, David. *Music Business Handbook and Career Guide,* 3rd ed. Los Angeles: Sherwood, 1982. 1v. $18.95. Overview of music in the marketplace from songwriting to copyright, licensing, agents, management, production, merchandising, records, music films, and career options and development. Appendix of sample business forms.

998. Krebeck, Benjamine, and

Firestone, Rod. *Start Me Up!: The Music Business Meets the Personal Computer.* Van Nuys CA: Mediac, 1986. 167p. $12.95. Explains applications of small computers to booking, tours, publicity as well as accounting, communications, and directories in the music business. Organization and operations discussed. Examples of businesses successfully employing computers.

999. Lambert, Dennis, and Zalkind, Ronald. *Producing Hit Records.* New York: Schirmer, 1980. 196p. $16.95. For the songwriter, record producer, or agent. Guide book outlining the key problems and questions which must be faced in producing a successful song or record.

1000. *Legal and Business Aspects of the Music Industry: Music, Videocassettes, and Records.* New York: Practicing Law Institute, 1980. 736p. $40. Articles, legal documents, and standard forms for contracts, copyright, and agreements in the music and recording industry. Textbook for Institute course.

1001. Livingston, Robert A. *Livingston's Complete Music Industry Business and Law Reference Book.* Cardiff by the Sea CA: La Costa Music Business Consultants, 1981. 346p. $27. Music business law from the prospective of the songwriter, musician, or performer. Articles on contracts, copyright, and agreements with laws and standard forms related. Provides different perspective for business owner, manager, or agent.

1002. Recording Industry Association of America. *State Laws Against Piracy of Sound Records: A Handbook for Enforcement and Prosecution.* New York. Biennial. Controlled distribution. Summary of state enactments plus association recommendations and procedures for eliminating piracy by groups and individuals.

1003. Shermel, Sidney, and Krasilousky, M. William. *More About This Business of Music,* 3rd ed. New York: Billboard, 1982. 214p. $14.95. Introduction to production and performance of music and the types of organizations and people involved. Examines the business of serious music, live performances, printed music, and transcriptions, and trade organizations and music law. The implication is that this work supplements *This Business of Music,* when, in actual fact, it examines many facets of the music business not within the scope of Shermel's earlier sourcebook (see **1004**).

1004. _____, and _____. *This Business of Music,* 4th ed. New York: Billboard, 1979. 596p. Out of print. Recognized as "the" music business text. Discusses the relationship of music creation to music production especially as it relates to recordings and the recording industry. Almost half of the book is devoted to industry forms for copyright and contracts.

1005. Stein, Howard, and Zalkind, Ronald. *Promoting Rock Concerts.* New York: Schirmer, 1979. 188p. $6.95. For concert agents. Guide book outlining the key problems and questions which must be faced in establishing an effective, successful program.

1006. Tobler, John, and Grundy, Stuart. *Record Producers.* New York: Saint Martin's, 1983. 248p. $10.96. Collection of interviews with 13 American and British rock record producers on the business of contacting for, producing, and marketing some of the biggest rock 'n' roll hits.

1007. Wall, Geoffrey, and Mitchell, Clare. *Community Impact of Symphony Orchestras.* Toronto, Canada: Association of Canadian Orchestras, 1984. 117p. $10. Survey of the economic as well as social impact. In addition to this general study, the authors have conducted specific studies, published separately by the Association ($5 each) on the impact of the Kitchener-Waterloo, Lethbridge, Quebec, and Toronto orchestras on these communities.

1008. Zalkind, Ronald. *Getting Ahead in the Music Business.* New York: Schirmer, 1979. 286p. $16.95. Basic survival strategies for beginning music business entrepreneurs. Guide book outlining key problems and questions. No solutions offered. Good beginning point but must be detailed through more in-depth reference sources.

Industry

1009. Canada. Statistics Canada. *Phonograph Records and Prerecorded Tapes in Canada.* Ottawa, Canada. Annual. $40. Statistics on establishments, production, and sales by region, monthly, and cumulated.

1010. Key Note Publications Ltd. *Records and Tapes,* 6th ed. London, 1987. 42p. $100. Analyzes industry structure and trends over a five-year span and compares companies in the last three. Financial ratios and future development examined. Market structure and potential for overseas tourists reviewed. Bibliography.

1011. Recording Industry Association of America. *Inside the Recording Industry: A Statistical Overview.* New York, 1985. 2v. Membership. Two-part examination of the industry. Part 1 is a broad look at the music business from recording through record production to merchandising. Part 2 contains extensive statistical charts and tables on production and sales.

Market

1012. Euromonitor. *Audio Report.* London, 1981. 57p. $325. Examination of the United Kingdom market, its growth and development in the past decade, and its prospects for the 1980s. Data on consumer demand, market share, and retail distribution. Examines music centres, radio music market, record and tape sales, and audio equipment purchases.

1013. Hope Reports, Inc. *Hope Reports 1986 Market Trends: A Special Report & General Forecast on AV Media Potential.* Rochester NY, 1986. 19p. $55. Charting audio-video production, growth, and sales potential. Based upon the *Hope Reports Industry Quarterly* market letter.

1014. Linear Group. *Bluegrass Audience 1984 Survey Results.* Owensboro KY: International Bluegrass Music Association, 1987. 3p. Membership. Summary results of survey of attendees at four major bluegrass festivals in June and July, 1984. Statistics by age, income, education, occupation, residency, marital status, gender, number of children, and other data. Also published in *International Bluegrass,* March/April 1987, p. 11.

1015. NPD Special Industry Services. *Consumer Purchasing of Records and Pre-recorded Tapes in the United States: Five Year Trend Report 1979–1983.* New York: Recording Industry Association of America, 1984. 12p. Controlled distribution. Primarily statistical tables and charts.

Periodicals

1016. American Music Festival Association. *American Music Fest.* Anaheim CA. Annual. Membership. Articles on music festivals in America, the performers and their works, and activities of the association.

1017. American Society of Composers, Authors, and Publishers. *ASCAP in Action.* New York. 3 issues. Membership. News and articles on music copyright legislation, cases, and licensing. Indexed in *Music Index.*

1018. American Symphony Orchestra League. *Symphony Magazine.* Washington DC. Bimonthly. $25. Official association publication. For orchestra managers, board members, conductors, and the symphony community. Profiles, programming, fund raising, management tips, industry trends, and technological developments featured. Special report: "North American Orchestra Directory" in each December issue. Calendar of symphonic events each issue. Indexed in *Music Index.*

1019. Association of Canadian Orchestras. *Orchestra Canada/Orchestras Canada.* Toronto: 10 issues. $6. Official association publication. News and profiles of the orchestras, music season, finance and management, and calendar of events.

1020. Association of Concert Bands. *ACB Newsletter.* Utica NY. 10 issues. Membership. Official association publication. News of the association, conferences, management, fund raising, and profiles.

1021. Association of Professional Vocal Ensembles. *APVE Voice.* Philadelphia PA. Bimonthly. Membership. Official association publication. Reports on endowments, funding legislation, state arts agencies, and association news. News of conferences, workshops, festivals, and other events.

1022. *Audio Publishing Reporter.* White Plains NY: Knowledge Industry. Monthly. $245. Articles on manufacturers, distributors, and the industry. Interviews and surveys. Financial, production, and market statistics.

1023. *Audio Times.* New York: International Thompson Retail. Monthly. $24. News and feature articles on business conditions, market developments, merchandising, and product trends in the United States. Column on audio technology.

1024. *Billboard.* New York: Billboard. Weekly. $148. News magazine of the music business. News of people, events, recordings, companies, and the economic condition of the industry. Indexed in *Music Index, Predicasts F&S Index: United States, Trade and Industry Index.*

1025. *Bluegrass Unlimited.* Broad Run VA: Bluegrass Unlimited. Monthly. $15. News and articles on bluegrass groups, performers, and clubs, appearance calendar, and discographies. Special reports: "Festival Guide" in each March issue and "Bluegrass Talent Directory" in each December issue.

1026. Canadian Independent Record Production Association. *CIRPA Newsletter.* Toronto, Canada. 8 issues. Membership. Official association publication. News of the association and the Canadian industry.

1027. *Canadian Musician.* Toronto, Canada: Norris. Bimonthly. $15. News and articles on groups, professional performances, and the Canadian music scene. Information on equipment, products, and instruction. *Canadian Music Trade* is a more important source of music and record industry statistics. Special reports: "Songwriter's Market Guide"

in each June issue and "Canadian Recording Studio Guide" in each October issue. Indexed in *Music Index.*

1028. *Cash Box: The International Music-Record Weekly.* New York: Cash Box. Weekly. $125. Primary industry source for record reviews, ratings, and lists. Information on the music video and music amusements fields. Current news, information on the economic state of the industry, and record marketing tips. Industry statistics. Special issue: *Cash Box Directory* (each July, $15). Indexed in *Music Index.*

1029. Chamber Music America. *Chamber Music Magazine.* New York. Quarterly. Membership. Articles on chamber music, musical groups, performance organization, management, and promotion.

1030. Country Music Association. *Close Up.* Nashville TN. Monthly. Membership. Official association publication. News of performers, industry, events, and record charts worldwide.

1031. *Entertainment Merchandising.* Cleveland OH: Harcourt Brace Jovanovich. Monthly. $24. Primarily a new audio, video, and compact disc product listing medium. Limited number of news and merchandising articles.

1032. Gospel Music Association. *Good News Newsletter.* Nashville TN. Irregular. Membership. Official association publication. News of the industry, broadcasting, association and its members, and calendar of events.

1033. *Grassometer: America's Bluegrass Indicator.* Olustee FL: Starlite Entertainment. Monthly. $12. News of the industry, producers and companies, statistics, broadcasting of bluegrass, events, personalities, and top recordings on radio.

1034. Hope Reports,Inc. *Hope Reports Industry Quarterly*. Rochester NY. Quarterly. $250. Statistics on manufacturing expenditures, costs, profits, production, and distribution of home audio and video recordings. Dollar and unit sales for over 150 products. Market information and forecasts.

1035. International Association of Independent Producers. *Communication Arts International*. Washington DC. Quarterly. $6. Official association publication. News on performing arts production and recording. Text in English with summaries in Chinese, French, German, and Spanish. Production techniques, management, law, patents, and industry and marketing statistics.

1036. International Bluegrass Music Association. *International Bluegrass*. Owensboro KY. Bimonthly. Membership. Business briefs, broadcasting news, foreign and regional news, industry statistics, and books and record reviews.

1037. International Society of Performing Arts Administrators. *Performing Arts Forum*. Austin TX. 7 issues. $15. Official association publication. News of the association, musical events and festivals, and members.

1038. International Tape/Disc Association. *ITA News Digest*. New York. Bimonthly. Membership. Official association publication. Contains news of the association and the industry.

1039. Jazz World Society. *Jazz World*. New York. Bimonthly. Membership. Official association publication. News of the jazz industry, the market and growth, bookings, recordings, festivals, and other events.

1040. *Leisure Time Electronics*. New York: CBS Magazines. Monthly. $24. For the high volume audiovideo retailer. Articles on new product marketing programs, consumer buying patterns, and retailer sales projections. Case histories of successful sales programs.

1041. *Music and Sound Electronics Retailer*. Carle Place NY: Professional Recording and Sound Publications, Inc. Monthly. Controlled circulation. News of products, firms, and the industry. Includes statistics. Tabloid format. Former title: *Sound Arts Merchandising Journal*.

1042. *Music Business Contacts*. Long Island City NY: Music-by-Mail. Bimonthly. $6. For songwriters. Information on new performance, publishing, and recording companies in the music business to which news music can be submitted.

1043. Music Industries Association of Canada. *MIAC Newsletter*. Toronto, Canada. Bimonthly. Membership. Official association publication. Association and industry news.

1044. *Music Video Retailer*. Chestnut Hill MA: Larkin-Pluznick-Larkin, Inc. Monthly. $20. Articles on merchandising records and tapes. Product news. Special reports: "Directory of (over 10,000) Record and Tape Stores" in May issue, "Music and Video Suppliers Directory" in October issue, and "Top 100 Retail Chains" in December issue. Former title: *Music Retailer*.

1045. National Association of Independent Record Distributors and Manufacturers. *NAIRDM Newsletter*. Pennsauken NJ. Irregular. Membership. Official association publications. News of the association and the industry.

1046. National Association of Recording Merchandisers. *NARM Sounding Board*. Marlton NJ. Bimonthly. Membership. Official association publication. News of the association and the industry.

1047. *Record Research*. Brooklyn NY. Bimonthly. $10 per 10 issues. Individual and collective statistics on phonorecord sales. Market information and analysis. Indexed in *Music Index*.

1048. Recording Industry Association of America. *RIAA Newsletter*. New York. Quarterly. Membership. Official association publication. News of the association and the industry.

1049. Small Independent Record Manufacturers Association. *SIRMA Newsletter*. Stamford CT. Quarterly. Membership. Official association publication. News of small black-owned recording companies, the roll of blacks in the recording industry, and activities of the association.

1050. *Up Beat*. Chicago: Maher. Monthly. $15. For the music retailer. News and articles on industry, market trends, sales promotion, products, management, finance, inventory control, and government regulations.

1051. Women's Independent Label Distribution Network. *WILD Newsletter*. Lansing MI. Monthly. Free. Official association publication. News of women in the recording industry, women's recording companies, and the association.

Databases

1052. Billboard Publications, Inc. *Billboard Information Network*. New York. Updated daily. $200. Articles and analysis. Music chart and paylist statistics from 600 broadcasting and entertainment outlets. Record, video, video game, and computer software sales and rental statistics from 600 outlets. Online 24 hours per day via Tymeshare.

1053. International Bluegrass Music Association. *Radio Stations Play Bluegrass Music*. Updated continuously. Membership. Directory. List of stations with address, phone, and contact. Not online.

1054. Jazz World Society. *Jazz Directories and Mailing Lists*. Updated continuously. Membership. Directory. Computerized mailing lists of jazz world organizations and individuals including bands, booking agencies, clubs that feature jazz, festivals, record producers, etc. Not online.

Bibliographies/Indexes

1055. Cooper, B. Lee. *Popular Music Handbook: A Resource Guide for Teachers, Librarians, and Media Specialists.* Littleton CO: Libraries Unlimited, 1984. 415p. $37.50. Designed for teaching popular music topics, biographical research, and discography study but contains references to music business topics. Bibliography of basic popular music reference books. Format is more oriented to teachers than research, but the thoroughness of its listings makes the work an excellent research source. Periodical and book citations. No abstracts. Subject index.

1056. Iwaschkin, Roman. *Popular Music: A Reference Guide.* New York: Garland, 1986. 658p. $80. Thousands of citations make this work one of the most comprehensive sourcebooks to the major segments of British and American music. General, reference, historical, biographical, instruction, professional technique, the music business (oriented to publishing and recording), literary works, and music periodicals. More valuable to the music researcher than the business investigator but still must be consulted.

1057. *Music Index.* Detroit MI: Information Coordinators. Monthly with biennial cumulation. $840. Citations to articles in over 350 music periodicals by author and subject. Extensive coverage of music industry information and reports. A must for any entertainment library or information center even though publication is five years behind.

Associations

1058. American Music Festival Association. 2323 W. Lincoln Ave., Suite 225, Anaheim CA 92801. (714) 535-7591. Federation of state and regional associations. Compiles statistics. Conducts research. Provides seminars. Publishes periodical.

1059. American Society of Composers, Authors, and Publishers. One Lincoln Plaza, New York NY 10023. (212) 595-3050. Association of music owners. Grants licenses and distributes royalties for commercial performances of copyrighted musical works of its members. Provides seminars. Publishes handbooks, periodical.

1060. American Symphony Orchestra League. 633 E St., N.W., Washington DC 20004. (202) 628-0099. Association of professional performing companies and supporting individuals and organizations. Compiles statistics. Conducts research. Provides management counsel, seminars. Maintains library. Publishes periodical.

1061. Association of British Orchestras. Francis House, Francis St., London, England SW1P 1DE. (01) 828-6913. Association of professional performing companies. Purpose is to represent management in negotiations with employees, unions, and governmental agencies.

1062. Association of Canadian Orchestras. 56 The Esplanade, Toronto, Ontario, Canada M5E 1A7. (416) 336-8834. Association of professional performing companies. Compiles statistics. Conducts research. Provides seminars. Publishes statistics, directory, periodical.

1063. Association of Concert Bands. 19 Benton Circle, Utica NY 13501. (315) 732-2738. Association of professional performing companies, business corporations, and individuals devoted to the development and growth of community and concert bands in America and abroad. Conducts research. Provides management counsel, seminars. Publishes handbooks, directory, periodical.

1064. Association of Professional Recording Studios. 23 Chestnut Ave., Chorleywood, Rickmansworth, Herts, England WD4 4HA. Rickmansworth 72907. Association of companies and nonprofit studios in the United Kingdom and overseas. Publishes handbooks, directory.

1065. Association of Professional Vocal Ensembles. 251 S. 18th St., Philadelphia PA 19103. (215) 545-4444. Association of professional performing companies and individuals supporting the growth of professional vocal music in America. Provides management counsel, seminars. Publishes periodical.

1066. Canadian Independent Record Production Association. 144 Front St., W. Suite 330, Toronto, Ontario, Canada M5J 2L7. (416) 593-1665. Association of companies. Publishes periodical.

1067. Canadian Recording Industry Association. 89 Bloor St., E. Toronto, Ontario, Canada M4W 1A9. (416) 967-7272. Association of companies.

1068. Chamber Music America. 545 Eighth Ave., New York NY

10018. (212) 244-2772. Association of conductorless professional ensembles, individuals, and professional schools. Compiles statistics. Conducts research. Provides management counsel, seminars. Publishes statistics, periodical.

1069. Country Music Association. P.O. Box 22299, Nashville TN 37202. (615) 244-2840. Association of organizations and individuals deriving income from producing and performing country music. Purpose is to promote country music. Provides seminars, trade shows. Maintains library. Publishes handbooks, periodical.

1070. Gay and Lesbian Association of Choruses. 4016 S.W. 57th St., Portland OR 97221. (503) 292-6442. Association of professional performing companies. Purpose is to promote the development and growth of choruses. Provides management counsel, seminars. Maintains library.

1071. Gospel Music Association. P.O. Box 23201, Nashville TN 37202. (615) 242-0303. Association of companies and individuals deriving income from producing and performing gospel music. Purpose is to promote gospel music worldwide. Compiles statistics. Provides seminars. Publishes handbooks, directory, periodical.

1072. Incorporated Society of Musicians. 10 Stratford Place, London, England W1N 9AE. (01) 629-4413. Association of solo performers and private teachers. Provides seminars. Publishes directory.

1073. International Association of Independent Producers. P.O. Box 2801, Washington DC 20013. (202) 638-5595. International association of companies and individuals involved in production of film, video, and recordings. Compiles statistics.

Provides management counsel, seminars. Publishes periodical.

1074. International Bluegrass Music Association. 326 Saint Elizabeth St., Owensboro KY 42301. (502) 926-1100. Association of companies and individuals deriving income from producing and performing bluegrass music. Purpose is to promote bluegrass music worldwide. Compiles statistics. Conducts research. Provides seminars, trade shows. Maintains database. Publishes statistics, periodical.

1075. International Federation of Phonogram and Videogram Producers. 123 Pall Mall, London, England SW1Y 5EA. (01) 930-1752. Federation of national associations. Purpose is primarily international copyright protection.

1076. International Society of Performing Arts Administrators. P.O. Box 200238, Austin TX 78720. (512) 346-1328. Association of local concert managers and promoters. Publishes periodical. Former name: International Association of Concert and Festival Managers.

1077. International Tape/Disc Association. Ten Columbus Circle, New York NY 10019. (212) 956-7110. Association of companies manufacturing audio and video tapes, home computers, software and optical/laser media. Compiles statistics. Provides seminars. Publishes standards, directory, periodical.

1078. Jazz World Society. P.O. Box 777, Times Sq. Station, New York NY 10109. (202) 939-0836. Association of professionals, fans, and companies. Purpose is to stimulate the growth of jazz worldwide. Provides seminars. Maintains library, database. Publishes directories, periodical.

1079. Music Trades Association. P.O. Box 249, London, England W4

5EX. (01) 459-6194. Association of companies in the audiovideo and musical instrument and sheet music industries. Provides seminars, trade shows.

1080. National Association of Independent Record Distributors and Manufacturers. 6935 Airport Highway Ln., Pennsauken NJ 08109. (609) 665-8085. Association of companies. Publishes periodical.

1081. National Association of Recording Merchandisers. 2 Eves Dr., Suite 307, Marlton NJ 08053. (609) 424-7404. Association of companies primarily servicing the large retailer. Compiles statistics. Publishes periodical.

1082. Professional Audiovideo Retailers Association. 9140 Ward Pkwy., Kansas City MO 64114. (816) 444-3500. Association of companies committed to promoting the sale of high quality audiovideo products. Compiles statistics. Provides seminars. Publishes directory, periodical. Certifies individuals.

1083. Recording Industry Association of America. 888 Seventh Ave., 9th Fl., New York NY 10106.

(212) 765-4330. Association of companies that manufacturer audio and video discs and tapes for the home market. Compiles statistics. Publishes standards, statistics, periodical.

1084. Small Independent Record Manufacturers Association. 2001 W. Main St., Suite 205E, Stamford CT 06902. (203) 358-9948. Association of black-owned companies grossing less than $250,000 per year. Provides management counsel, seminars. Publishes periodical.

1085. Tape Manufacturers Group. Hesketh House, Portman Sq., London, England W1H 9FG. (01) 486-9021. Association of companies in Great Britain manufacturing blank audio and video tapes.

1086. Women's Independent Label Distribution Network. P.O. Box 14224, Lansing MI 48906. (517) 323-4325. Association of companies owned and operated by women. Purpose is to advance the role of women in the recording industry. Provides management counsel, seminars. Publishes periodical.

20. The Professional Sports Industry

SIC Code: 7941.

Enterprises providing professional team athletic entertainment.

Directories

1087. American League of Professional Baseball Clubs. *American League Red Book.* Saint Louis MO: Sporting News. Annual. $9.95. Clubs, rosters, club and player statistics, records, newsworthy professional baseball events, League and World series, chronology, and history. Each club listing gives name, address, phone, key personnel, and stadium information.

1088. *Baseball Blue Book.* Saint Petersburg FL: Baseball Blue Book. Annual. $35. Lists professional and amateur leagues and teams giving name, address, phone, and key personnel. Arrangement is by league with club name and personal name index.

1089. Major Indoor Soccer League. *MISL Guide.* New York. Annual. $10. Owners, managers, and rosters of the League's 12 clubs. Club and player statistics past and present. League history to date. Each club listing gives name, address, phone, key personnel, and stadium information.

1090. National Basketball Association. *NBA Guide.* Saint Louis MO: Sporting News. Annual. $9.95. Clubs, rosters, club and player statistics, records and rankings, newsworthy professional basketball events, playoffs and national championship, chronology, and history. Each club listing gives name, address, phone, key personnel, and arena information.

1091. National Football League. *NFL Record and Fact Book.* New York. Annual. $12.95. Clubs, rosters, club and player statistics, records and rankings, newsworthy professional football events, playoffs and Superbowl, chronology, and history. Each club listing gives name, address, phone, key personnel, and stadium information.

1092. National Hockey League. *Hockey Guide.* Saint Louis MO: Sporting News. Annual. $9.95. Professional and amateur clubs and leagues, rosters, club and player statistics, records and rankings, newsworthy professional basketball events, playoffs, championships, and Stanley Cup, chronology, and history. Each club listing gives name, address, phone, key personnel, and arena information.

1093. National League of Professional Baseball Clubs. *National League Green Book.* Saint Louis MO: Sporting News. Annual. $9.95. Clubs, rosters, club and player statistics, records, events, League and World series, chronology, and history. Each club listing gives name, address, phone, key personnel, and stadium information.

Management

1094. Berry, Robert C.; Gould, William B.; and Staudohar, Paul D. *Labor Relations in Professional Sports.* Dover MA: Auburn House, 1986. 289p. $35. Law, cases, and legal analysis. Contracts, privacy, leagues, player-club issues, player-agent relationship, unions, collective bargaining, and arbitration.

1095. _____, and Wong, Glenn M. *Law and Business of the Sports Industries.* Dover MA: Auburn House, 1986. 2v. $90. Law, cases, and legal analysis. Volume one examines "Professional Sports Leagues."

1096. Byrne, Jim. *League: The Rise and Fall of the* USFL. New York: Prentice Hall, 1987. 352p. $17.95. Story of an ill-fated United States professional football league as recorded by its chief press agent. Drafting competitions, excessive salaries, TV contracts, and under-financing are chronicled.

1097. Klein, Gene, and Fisher, David. *First Down and a Billion: The Funny Business of Pro Football.* New York: Morrow, 1987. 300p. $17.95. Insights and recollections on ownership, management, and the owners of professional football clubs by the former owner of the San Diego Chargers.

1098. Maryland. Dept. of Economic and Community Development Research Division. *Economic Impact of Professional Sports on the Maryland Economy.* Annapolis MD, 1985. 71p. Free. Study and statistics on the expenditure by professional sports organizations, government, and consumers prepared for the Maryland Special Advisory Commission on Professional Sports and the Economy.

1099. Maryland. Special Advisory Commission on Professional Sports and the Economy. *Report on Professional Sports and the Economy.* Annapolis MD, 1985. 91p. Free. Analysis and recommendations on a "Professional Sports Action Plan" for the State of Maryland involving state and local financial support. Bibliography.

1100. Osbourn, Kevin. *Efforts to Attract Professional Sports as a Source of Revenue.* Lexington KY: Council of State Governments, 1986. 6p. Free. General introduction to the economics of professional sports, sports francises, and state financial and administrative involvement in recruitment. Bibliography.

1101. Staudohar, Paul D. *Sports Industry and Collective Bargaining.* Ithaca NY: ILR Press, 1986. 195p. $22.50. Study of the history and processes of labor relations and player-owner negotiations in all professional sports. Bibliography and subject index.

1102. Tischler, Steven. *Footballers and Businessmen: The Origins of Professional Soccer in England.* New York and London: Holmes & Meier, 1981. 154p. $29.50. Examines the complex structure and role of businessmen in the development of soccer clubs and professional soccer players in the United Kingdom.

1103. Touche Ross and Co. *Professional Sports Action Plan: Final Report.* Newark NJ, 1985. 2v. Controlled distribution. Summary and detailed program recommended to the Maryland Special Advisory Commission on Professional Sports and the Economy on State of Maryland support of professional sports.

1104. Yasser, Raymond L. *Sports Law: Cases and Materials.* Lanham MD and London: University Press of America, Inc., 1985. 642p. $45. Landmark cases analyzed with notes and bibliography. Contains professional sports cases.

1105. _____. *Torts and Sports: Legal Liability in Professional and Amateur Athletics.* Westport CT and London: Greenwood, 1985. 424p. $35. Landmark cases analyzed with notes and bibliography.

Market

1106. Market Facts, Inc. *Chicago Cubs Survey.* Chicago, 1985. 3v. Controlled distribution. Market survey and study of the general public, season ticket holders, and neighborhood residents on various aspects of the team, promotion and marketing, the operation of the club, and the Wrigley Field environment.

Periodicals

1107. Continental Basketball Association. *CBA Newsweekly.* Denver CO. Weekly. Controlled distribution. Official association publication. News of the league, its teams and players, the parent NBA, and professional basketball. Game and season statistics.

1108. *Edelstein Pro Football Letter.* Wilmington DE: Associates International. Weekly. $75. Newsletter of management, player, and governmental happenings in the United States.

1109. Kagen, Paul, Associates, Inc. *Pay TV Sports.* Carmel CA. Monthly. $425. Newsletter on the economics of national and regional cable and pay TV and professional sports in the United States.

1110. Major Indoor Soccer League. *Missile.* New York. Bimonthly. Controlled distribution. Official association publication. News of the league, its member teams, and soccer activities, events, and seminars. Game and season statistics.

1111. Major Indoor Soccer League Players Association. *Kick-Off Newsletter.* Washington DC. Biweekly. Membership. Official association publication. Monitors MISL management, financial status, and activities. Information on negotiations, contracts, grievances, and arbitrations. News of the association, members, and events.

1112. National Association of Professional Baseball Leagues. *Baseball News.* Saint Petersburg FL. 10 issues. Membership. Official association publication. News of minor league baseball, member leagues, the major league, baseball events, and the association. Statistics from league play.

1113. National Basketball Association. *Hoop.* New York: Professional Sports Publications. Monthly. Controlled distribution. Official association publication. News of the league, its member teams, basketball activities and events, professional sports, and related governmental activities. Game and season statistics.

1114. National Basketball Players Association. *Time Out.* New York. Monthly. Membership. Official association publication. Monitors NBA operations. Information on negotiations, contracts, arbitrations, and grievances. News of the association, its members, and events.

1115. National Football League Players Association. *Audible.* Washington DC. Monthly. Membership.

Official association publication. Monitors NFL activities. Information on negotiations, contracts, free agency, grievances, and arbitrations. News of the association, members, and events.

1116. _____. *Laudible*. Washington DC. Monthly. $150. For agents and attorneys of NFL players. Leaguewide salary, compensation, bonus, and other financial information with analysis.

1117. *Sports Industry News*. Camden ME: Game Point. Weekly. $227. Professional and major amateur sports. News and articles on leagues, sales, television and player contracts, labor relations, concessions, endorsements, and legal problems and solutions. Statistics on attendance, salaries, income, and expenditures. Indexed in *Predicasts F&S Index: United States*.

Bibliographies/Indexes

1118. Smith, Myron J., comp. *Baseball: A Comprehensive Bibliography*. Jefferson NC and London: McFarland, 1986. 915p. $55. Contains 21,251 citations to books and articles. Section on "Professional Leagues and Teams" is valuable for its background, not its business information.

Associations

1119. American Hockey League. 218 Memorial Ave., West Springfield MA 01089. (413) 781-2030. Association of minor league teams in the United States and Canada. Compiles statistics. Publishes player and game statistics but no industry or market data. Affiliated with the National Hockey League.

1120. American League of Professional Baseball Clubs. 350 Park Ave., New York NY 10022. (212) 371-7600. Association of major league teams in the United States and Canada. Compiles statistics. Maintains library. Publishes player and game statistics but no industry or market data, directory.

1121. Canadian Football League. 1200 Bay St., 12th Fl., Toronto, Ontario, Canada M5R 2A5. (416) 928-1200. Association of league teams in Canada.

1122. Continental Basketball Association. 425 S. Cherry St., Suite 230, Denver CO 80222. (303) 331-0404. Association of minor league teams in the United States. Compiles statistics. Publishes, player and game statistics, handbooks, periodical. Affiliated with the National Basketball Association.

1123. Federation of Professional Athletes. 2021 L St., N.W., Washington DC 20036. (202) 463-2200. Association professionally affiliated with sports labor unions in the United States. Compiles statistics. Conducts research. Provides seminars. Maintains library. Affiliated with the American Federation of Labor and Congress of Industrial Organizations. Former name: Professional Athletes International.

1124. International League of Professional Baseball Clubs. P.O. Box 608, Grove City OH 43123. (614) 871-1300. Association of minor league teams in the United States. Compiles statistics. Publishes player and game statistics but no industry or market data.

1125. International Table Tennis League. 1218 Third Ave., N., Seattle WA 98109. (206) 282-6449. Association of professional teams worldwide. Purpose is to organize and promote team competition.

1126. Major Indoor Soccer League. 757 Third Ave., Suite 2305, New York NY 10017. (212) 486-7070. Association of league teams in the United States. Compiles statistics. Provides seminars. Publishes game and player statistics, directory, periodical.

1127. Major Indoor Soccer League Players Association. 1300 Connecticut Ave., N.W., Suite 407, Washington DC 20036. (202) 463-2200. Labor union. Publishes periodical. Affiliated with Federation of Professional Athletes.

1128. Major League Baseball Players Association. 805 Third Ave., New York NY 10022. (212) 826-0808. Labor union. Unaffiliated.

1129. National Association of Professional Baseball Leagues. 201 Bayshore Dr., S.E., Box A, Saint Petersburg FL 33731. (813) 822-6937. Federation of 18 minor leagues in the United States, Canada, and Latin America. Purpose is promotion of minor league baseball. Compiles statistics. Provides management counsel, seminars. Publishes game and player statistics, handbooks, periodical.

1130. National Basketball Association. 645 Fifth Ave., New York NY 10022. (212) 826-7000. Association of league teams in the United States. Compiles statistics. Publishes play and game statistics, handbooks, directory, periodical.

1131. National Basketball Players Association. 15 Columbus Circle, New York NY 10023. (212) 541-7118. Labor union. Compiles statistics. Provides seminars. Publishes periodical. Unaffiliated.

1132. National Football League. 410 Park Ave., New York NY 10022. (212) 758-1500. Association of league teams in the United States. Compiles statistics. Publishes player and game statistics but no industry or market data, directory.

1133. National Football League Players Association. 1300 Connecticut Ave., N.W., Washington DC 20036. (202) 463-2200. Labor union. Compiles statistics. Conducts research. Provides seminars. Publishes handbooks, periodical. Affiliated with Federation of Professional Athletes.

1134. National Hockey League. 960 Sun Life Bldg., 1155 Metcalfe St., Montreal, Quebec, Canada H3B 2W2. (514) 871-9220. Association of league teams in the United States and Canada. Compiles statistics. Publishes play and game statistics but no industry or market data, directory.

1135. National Hockey League Players Association. 65 Queen St., W., Suite 210, Toronto, Ontario, Canada M5H 2H5. (416) 868-6574. Labor union. Unaffiliated.

1136. National League of Professional Baseball Clubs. 350 Park Ave., New York NY 10022. (212) 371-3700. Association of major league teams in the United States and Canada. Compiles statistics. Maintains library. Publishes player and game statistics but no industry or market data, directory.

1137. Women's American Basketball Association. 19 N. Cooper, Memphis TN 38104. (901) 278-4953. Association of owners of teams in the United States. Purpose is to create a professional league. Successor to the defunct Women's Professional Basketball League.

21. The Professional Racing Industry

SIC Code: 7948.

Enterprises providing professional racing entertainment.

Directories

1138. American Greyhound Track Operators Association. *Track Facts.* North Miami FL. Annual. Free. Lists member racetracks giving name, location, address, phone, officers, officials, operating data, track and facilities information, and record attendance. Arrangement is alphabetical. Also lists greyhound government supervisory agencies and track suppliers.

1139. American Horse Council. *Horse Industry Directory.* Washington DC. Annual. $5. Horse industry organizations such as breed registries, licensing and health agencies, racing bodies, shows, and clubs. Statistical data on breed registration and equine population by state. Each listing gives name, address, and phone. Arrangement is alphabetical.

1140. Championship Auto Racing Teams. *CART Media Guide.* Bloomfield Hills MI. Annual. Controlled distribution. Racing teams, race and car statistics, newsworthy automobile racing data, track information, and history. Each team listing gives owner, drivers, pit crew, car data, and record.

1141. Harness Horsemen International. *This is HHI.* Rocky Hill CT. Annual. Membership. Lists regional groups giving location, address, phone, officers, and activity information. Arrangement is alphabetical. Also lists headquarter's officers and staff giving name, phone, and responsibilities. Association data and history.

1142. Harness Tracks of America. *HTA Directory.* Morristown NJ. Annual. Membership. Lists member racetracks giving name, location, address, phone, officers, officials, operating data, track and facilities information. Arrangement is alphabetical.

1143. International Motor Sports Association. *IMSA Yearbook.* Bridgeport CT. Annual. Controlled distribution. Association staff, drivers, racetracks, races and order of finish, and historical data. Racetrack listings give name, address, phone, key personnel, and description. Arrangement is geographical.

1144. National Hot Rod Association. *NHRA Yearbook.* Glendora CA. Annual. Controlled distribution. Association staff, drivers, racetracks, races and order of finish, and historical data. Racetrack listings give name, address, phone, key personnel, and description. Arrangement is geographical.

1145. *National Speedway Directory.* Marne MI: Slideways. Annual. $6. Lists automobile racetracks in the United States and Canada giving name, address, phone, location, size, surface, operating hours, key officials, and sanctioning. Arrangement is geographical. Former title: Midwest Auto Racing Guide.

1146. Pickering, Martin, ed. *Directory of the Turf.* London: Pacemaker; Lexington KY: MacLeod & Hopper. Annual. $49.95. Racetracks and owners, trainers, and jockeys of thoroughbred race horses in Great Britain. Track listings give name, location, address, phone, officers, officials, and description. Personal listings give name, address, phone, and biographical and horse-related details. Arrangement is classified then alphabetical.

1147. Thoroughbred Racing Associations of North America. *TRA Directory and Record Book.* Lake Success NY. Annual. Free. Lists racetracks in the United States and Canada giving corporate name, name of track, location, address, phone, officers, officials, track information and facilities, prices, and history of the track. Non-member track listings omit description data and history. Arrangement is alphabetical. Industry racing dates for the coming year and statistics for past three years.

1148. United States Auto Club. *USAC Media Guide/Yearbook.* Indianapolis IN. Annual. Controlled distribution. Association staff, drivers, racetracks, races and order of finish, purses, and historical data. Racetrack listings give name, address, phone, key personnel, and description. Arrangement is geographical.

1149. United States Trotting Association. *Racing, Farm, Corporate, and Stable Names Registered with USTA.* Columbus OH. Annual. $10. Each listing gives name, address,

phone, officers, stockholders, and description of property. Arrangement is alphabetical.

1150. _____. *USTA Year Book.* Columbus OH. Annual. $15. Lists harness race horses giving name, owner, breeding, earnings, and records. Arrangement is alphabetical.

Management

1151. American Quarter Horse Association. *Introduction to Quarter Horse Racing.* Amarillo TX, 1986. 31p. Free. Origin of quarter horse racing, equipment, the race, state rules and regulations on horse racing, and organization and management procedures. Glossary of terms.

1152. Connors, Jerry. *Handicapping Beyond the Basics: Theory and Practice for the Intermediate Handicapper.* Columbus OH: United States Trotting Association, 1986. 78p. $3.50. Handicapping the harness race. Cites 80 examples using actual races from tracks around North America.

1153. Davis, Thomas A. *Horse Owners and Breeders Tax Manual.* Washington DC: American Horse Council, 1987. 1v. $90. Guide to federal tax laws affecting horse operations. Sections on business vs. hobby, purchases and sale, account rules, record keeping, depreciation, expenses, and tax credits. IRS regulations and forms. Looseleaf format.

1154. Thoroughbred Owners and Breeders Association. *Thoroughbred Ownership: A Guide for Potential Owners and Breeders.* Elmont NY, n.d. 56p. Free. For the individual entrepreneur, investing, acquiring, incorporating, managing, and registering a thoroughbred race horse.

Industry

1155. American Greyhound Track Operators Association. *AGTOA Annual Report.* North Miami FL. Annual. Free. Individual member track statistics on attendance and pari-mutuel money handled for current and past two years. Comparative data and ten-year summaries for industry attendance, p/m money, and revenue. Stake purses, champions, and records. Review of industry events for the past year and other historical data.

1156. _____. *Summary of State Pari-mutuel Tax Structures.* North Miami FL. Annual. Membership. State by state summary of taxes imposed on tracks with percentage rates and related regulations. Law as to underpayments, legal age, and fines for each state in which a track is operated. Track and industry data on attendance, revenue to government units, and pari-mutuel money handled.

1157. National Association of State Racing Commissioners. *Statistical Reports on Greyhound Racing.* Lexington KY. Annual. $15. Statistics on pari-mutuel betting and revenue to U.S. states, Canada, the Bahamas, and Puerto Rico. Current and retrospective data. Summary of taxing methods used by each state.

1158. _____. *Statistical Reports on Horse Racing.* Lexington KY. Annual. $15. Statistics on pari-mutuel betting and revenue to U.S. states, Canada, the Bahamas, and Puerto Rico. Current and retrospective data. Summary of taxing methods used by each state.

1159. United State Trotting Association. *Trotting and Pacing Guide.* Columbus OH. Annual. $7.50. For the racing reporter. Brief statistics on horses, tracks, and the industry as a whole. Current and retrospective data.

Periodicals

1160. American Horse Council. *AHC Business Quarterly.* Washington DC. Quarterly. Membership. Official association publication. In-depth articles on current industry and operations topics by recognized experts.

1161. _____. *AHC Newsletter.* Washington DC. Monthly. Membership. Official association publication. Focuses on Washington legislation and national political trends affecting the horse industry.

1162. _____. *AHC Tax Bulletin.* Washington DC. Monthly. Membership. Official association publication. Information on laws and regulations, court cases, and industry implications.

1163. American Hot Rod Association. *Drag World.* Spokane WA. Monthly. Membership. Official association publication. News of competitions, cars and drivers, equipment, and the association. Statistics and race results.

1164. Championship Auto Racing Teams. *Fastlanes.* Bloomfield Hill MI. Quarterly. Membership. Official association publication. For members as well as "Winner's Circle Club" members. Emphasis is on race cars and races more than on business.

1165. Harness Horsemen International. *News from HHI.* Rocky Hill CT. 17 issues. Membership. Official association publication. News of racing, races, purses, horses and riders, and standards for racing. Articles on government regulations, insurance, and financial matters. Race statistics.

1166. Harness Tracks of America. *Track Topics.* Morristown NJ.

Weekly. Membership. Official association publication. News and articles on track operations, track improvements, promotional ideas, pari-mutuel betting, and legislation and legal matters. Summaries of association track studies.

1167. Horsemen's Benevolent and Protective Association. *Horsemen's Journal.* New Orleans LA. Monthly. $24. Official association publication. News of sales, races, and racing industry. Articles on business management, legislations, and health issues. Features on horses, owners, and trainers.

1168. International Hot Rod Association. *Drag Review.* Bristol TN. Weekly. Membership. Official association publication. News of races, cars, racetracks, and drivers. Competition statistics.

1169. Jockey Club. *Jockey Club News.* New York. Bimonthly. Membership. Official association publication. Announcement of rules and regulations, research, statistics, and racing developments of thoroughbred horses.

1170. Jockeys' Guild. *Jockey News.* New York. Monthly. Membership. Official association publication. Monitors professional horse racing. Reports on tracks, races, racing commissions, rules, and regulations.

1171. Motorsports Marketing Association. *MMS News.* Langhorne PA. Monthly. $60. News and reports of market research, promotions, public relations, publicity, and advertising of motorsports and motor racing competitions.

1172. National Association for Stock Car Auto Racing. *NASCAR Newsletter.* Daytona Beach FL. Semimonthly. Membership. Official association publication. News of the auto racing industry in the United States

and Canada. Calendar of upcoming races and other racing events. Statistics on races and drivers.

1173. National Association of State Racing Commissioners. *NASRC Weekly News Bulletin.* Lexington KY. Weekly. Membership. Official association publication. Emphasis on the gambling aspects of the racing industry. News of wagering law, legislation, and administrative rulings, conferences, reports, and meetings.

1174. National Greyhound Association. *Greyhound Review.* Abilene KS. Monthly. $20. Official association publication. News of breed development and improvement, racers, racetracks, and the racing industry, breeders, and the association. Breed charts and stud information.

1175. National Hot Rod Association. *National Dragster.* North Hollywood CA. Weekly. Membership. Official association publication. News of races, drivers, and auto racing industry. Statistics on races and drivers.

1176. Standardbred Owners Association. *Horse Sense.* Westbury NY. Bimonthly. Membership. Official association publication. News of harness racing, the relationships between owners and track operators, rules, and regulations. Features on breeders, health and safety, and racing events.

1177. *Thoroughbred Business.* Lexington KY: Lexington Publishers. Bimonthly. $18. Articles on financial, legal, tax, investment, and marketing aspects of the race horse industry.

1178. Thoroughbred Owners and Breeders Association. *Blood-Horse.* Lexington KY: Blood-Horse. Weekly. $68.75. Official association publication. Horse breeding and earnings charts. News of horses, sales, tracks, and people. Articles on finance, management and regulations. Calendar of events.

1179. Thoroughbred Racing Associations of North America. *TRA Newsletter.* Lake Success NY. Monthly. Membership. Official association publication. News of tracks, management, and gambling and horse regulations. Racing statistics and calendar òf events.

1180. United States Auto Club. *USAC News.* Indianapolis IN. Bimonthly. $7. Official association publication. News of races, drivers, and auto racing industry. Statistics on races and drivers.

1181. United States Trotting Association. *Hoof Beats.* Columbus OH. Monthly. $18. Official association publication. News on harness racing, rules, licensing, registration of horses, people, and events. Articles on breeders, tracks, and management. Race, horse, and driver statistics.

1182. United Thoroughbred Trainers of America. *Backstretch.* Detroit MI. Quarterly. $6. Official association publication. News of training methods, stable management, racing rules and regulations, and people and events. Features on farms and stables.

Bibliographies/Indexes

1183. Ebershoff-Coles, Susan, and Leibenguth, Charla Ann. *Motorsports: A Guide to Information Sources.* Detroit MI: Gale Research, 1979. 193p. $62. English language books and articles published from 1965 through 1978. Many racing industry references. Directory of major racing organizations functioning during that period and list of race driver schools.

Associations

1184. American Greyhound Track Operators Association. 1065 N.E. 125th St., Suite 219, North Miami FL 33161. (305) 893-2101. Association owners and operators of pari-mutuel racetracks in the United States. Compiles statistics. Maintains library. Publishes handbooks, statistics, directory.

1185. American Horse Council. 1700 K St., N.W., Suite 300, Washington DC 20006. (202) 296-4031. Association of commercial organizations in the horse industry. Compiles statistics. Conducts research. Provides management counsel, seminars. Publishes handbooks, directory, periodicals.

1186. American Hot Rod Association. 111 Hayford Rd., Spokane WA 99204. (509) 244-2372. Association of professionals and amateurs in the United States and Canada. Purpose is to sponsor national drag racing championship competitions. Compiles statistics. Provides seminars. Publishes standards, handbook periodical. Sanctions competitions.

1187. American Motorcyclists Association. P.O. Box 6114, Westerville OH 43081. (614) 818-2425. Association of professional and amateur racers and other motorcyclists. Compiles statistics. Publishes periodical. Sanctions competitions. Affiliated with the Federation Internationale Motorcycliste.

1188. Association Internationale des Organisateurs de Courses Cyclistes. 10 Rue Faubourg, Montmartre, Paris, France F 75438. 1 246 9233. Association of cycle racetrack owners and organizers. Purpose is to develop professional and amateur cycling competition worldwide.

1189. Automobile Competition Committee for the United States.

1500 Skokie Blvd., Suite 101, Northbrook IL 60062. (312) 272-0090. Federation of five United States automobile racing associations. Purpose is to coordinate activities between the member organizations and the Federation Internationale de l'Automobile. Certifies United States international race drivers.

1190. Canadian Greyhound Racing and Breeders Association. Alexander Blvd., Baldwin, Ontario, Canada L0E 1A0. (416) 722-5394. Association of individuals breeding for racing and sale.

1191. Canadian Racing Drivers Association. P.O. Box 5310, Stn. A, Toronto, Ontario, Canada M5W 1N6. (416) 924-0533. Association of certified race car drivers.

1192. Championship Auto Racing Teams. 390 Enterprise Ct., Bloomfield Hills MI 48013. (313) 334-8500. Association of race car owners, drivers, and mechanics who compete in Indianapolis type auto races and fans (associate members). Compiles statistics. Publishes standards, directory, statistics on races and cars, periodical. Sanctions competitions.

1193. Harness Horsemen International. 1800 Silas Deane Hwy., Suite 220, Rocky Hill CT 06067. (203) 563-1910. Association of owners, drivers, trainers, and breeders engaged in harness racing. Publishes directory, periodical.

1194. Harness Tracks of America. 35 Airport Rd., Morristown NJ 07960. (201) 285-9090. Association of pari-mutuel racetracks in the United States. Compiles statistics. Conduct research. Provides management counsel, seminars. Publishes standards, handbooks, statistics, directory, periodical.

1195. Horsemen's Benevolent and Protective Association. 2800 Grand Route Saint John, New Orleans LA 70119. (504) 945-4500. Association of thoroughbred race horse owners and trainers. Compiles statistics. Publishes periodical.

1196. International Association of Permanent Motor Racing Circuits (Association Internationale des Circuits Permanents). 21 Autodromo Nazionale, Monza, Italy I-20052. 39 22366. Association of auto and motorcycle racetracks. Sanctions competitions.

1197. International Hot Rod Association. P.O. Box 3029, Bristol TN 37620. (615) 764-1164. Association of professional and sports drivers. Compiles statistics. Publishes handbooks, periodical. Sanctions competitions.

1198. International Motor Contest Association. 421 First Ave., Vinton IA 52349. (319) 472-4713. Association of race car owners, drivers, and mechanics. Sanctions competitions east of the Rocky Mountains.

1199. International Motor Sports Association. P.O. Box 3465, Bridgeport CT 06605. (203) 336-2116. Association of race car owners, drivers, mechanics, and racetrack owners. Compiles statistics. Publishes directory, statistics on races and cars, periodical. Sanctions competitions.

1200. Jockey Club. 380 Madison Ave., New York NY 10017. (212) 687-7746. Service organization acting as the official breed registry for United States and Canadian thoroughbred horses. Compiles statistics. Conducts research. Provides information to breeders and researchers. Publishes periodical.

1201. Jockey's Guild. 20 E. 46th St., New York NY 10017. (212) 687-7746. Association of United States state-licensed flat-riding jockeys. Purpose is financial and medical aid to members and families. Publishes periodical.

1202. Motorsports Marketing Association. 1448 Hollywood Ave., Langhorne PA 19047. (215) 752-7797. Association of people involved in promotion, public relations, publicity, and advertising. Purpose is to professionalize motorsports marketing. Publishes periodical.

1203. National Association for Stock Car Auto Racing. P.O. Box K, Daytona Beach FL 32015. (904) 253-0611. Association of race car owners, drivers, mechanics, racetrack owners, and fans (associate members) in the United States and Canada. Compiles statistics. Publishes periodical. Sanctions competitions.

1204. National Association of State Racing Commissioners. 535 W. Second St., Suite 300, Lexington KY 40508. (606) 254-4060. Federation of government regulatory agencies in the United States, Canada, the Bahamas, and Puerto Rico. Compiles statistics. Conducts research. Publishes statistics, periodical.

1205. National Greyhound Association. P.O. Box 543, Abilene KS 67410. (913) 263-4660. Association of greyhound breeders. Purpose is breed improvement, and racing promotion. Publishes periodical. Breed registry.

1206. National Hot Rod Association. P.O. Box 150, North Hollywood CA 91603. (818) 985-6472. Association of professional and amateur dragster drivers, mechanics, dragstrip owners, and fans. Compiles statistics. Conducts research. Provides seminars. Publishes standards, directory, statistics, periodical. Sanctions competitions.

1207. Racetracks of Canada. 555 Burnhamthorpe Rd., Suite 216, Etobicoke, Ontario, Canada M9C 2Y3. (416) 562-6561. Association of owners.

1208. Standardbred Owners Association. 539 Old Country Rd., Westbury NY 11590. (516) 333-5663. Association of owners, trainers, and drivers. Purpose is to promote harness racing in the United States. Compiles statistics. Conducts research. Provides management counsel, seminars. Publishes handbooks, periodical.

1209. Thoroughbred Club of America. P.O. Box 8098, Lexington KY 40533. (606) 254-4282. Association of owners, breeders, and trainers in the United States, Canada, and Europe. Maintains library.

1210. Thoroughbred Owners and Breeders Association. P.O. Box 358, Elmont NY 11003. (516) 488-2260. Association of owners and breeders in the United States and Canada. Purpose is to maintain bloodline records. Compiles statistics. Conducts research. Provides seminars. Publishes handbooks, directory, periodical.

1211. Thoroughbred Racing Associations of North America. 3000 Marcus Ave., Suite 2W4, Lake Success NY 11040. (516) 328-2660. Association of racetracks. Compiles statistics. Publishes statistics, directory, periodical.

1212. U.S. Professional Cycling Federation. P.O. Box 130, R.D. 1, New Tripoli PA 18066. (215) 298-3262. Association of racers. Compiles statistics. Provides seminars. Sanctions competitions. Affiliated with the Union Cycliste Internationale.

1213. United States Auto Club. 490 W. 16th St., Indianapolis IN 46224. (317) 247-5151. Association of race car owners, drivers, mechanics, manufacturer's representatives, and fans. Compiles statistics. Publishes standards, directory, statistics on races and cars, periodical. Certifies individuals. Sanctions competitions.

1214. United States Trotting Association. 750 Michigan Ave., Columbus OH 43215. (614) 224-2291. Association of owners, trainers, and drivers of standardbred race horses, harness track owners and managers, and officials. Compiles statistics. Publishes statistics, directory, periodical. Certifies drivers.

1215. United Thoroughbred Trainers of America. 19363 James Couzens Hwy., Detroit MI 48235. (313) 342-6144. Association of individuals. Purpose is to promote professional standard, licensure, and thoroughbred racing. Publishes periodical. Former name: National Thoroughbred Trainers Guild.

22. The Professional Tournament Industry

SIC Code: 7999.

Enterprises providing organized individual athletic competition for certified professionals.

Directories

1216. American Horse Shows Association. *AHSA Rule Book.* New York. Biennial. $50. Lists horse shows in the United States and Canada giving name, sponsor, location, address, phone, and activity details. Includes procedures and guidelines for tournament organization, rules, classes, judging, and scoring.

1217. Ladies Professional Bowlers Tour. *LPBT Program Book.* Rockville IL. Annual. Controlled distribution. Tournaments, players, records, and statistics. Current and retrospective.

1218. Ladies Professional Golf Association. *LPGA Player Guide.* Sugar Land TX. Annual. Controlled distribution. Tournaments, players, records, rules, and purses.

1219. Professional Bowlers Association of America. *PBA Tournament Tour Press-Radio-TV Guide.* Akron OH. Annual. $3.50. Lists national and regional tournaments giving location, winners, rankings, records, and statistics. Current and retrospective data.

1220. Professional Putters Association. *Fact and Membership.* Fayetteville NC. Annual. Controlled distribution. Tournaments, players, rankings, rules, and statistics.

1221. Professional Rodeo Cowboys Association. *PRCA Media Guide.* Colorado Springs CO. Annual. Controlled distribution. Lists national and regional tournaments giving location, sponsor, contestants, bucking stock, rules, categories, and statistics.

1222. Women's International Tennis Association. *WITA Media Guide.* Miami FL. Annual. Controlled distribution. Lists tournaments giving location and statistics. Players giving biographical data and tournament statistics. Current and retrospective data.

1223. World Professional Squash Association. *WPSA Pro Tour Program.* Toronto, Canada. Annual. Controlled distribution. Tournaments, players, standings, and schedule. Promotional tips for tournament managers.

Management

1224. American Platform Tennis Association. *How to Conduct a Tournament Draw.* Upper Montclair NJ, 1973. 9p. Free. Rules, calculations, seeding, and schedule illustrations with "bye" instructions.

1225. Blackburn, Lois H. *Handbook for Planning and Conducting Tennis Tournaments.* Princeton NJ: United States Tennis Association Center for Education and Recreational Tennis, 1986. 95p. $4.50. For the amateur contest but generally applicable as an outline for organizing a pro tournament. Planning, policy, rules, decisions, schedules, and recognition procedures.

1226. Cooper, Leslie C. *Horse Show Organization.* London: J.A. Allen; New York: Sporting Book Center, 1979. 180p. $9.95. British approach to show organization and operation. Emphasis on activities more than management.

1227. International Professional Rodeo Association. *IPRA Official Rules.* Pauls Valley OK, 1986. 112p. Free. Association constitution, bylaws, but, primarily, rules for organization, sanction, contests, conduct, and point scoring for a rodeo.

1228. Ladies Professional Bowlers Tour. *LPBT Tournament Rule Book.* Rockford IL. Annual. Controlled distribution. Rules, procedures, decisions, organization, scheduling, and point awards.

1229. Phillips, Alfred N. *Horse Shows: How to Organize and Run.* Danville IL: Interstate Printers & Publishers, 1956. 1v. $5. Old and with emphasis on local, do-it-yourself approach; nevertheless, covers the basics in detail. Recommended. And the price is right.

1230. Professional Rodeo Cowboys Association. *PRCA Articles of Incorporation, By-Laws and Rules.* Colorado Springs CO, 1986. 116p. Free. Primarily rules governing rodeo organization, activities, contests, conduct, grievances, points, and sanctioning.

1231. _____. *PRCA Rodeo Committee Guide.* Colorado Springs CO, 1983. 108p. Controlled distribution. Tournament planning manual. Organization, sanctioning, publicity, sponsorship, and stock and personal contracts outlined and discussed with sample forms.

Industry

1232. American Horse Council. *Spotlights on Showing: Study of the Economic Impact of Horse Shows.* Washington DC, 1980. 4p. Free. Number of national and local sanctioned shows in the United States, classification of type, size, and purse. Statistics on income, expenses, revenue, employees, and donations.

1233. Simkins, Jean. *Sponsorship,* 3rd ed. London: Economist, 1986. 115p. $100. Data on sponsorship, promotion, and publicity of special events in the United Kingdom.

Periodicals

1234. American Horse Shows Association. *Horse Show.* New York. Monthly. Membership. Official association publication. News of shows and tournaments, tournament results, riders and horses, association activities, and the horse world.

1235. Association of Professional Bridge Players. *APBP Newsletter.* Berkeley CA. Quarterly. Membership. Official association publication. News of tournaments, tournament organization, and contract bridge. Tips on securing financing, management, and organizing play. Discussions of rules and decisions.

1236. Association of Tennis Professionals. *International Tennis Weekly.* Arlington TX. Weekly. $30. Official association publication. News of tournaments, players, and the tennis world. Tournament results, point standings, and rankings. Articles evaluating play and players. Calendar of events.

1237. International Professional Rodeo Association. *Rodeo News.* Pauls Valley OK. 11 issues. $15. Official association publication. News of events, rules, contestants, and rodeo management. Calendar of scheduled rodeos and standings.

1238. Professional Golfers' Association of America. PGA *Magazine.* Palm Beach Gardens FL. Monthly. $12. Official association publication. Articles and news on the Tour and other professional tournaments. Standings and tournament statistics. Information on course operations and management, new equipment and supplies.

1239. Professional Pool Players Association. PPPA *Newsletter.* Elizabeth NJ. Monthly. Membership. Official association publication. News of tournaments, progress on establishment of the tour, and plays. Tournament results and player points and rankings. Reports on players, facilities, and equipment.

1240. Professional Putters Association. *Putt-Putt World.* Fayetteville NC. Quarterly. Membership. Official association publication. News of events, people, and courses. Tournament results. Course management and operations.

1241. Professional Rodeo Cowboys Association. *Prorodeo Sports News.* Colorado Springs CO. Biweekly. $15. Official association publication. News of PRCA approved rodeos, rules, contestants, and standings. Features on rodeo winners. Calendar of events.

1242. *US Archer.* Tucson AZ: US Archer. Bimonthly. $13.50. Official association publication of the National Archery Association and Professional Archers Association. News of tournaments, competitions, meetings, equipment, and people. Tournament results and standings.

1243. Women's International Tennis Association. *Inside Women's Tennis.* Miami FL. Monthly. Membership. Official association publication. News of tournaments, players, and professional women's tennis. Tournament and player results, point totals, and player rankings. Articles on individual players.

1244. Women's Professional Rodeo Association. WPRA *News.* Blanchard OK. Monthly. $5. Official association publication. News of PRCA tournaments, results, clinics, and the activities of the association.

1245. World Professional Squash Association. WPSA *Newsmagazine.* Toronto, Canada. Monthly. Membership. Official association publication. News of tour, players, standings, and schedule. Promotional tips.

Associations

1246. American Golf Sponsors. Box 41, Golf IL 60029. (312) 724-4600. Association of PGA Tour tournament sponsors. Former name: International Golf Sponsors Association.

1247. American Horse Shows Association. 220 E. 42nd St., New York NY 10017. (212) 972-2472. Association of horse shows and individuals. Provides seminars. Publishes standards, periodical. Sanctions tournaments.

1248. Association of Professional Bridge Players. P.O. Box 7104, Berkeley CA 94707. (415) 548-0862. Association of professional members of the American Contract Bridge League and bridge tournament organizers. Provides management counsel. Publishes periodical.

1249. Association of Tennis Professionals. 611 Ryan Plaza Dr., Arlington TX 76011. (817) 860-1166. Association of individuals. Purpose is to promote and improve spectator tennis. Publishes periodical.

1250. Canadian Professional Rodeo Association. 2116 27th Ave., N.E., Calgary, AB, Canada T2E 7A6. (403) 250-7440. Association of performers, stock contractors, and producers. Sanctions tournaments.

1251. International Professional Rodeo Association. P.O. Box 615, Pauls Valley OK 73075. (405) 238-6488. Association of performers, stock contractors, and producers. One of two governing bodies for professional rodeo. (See Professional Rodeo Cowboys Association.) Compiles statistics. Publishes standards, handbooks, periodical. Sanctions tournaments.

1252. Ladies Professional Bowlers Tour. 7171 Cherryvale Blvd., Rockford IL 61112. (815) 332-5756. Association of touring professionals. Compiles statistics. Provides management counsel. Publishes standards, directory, periodical. Sanctions tournaments. Former name: Women Professional Bowlers Association.

1253. Ladies Professional Golf Association. 4675 Sweetwater Blvd., Sugarland TX 77479. (703) 980-5742. Association of tournament players and teachers. Compiles statistics. Publishes directory. Certifies professionals. Sanctions tournaments. Former name: Women's Professional Golf Association.

1254. Professional Archers Association. 7315 N. San Anna Dr., Tucson AZ 85704. (602) 742-5846. Association of competitors and teachers.

Purpose in to promote professional tournaments. Provides management counsel. Publishes periodical. Sanctions tournaments.

1255. Professional Bowlers Association of America. 1720 Merriman Rd., Akron OH 44313. (216) 836-5568. Association of certified professionals. Compiles statistics. Provides management counsel, seminars. Maintains library. Publishes handbooks, directory. Certifies professionals. Sanctions tournaments.

1256. Professional Golfers' Association. Apollo House, The Belfry, Sutton Coldfield, West Midlands, England B76 9PT. 06-757-0333. Association of certified professionals in Great Britain. Compiles statistics. Provides seminars. Maintains library. Publishes handbooks, directory, periodical. Certifies professionals. Sanctions tournaments.

1257. Professional Golfers' Association of America. 100 Avenue of Champions, Palm Beach Gardens FL 33418. (305) 626-3600. Association of professionals and apprentices. Provides seminars. Maintains library. Publishes periodical. Certifies professionals. Sanctions tournaments.

1258. Professional Pool Players Association. 422 N. Broad St., Elizabeth NJ 07206. (201) 355-1302. Association of professionals, apprentices, pool hall owners, and manufacturers. Purpose is to organize a professional pool tour. Provides management counsel. Publishes periodical. Certifies professionals. Sanctions tournaments.

1259. Professional Putters Association. P.O. Box 35237. Fayetteville NC 28303. (919) 485-7131. Association of individuals competing in national putting tournaments sanctioned by the PPA, "putt putt" golf course owners, managers, and suppliers.

Compiles statistics. Publishes directory, periodical. Sanctions tournaments.

1260. Professional Rodeo Cowboys Association. 101 Pro Rodeo Dr., Colorado Springs CO 80919. (719) 593-8840. Association of performers, stock contractors, and producers. One of two governing bodies for professional rodeo. (See International Professional Rodeo Association.) Compiles statistics. Publishes standards, handbooks, periodical. Sanctions tournaments.

1261. United Professional Horsemen's Association. 181 Mill St., Lexington KY 40507. (606) 252-6888. Association of trainers, breeders, and owners of show horses. Purpose is to promote horse shows.

1262. United States Professional Cycling Federation. R.D. 1, Box 130, New Tripoli PA 18066. (215) 298-3262. Association of individuals. Purpose is to promote cycling competitions. Provides management counsel. Certifies professionals. Sanctions tournaments.

1263. Women's International Tennis Association. Grand Bay Plaza, 2665 South Bayshore Dr., Suite 1002, Miami FL 33133. (305) 856-4030. Association of professionals. Purpose is to organize professional women's tennis tournaments. Publishes, standards, handbooks, directory, periodical. Sanctions tournaments.

1264. Women's Professional Rodeo Association. R.D. 5, Box 698, Blanchard OK 73010. (405) 485-2277. Association of women competing in tournaments sanctioned by the Professional Rodeo Cowboys Association. Publishes periodical. Former names: Girls Rodeo Association, Professional Women's Rodeo Association.

1265. World Professional Squash Association. 12 Sheppard St., Suite 401, Toronto, Ontario, Canada M5H 3A1. (416) 869-3499. Association of professionals and teachers. Purpose is promoting World Professional Squash Association Pro Tour. Provides management counsel, seminars. Publishes standards, handbooks, directory, periodical. Former name: North American Professional Squash Racquets Association.

23. The Public Amusements Industry

SIC Codes: 7993, 7996, 7999.

Enterprises providing a public setting and devices for recreation and/or entertainment. For arenas, athletic fields, and stadiums see Chapter 20, The Professional Sports Industry. For racetracks see Chapter 21, The Professional Racing Industry. For physical fitness centers see Chapter 1, The Fitness Industry. For motion picture theatres see Chapter 18, The Motion Picture Industry. For gambling casinos or parlors see Chapter 24, The Gambling Industry. For enterprises whose primary emphasis is live theatrical or music entertainment in a festival setting see Chapter 19, The Music Industry, or Chapter 17, Show Business.

Directories

1266. Amusement and Music Operators Association. *Who's Who in the Amusement and Music Operators Association.* Chicago. Annual. $150. Lists companies in the coin-operated amusement and music business giving name, address, phone, and key executives. Arrangement is alphabetical.

1267. *Amusement Industry Buyers Guide.* Nashville TN: Billboard. Annual. $15. Manufacturers, import-ers, and suppliers of games, rides, and merchandise in the United States. Arrangement is classified.

1268. *AudArena Stadium Guide.* Nashville TN: Billboard. Annual. $50. Arenas, auditoriums, stadiums, theaters, performing arts centers, exhibition halls, and coliseums in the United States, Canada, and a few elsewhere. Each listing gives name, owner, contact, address, phone, and description of facility, capacity, and services. Arrangement is geographical.

1269. Bedford, Bruce. *Underground Britain: A Guide to the Wild Caves and Show Caves of England, Scotland and Wales.* London: Willow; Topsfield MA: Merrimack, 1985. 176p. $16.95. Separate sections for wild and show caves. Latter described generally and specifically by features. Introduction details cave formation. Not truly a directory but excellent background for the prospective show cave entrepreneur.

1270. *Book of Festivals Series.* South Bend IN: Icarus, 1985- . $10.95. Publications on the Midwest, California, Hawaii, and Nevada inaugurated this series. More detailed than the *Festivals Sourcebook* (see **1290**). Each listing gives name, location, theme, description, history, name, address, and phone of contact, fees, attendance, and accommodations for the traveler. Arrangement is by state and then alphabetical.

1271. *Directory of International Film and Video Festivals.* London, England: British Council. Biennial. $20. Film, television, and video festivals worldwide. Each listing gives name, location, dates, fees, and contact. Arrangement is geographical. Previous title: *International Film Festivals Directory.*

1272. *Directory of North American Fairs, Festivals, and Expositions.* Nashville TN: Billboard. Annual. $40. Fairs, festivals, and expositions in the United States and Canada running three days or more giving location, name, address, manager, demographics, and size of grounds or budget. Chronological index.

1273. *Facilities Supplies Sourcebook.* Nashville TN: Billboard. Annual. $17.50. Lists manufacturers and suppliers in the mass entertainment industry giving name, address, phone, and product or service. Arrangement is classified by product/service. Former title: *Buyer's Guide for the Mass Entertainment Industry.*

1274. *FunParks Directory.* Nashville TN: Billboard. Annual. $40. Lists theme, amusement, and water parks as well as suppliers giving name, key executives, address, phone, and description of park, product, or service. Arrangement is geographical with classified index.

1275. Home and Garden Show Executives International. *Date Folder.* Milwaukee WI. Annual. Free. Lists shows giving location, date, contact, and brief description of activities. Background and historical data.

1276. Independent Dealers Association of America. *Dealer's Desk Reference.* Arnold MO. Annual. $25. Lists fairs, shows, and events which rent booths to vendors giving name, sponsor, address, phone, contact, rates, attendance, number of vendors, and facilities and attractions. Former title: *Fair Book.*

1277. International Association of Amusement Parks and Attractions. *IAAPA Address and Telephone Directory.* Alexandria VA. Annual. Membership. Lists park, attraction, and supplier members giving name, address, phone, and key executives. Arrangement is alphabetical with personal name index.

1278. International Association of Auditorium Managers. *IAAM Membership Directory.* Chicago. Annual. Membership. Lists members giving name, name of facility managed, address, phone, and brief description of facility. Arrangement is alphabetical with geographic index.

1279. International Association of Fairs and Expositions. *IAFE Directory.* Springfield MO. Annual. $50. Lists member agricultural fairs and state fair associations in the United States and Canada giving name, address, phone, key executives, and description of fairgrounds. Arrangement is classified by activity then alphabetical by name. Last name index.

1280. International Council of Air Shows. *ICAS Membership Directory.* Jackson MI. Annual. Free. Lists sponsors, producers, associates, performers, government agencies, and association officers giving name, address, phone, and position or specialty. Arrangement is classified by activity then alphabetical by name. Last name index.

1281. International Festivals Association. *IFA Directory of Members.* Saint Petersburg FL. Annual. $50. Lists local festivals giving name, location, sponsor, manager, address, phone, and dates. Arrangement is alphabetical with city index.

1282. National Association of Canoe Liveries and Outfitters. *Let's Go Paddling Directory.* Atlanta GA. Annual. Free. Lists members giving name, address, phone, owners, and description of services. Arrangement is geographical with alphabetical name index. Includes alphabetical list of associate members.

1283. National Caves Association. *Caves and Caverns Directory.* McMinnville TN. Annual. Free. Lists member commercial show caves giving name, address, and phone. Arrangement is geographical. United States map with cave locations appendixed.

1284. Norris, John, and Norris, Joann. *Amusement Parks: An American Guide.* Jefferson NC and London: McFarland, 1986. 128p. $19.95. Lists major United States theme and amusement parks giving name, location, address, phone, brief history, season, hours and best times to attend, ticket information, and description. Arrangement is geographical.

1285. Shemanski, Frances. *Guide to Fairs and Festivals in the United States.* Westport CT: Greenwood, 1984. 339p. $35. Lists recurring events giving place, name, time of year occurring, type and theme, and narrative description. Arrangement is geographical by state with type and calendar index by state.

1286. Shemanski, Frances. *Guide to World Fairs and Festivals.* Westport CT: Greewood, 1985. 320p. $29.95. Lists recurring events in 72 countries outside the United States. Organized similar to United States directory above (see **1285**).

1287. *Showman's Directory.* Godalming, England: Stephen & Jean Lance. Annual. $10. Fairs and festivals in Great Britain and show companies seeking to perform at these gatherings. For fairs and festivals, gives name, location, dates, expected attendance, and name, address, and phone of contact. For companies, gives name, address, and phone.

1288. *Steam Passenger Service Directory.* Middletown NY: Empire State Railway Museum. Annual. $6. Lists tourist railroads and trolleys in the United States and Canada giving name, location, gauge, description of operations, equipment, schedule, cost, address, and phone. Arrangement is geographical.

1289. Ukman, Lisa, ed. *Official International Directory of Special Events and Festivals.* Chicago: Special Events Report, 1984. 406p. $100. Recreation and entertainment events and festivals in the United States, Canada, and, some worldwide, available for corporate sponsorship and companies servicing these activities. Each listing gives name, location, dates, contact, address, phone, description, sponsorship availability, budget, attendance, audience demographics, and whether for profit or non-profit. Arrangement is geographical with name, location, date indexes. Updated by *Special Events Report.* (See **1322**.) Includes a list of "Publications and Directories" on the fair and festival industry.

1290. Wasserman, Paul, and Applebaum, Edmond. *Festivals Sourcebook.* Detroit MI: Gale Research, 1984. 725p. $130. Lists festivals and fairs giving location, name, dates, contact, address, and description. Arrangement is classified by theme then subarranged geographically by state. Chronological, event name, geographic, and subject indexes.

Management

1291. American Entrepreneurs Association. *Pinball and Video*

Games Arcade. Los Angeles, 1984. 148p. $39.50. Guide to establishing and operating a small business. Chapters on legal, management, marketing, operating, and financial procedures. Supplier addresses and a bibliography. Looseleaf format.

1292. Hassan, Yahya Abdel Kader. *Design Model for the Development of a Prototype Theme/ Amusement Center to Be Located at the Suez Canal Region, The Arab Republic of Egypt.* PhD. Thesis, University of Tennessee, 1983. 135p. In developing the model, the author identified need based upon use of a United States formulated questionnaire which he sent to 1,000 Egyptian families. Development plan appendixed.

1293. International Council of Air Shows. *ICAS Air Show Manual,* 3rd ed. Jackson MI, 1987. 66p. Membership. Checklist for planning, organizing, financing, promoting, and operating a show. Performer and certification section provides sample forms for contracts and federal and state aviation and safety approval. FAA and Canadian governmental airshow coordinators listed with address and phone.

1294. Jackson, John J. *Leisure and Sports Center Management.* Springfield IL: Charles C. Thomas, 1984. 200p. $22.75. Case studies in management and cost control for public sports and amusement facilities.

1295. Kaiser, Ronald A. *Liability and Law in Recreation, Parks, and Sports.* Englewood Cliffs NJ: Prentice Hall, 1986. 271p. $26.95. Textbook on background, law, cases, and analysis. Emphasis on liability of owner/manager of park and recreation facility. List of immunity laws, glossary, and subject index.

1296. Tourism and Recreation

Research Unit, Edinburgh. *Recreation Site Survey Manual.* London; New York: E & F.N. Spon, 1983. 146p. $25. Methods and techniques for conducting visitor surveys of park and recreation facilities. Procedures and techniques, forms and analysis.

1297. Wilson, Joe, and Udall, Lee. *Folk Festivals: A Handbook for Organization and Management.* Knoxville TN: University of Tennessee Press, 1982. 278p. $16. Background, planning, sponsorship, budgeting, management, and promotion. Procedures and forms. Bibliography and index.

Industry

1298. Gupla, Shiv K., ed. *Economic and Cultural Impact Study of the Amusement Park and Attraction Industry.* Philadelphia PA: Wharton Applied Research Center, 1977. 127p. Controlled distribution. (Summary available from IAAPA.) Study prepared for International Association of Amusement Parks and Attractions. Analyzes industry revenue generation and financing, employment, cultural/social aspects, and safety record. Extensive and detailed statistics and charts. Report presented as the basis for further industry analysis.

1299. International Association of Fairs and Expositions. *IAFE Statistical Report.* Springfield MO. Annual. Membership. Industry balance sheet, cost analysis, and attendance data.

Market

1300. U.S. Travel Data Center. *Amusement Parks and Tourist At-*

tractions Consumer Survey, 1986. Not published. Report available through the International Association of Amusement Parks and Tourist Attractions. Analysis and statistics on the influence of the location of an amusement park or tourist attraction on the destination choice of vacationers.

Periodicals

1301. American Pyrotechnics Association. *APA Bulletin.* Chestertown MD. Monthly. Membership. Official association publication. News of products, regulations, safety, displays, and the association.

1302. Amusement and Music Operators Association. *Location.* Chicago IL. Monthly. Membership. Official association publication. News of the association, the music and amusements industry, people, legislative matters, seminars and trade shows, and calendar of events.

1303. *Amusement Business.* Nashville TN: Billboard Publications, Inc. Weekly. $60. News from the entire spectrum of mass entertainment and public amusements industry. Numerous special directory lists. Special reports: "Managing the Leisure Facility" in each February, May, August, and December issue. Indexed in *Business Index, Trade and Industry Index.*

1304. *Amusement Park Journal.* Natrona Heights PA: Amusement Park Club International. Monthly. $30. Articles on parks, rides, and people. Management and promotional information. Historical and bibliography sources. Special report: "Park Directory" in each May issue.

1305. Canadian Parks/Recreation Association. *Recreation Canada.* Vanier, Canada. 5 issues. $35.

Official association publication. For the key decisionmakers in the recreation field across Canada. Emphasis on planning and management of parks. Articles on design, construction, landscaping, financing, regulating, and professional standards and development.

1306. *From the State Capitals: Tourist Business Promotion.* New Haven CT: Wakeman/Walworth. 12 issues. $75. Newsletter analyzing state and municipal actions affecting recreation, entertainment, and tourism businesses. Emphasizes state promotion, tourism legislation, and regulation. Discusses finance, support, and construction of recreation and entertainment facilities with state and local funds.

1307. Independent Dealers Association of America. *Fair Times.* Arnold MO. Monthly. $30. Official association publication. Calendar of fair, festival, market, show, and exhibition events with location, name, address, and contact for each. News of the independent vendor circuit.

1308. Institute of Leisure and Amenity Management. *Leisure Manager.* Cambridge, England: John S. Turner. Monthly. $60. Official association publication. For the park and recreation executive. Emphasis on management concerns. Indexed in *Leisure, Recreation and Tourism Index.*

1309. International Association of Amusement Parks and Attractions. *Funworld.* Alexandria VA. 11 issues. $30. Official association publication. News of the association, members, Washington scene, products, and events. Articles on management, promotion, safety, and parks. Industry statistics.

1310. International Association of Auditorium Managers. *Facility Manager.* Chicago. Quarterly. $20.

Official association publication. Analyzes industry trends, documents case histories, provides industry and market statistics, and reviews new products and services. Special feature each month, e.g. "Marketing Your Facility," "Politics of Facility Management."

1311. International Association of Fairs and Expositions. *Fairs and Expositions.* Springfield MO. Monthly. Membership. Official association publication. Management information and statistics. News and calendar of events.

1312. International Council of Air Shows. *ICAS News.* Jackson MI. Quarterly. $10 to qualified persons. Official association publication. News and articles on shows, management and promotion, and market surveys and statistics. Calendar of events and directory updates.

1313. International Festivals Association. *Festivals International.* Saint Petersburg FL. Quarterly. Membership. Official association publication. News of festivals, management, and the industry. Calendar.

1314. National Association of Canoe Liveries and Outfitters. *NACLO News.* Atlanta GA. Monthly. Membership. Official association publication. News of members, association activities, regulations, insurance, and products.

1315. National Caves Association. *NCA Cave Talk.* McMinnville TN. Bimonthly. Membership. Official association publication. News of cave shows, tourism developments, the association, and members. Articles on legislation, economics of cave operations, management, preservation, and safety.

1316. National Recreation and Park Association. *Journal of Leisure Research.* Alexandria VA. Quarterly.

$20. Of the two major research journals in leisure recreation, this is the most business oriented. Research articles, consumer surveys, and cost-benefit analyses are regularly reported. Well documented and referenced. Indexed in *CIJE,* Social Science Index.

1317. National Recreation and Park Association. *Parks and Recreation.* Alexandria VA. Monthly. $18. Official association publication. For the executive, public officials, and community leaders responsible for park and recreation development and management. Regular columns include "Washington Report," "Product Report," and "Coming Events." Indexed in *CIJE, PAIS, Readers' Guide, Real Estate Index.*

1318. Outdoor Amusement Business Association. *OABA Newsletter.* Minneapolis MN. Monthly. Membership. Official association publication. News of members, products, regulations, and the industry.

1319. *Park Maintenance.* Appleton WI: Madison. Monthly. $12. Articles on planning, financing, and management of public amusement parks and attractions. Emphasis on grounds and physical facilities.

1320. *Recreation Executive Report.* Washington DC: Leisure Industry/Recreation News. 24 issues. $65. For managers and policy makers. Resumes of news articles and reports. Newsletter format and extensive use of statistics.

1321. *Recreation, Sports and Leisure.* Minneapolis MN: Lakewood. 9 issues. $18. For managers of parks, public amusements, resorts, club, and fitness facilities. Emphasis on equipment purchase, use, and management.

1322. *Special Events Report.* Chicago: Special Events Report. Biweekly. $140. Updates *Official*

International Directory of Special Events and Festivals. News and directory data on corporate sponsored events including information on who to contact.

1323. *Tourist Attractions and Parks.* Philadelphia PA: Kane Communications. 6 issues. $24. Articles emphasize management and marketing. Special reports: "Arena Directory" in each July/August issue and "Preconventions" in each September/October issue.

1324. *World Airshow News: The Airshow Industry Magazine.* Oregon WI: Flyer. Quarterly. $10. News of shows, sponsorship, organization, management, and regulations. Articles on specific airshows, acts, and performers. Attendance and financial statistics.

Bibliographies/Indexes

1325. Starbuck, James C. *Theme Parks.* Monticello IL: Council of Planning Libraries, 1976. Books and articles.

Associations

1326. American Amusement Machine Association. 205 The Strand, Suite 3, Alexandria VA 22314. (703) 548-8044. Association of manufacturers, distributors, and suppliers of coin-operated devices. Former name: Amusement Game Manufacturers Association.

1327. American Pyrotechnics Association. P.O. Box 213, Chestertown MD 21620. (301) 778-6825. Association of manufacturers, importers, and distributors of commercial fireworks for public displays. Provides seminars. Publishes handbooks, periodical.

1328. American Recreational Equipment Association. P.O. Box 557, Delaware OH 43015. (614) 363-9715. Association of manufacturers and suppliers of amusement rides and devices. Conducts research. Provides seminars. Publishes standards.

1329. Amusement and Music Operators Association. 111 E. Wacker Dr., Suite 600, Chicago IL 60601. (312) 644-6610. Association of suppliers and servicers of coin-operated devices in the United States and Canada. Compiles statistics. Conducts research. Provides management counsel, seminars, trade shows. Publishes directory, periodical.

1330. Association of Exhibition Organizers. 17 Castle St., High Wycombe, Bucks, England HP13 6RU. (04) 943-0430. Association of companies producing exhibitions in Great Britain. Compiles statistics. Provides seminars.

1331. Canadian Parks/Recreation Association. 333 River Rd., Vanier, Ontario, Canada K1L 8H9. (613) 748-5651. Individuals dedicated to park and recreation improvement in Canada through improved management policies. Compiles statistics. Conducts research. Provides seminars, trade shows. Publishes standards, periodicals.

1332. Carnival Guild. 15 Viscount Ct., Eaton Socon, Hunt, England PE19 3DJ. Association of carnivals in Great Britain. Compiles statistics. Conducts research. Provides management counsel, seminars.

1333. Home and Garden Show Executives International. 6111 W. Bluemound Rd., Milwaukee WI 53213. (414) 774-4343. Association of managers of shows in the United States and Canada. Purpose is to exchange information. Publishes directory.

1334. Independent Dealers Asso-

ciation of America. 3630 Jeffco Blvd., Arnold MO 63010. (314) 464-2595. Association of fair, festival, flea market, and exhibition venders in the United States. Publishes directory, periodical.

1335. Institute of Leisure and Amenity Management. The Grotto, Lower Basildon, Reading, Berks, England RG8 9NE. (049) 187-3558. Association of managers and officials of British parks and recreation facilities. Provides seminars, trade shows. Maintains library. Publishes standards, periodical.

1336. International Association of Amusement Parks and Attractions. 4230 King St., Alexandria VA 22302. (703) 571-5800. Association of companies in the United States and Canada. Compiles statistics. Conducts research. Provides management counsel, seminars, trade shows. Publishes handbooks, statistics, directory, periodical.

1337. International Association of Auditorium Managers. 500 N. Michigan Ave., Suite 1400, Chicago IL 60611. (312) 661-1700. Association of public facility executives. Compiles statistics. Conducts research. Provides management counsel, seminars. Publishes statistics, directory, periodical. Former name: Auditorium Managers Association.

1338. International Association of Fairs and Expositions. P.O. Box 985, Springfield MO 65801. (417) 862-5771. Association of state and local agricultural fairs and expositions in the United States and Canada. Compiles statistics. Conducts research. Provides seminars. Maintains library. Publishes handbooks, statistics, directory, periodical.

1339. International Auto Show Producers Association. 32365 Mally Dr., Madison Heights MI 48701.

(313) 588-5568. Association of organizers of displays of customized cars in the United States and Canada. Provides management counsel.

1340. International Council of Air Shows. P.O. Box 1105, Jackson MI 49204. (517) 782-2424. Association of sponsors, producers, and performers in the United States and Canada. Compiles statistics. Conducts research. Provides management counsel, seminars. Publishes standards, handbooks, statistics, directory, periodical.

1341. International Federation of Boat Show Organizers. 353 Lexington Ave., New York NY 10016. (212) 684-6622. Association of sponsors and managers in the United States. Purpose is to interchange information.

1342. International Federation of Festival Organizations (Federation Internationale des Organisateurs de Festivals). P.O. Box 370, Split, Yugoslavia YU-500. (58) 515014. Federation of national associations. Purpose is to coordinate among festivals worldwide.

1343. International Festivals Association. P.O. Box 1828, Saint Petersburg FL 33731. (813) 898-1828. Association of community festivals in the United States, Canada, and a few elsewhere. Provides management counsel, seminars. Maintains library. Publishes periodical.

1344. National Association of Canoe Liveries and Outfitters. P.O. Box 88866, Atlanta GA 30356. (404) 393-8171. Association of renters in the United States with suppliers as associate members. Provides seminars. Maintains library. Publishes standards, directory, periodical.

1345. National Caves Association. Rt. 9, Box 106, McMinnville TN 37110. (615) 668-3925. Association of commercial show caves in the

United States. Compiles statistics. Conducts research. Provides management counsel, seminars. publishes standards, directory, periodical.

1346. National Recreation and Park Association. 3101 Park Center Dr., Alexandria VA 22302. (703) 820-4940. Association of individuals dedicated to park and recreation improvement in the United States through improved management policies. Compiles statistics. Conducts research. Provides seminars, trade shows. Maintains library. Publishes standards, handbooks, periodicals.

1347. National Showman's Association. P.O. Box 662, East Northport NY 11731. (516) 261-2417. Association of owners of traveling carnivals and amusement rides in the United States and Canada. Compiles statistics.

1348. Outdoor Amusement Business Association. 4600 W. 77th St., Minneapolis MN 55435. (612) 831-4643. Association of owners and employees of carnivals, entertainment concessions, traveling amusements, and equipment suppliers in the United States and Canada. Compiles statistics. Provides seminars. Publishes standards, handbooks, periodical.

1349. World Waterpark Association. 7474 Village Dr., Prairie Village KS 66208. (913) 362-9440. Association of parks and park suppliers in the United States.

24. The Gambling Industry

SIC Codes: 7993, 7999.

Enterprises providing opportunity for wagering.

Directories

1350. American Greyhound Track Operators Association. *Track Facts.* North Miami FL. Annual. Free. Lists member racetracks giving name, location, address, phone, officers, officials, operating data, track and facilities information, and record attendance. Arrangement is alphabetical. Also lists greyhound government supervisory agencies and track suppliers.

1351. *Gaming and Wagering Business Directory.* New York: BMT. Annual. $25. Lists gambling and wagering establishments, racetracks, jai alai frontons, and state racing, lottery, and gambling commissions giving name, address, phone, and key executives. Arrangement is classified by type of business or activity then alphabetical by name.

1352. *Gaming and Wagering Supplier Directory.* New York: BMT. Annual. $25. Gaming device manufacturers and distributors, producers of products for gambling, and gaming servicers giving name, address, phone, key executives, clientele, and products or services. Arrangement is classified by type of business or activity then alphabetical by name.

1353. Harness Tracks of America.

HTA Directory. Morristown NJ. Annual. Membership. Lists member racetracks giving name, location, address, phone, officers, officials, operating data, and track and facilities information. Arrangement is alphabetical.

1354. North American Association of State and Provincial Lotteries. *NAASPL Directory.* South San Francisco CA. Annual. Membership. Each listing gives name, address, phone, and key executives. Arrangement is geographical.

1355. Thoroughbred Racing Associations of North America. *TRA Directory and Record Book.* Lake Success NY. Annual. Free. Lists racetracks in the United States and Canada giving corporate name, name of track, location, address, phone, officers, officials, track information and facilities, prices, and history of the track. Nonmember track listings omit description data and history. Arrangement is alphabetical. Industry racing dates for the coming year and statistics for past three years.

Management

1356. American Entrepreneurs Association. *Bingo in America.* Los Angeles, 1984. 47p. $19.50. Examines the possibility of establishing and operating a privately owned bingo parlor, its financial and legal implications and government controls.

Lists agency addresses and a bibliography. Looseleaf format.

1357. Connors, Jerry. *Handicapping Beyond the Basics: Theory and Practice for the Intermediate Handicapper.* Columbus OH: United States Trotting Association, 1986. 78p. $3.50. Handicapping the harness race. Eighty examples using actual races from tracks around North America.

1358. Demos, Peter. *Casino Supervision: A Basic Guide.* Atlantic City NJ: CSI, 1983. 160p. $24.95. For the prospective casino floor manager. Textbook of questions and situations that arise during day-to-day casino operations.

1359. Eadington, William R., ed. *Gambling Papers: Conferences on Gambling, University of Nevada.* Reno NV: University of Nevada Bureau of Business, 1974– . (Still in print: 1982. 13v. $380; 1985. 5v. $180.) Six conferences have been held through 1985. The papers presented represent all aspects and viewpoints of gambling with somewhat of a Nevada emphasis. Well researched, controversial, and informative, this collection is one of the best ways to keep informed on the gambling industry.

1360. Friedman, Bill. *Casino Management,* Rev. ed. Secaucus NJ: Lyle Stuart, 1982. 384p. $125. Textbook for course. Describes legalized gambling from the standpoint of structure, casino organization, management, accounting, and government regulation. Discusses casino games from the management prospective.

1361. Goodwin, John R. *Gambling Control Law: The Nevada Model.* Columbus OH: Publishing Horizons, 1985. 198p. $39.95. Principles, statutes, and cases on gambling in Nevada. Discusses the ra-

tionales for gambling and analyzes the results in terms of laws and judicial decisions.

1362. Sternlieb, George, and Hughes, James W. *Atlantic City Gamble.* Cambridge MA: Harvard University Press, 1983. 256p. $16.50. For the city contemplating legalized gambling Atlantic City style by the director of the Center for Policy Research at Rutgers University. Examines the process and impact on city taxes, real estate, employment, and crime. Concludes that costs exceeded income.

1363. U.S. Commission on the Review of the National Policy Toward Gambling. *Gambling in America.* Washington DC: U.S. Government Printing Office, 1976. 4v. $30. Probably the most comprehensive and detailed look at gambling in the United States in recent times. Final report reflects the conservative thinking of the time but appendices present papers, Kallick et al. Survey (see **1372**), a review of two gambling studies, and a summary of the hearings of the Commission which give a more contemporary picture.

1364. U.S. Senate Committee on Governmental Affairs. Subcommittee on Intergovernment Relations. *State Lotteries: An Overview.* Washington DC: U.S. Government Printing Office, 1985. 628p. Hearings, October 3, 1984. Testimony and exhibits by state lottery commissioners and officials, opponents, and other interested individuals and federal and state officials. Excellent introduction to the growth of state sponsored lotteries in the United States.

1365. U.S. Senate Select Committee on Indian Affairs. *Establishing Federal Standards and Regulations for Conduct of Gaming Activities*

Within Indian Country. Washington DC: U.S. Government Printing Office, 1986. 673p. Hearings, June 17, 1986, on Senate Bill 902 and related bills. Testimony and exhibits from several tribes of native Americans, the Bureau of Indian Affairs, states, and others on efforts to control the growth and effects of gaming on federally supervised lands. Excellent survey of existing gaming activities.

Industry

1366. American Greyhound Track Operators Association. *AGTOA Annual Report.* North Miami FL. Annual. Free. Individual member track statistics on attendance and pari-mutuel money handled for current and past two years. Comparative data and ten-year summaries for industry attendance, p/m money, and revenue. Stake purses, champions, and records. Review of industry events for the past year and other historical data.

1367. _____. *Summary of State Pari-Mutuel Tax Structures.* North Miami FL. Annual. Membership. State by state summary of taxes imposed on tracks with percentage rates and related regulations. Law as to underpayments, legal age, and fines for each state in which a track is operated. Track and industry data on attendance, revenue to government units, and pari-mutuel money handled.

1368. Key Note Publications Ltd. *Betting and Gambling.* London, 1987. 26p. $75. Analyzes British development and industry structure, wagering establishment income, financial ratios, and market for the past five years. Projects future trends.

1369. Laventhol and Horwath. *Study of Financial Results and Reporting Trends in Gaming.* Philadelphia PA. Annual. $50. Narrative and statistical analysis based upon data supplied by gambling and gaming establishments in the United States. Composite statistics and ratios. Brief reports on gambling industry in individual states and cities. Former title: *U.S. Gaming Industry.*

1370. National Association of State Racing Commissioners. *Statistical Reports on Greyhound Racing.* Lexington KY. Annual. $15. Statistics on pari-mutuel betting and revenue to U.S. states, Canada, the Bahamas, and Puerto Rico. Current and retrospective data. Summary of taxing methods used by each state.

1371. _____. *Statistical Reports on Horse Racing.* Lexington KY. Annual. $15. Statistics on parimutuel betting and revenue in the United States, Canada, the Bahamas, and Puerto Rico. Current and retrospective data. Summary of taxing methods used by each state.

Market

1372. Kallick, Maureen, et al. *Survey of American Gambling Attitudes and Behavior.* Ann Arbor MI: Institute of Social Research, 1979. 560p. $25. 1975 sampling of 2,000 Americans to determine the extent of gambling activity in the United States. This study was part of a major examination of gambling by the U.S. Commission on the Review of the National Policy towards Gambling (see **1363**).

1373. Martinez, Tomas M. *Gambling Scene: Why People Gamble.* Springfield IL: Charles C. Thomas, 1983. 248p. $24.50. Introduction to the world of the gambler, description of the compulsive addict, study of the Nevada gambling scene, interviews with gamblers and casino owners, and the psychology of gambling. Historical information and a lexicon. Research methodology appendix.

Periodicals

1374. *Atlantic City Action.* Atlantic City NJ: Glasco. Bimonthly. $100. News and information magazine for the Atlantic City, New Jersey, casino industry. Report and statistics, events and activities, and reports on individual casinos.

1375. *Bingo Operator Newsmagazine.* Saint Louis MO: Bingo Science. 10 issues. $75. For organizations operating legal bingo establishments. Articles on bingo operations, management, personnel, finance and payoffs, and how to prevent cheating. Features on new games, variations, and innovations in the use of proceedings. News on federal and state laws and regulations, equipment, facilities, and security systems.

1376. *Casino Chronicle.* Cinnaminson NJ: Ben A. Borowsky. Weekly. $135. Newsletter focusing on developments in gambling in Atlantic City, New Jersey. Articles and news on casinos, profits, financing, laws and regulations, transportation, and labor relations.

1377. *Casino World.* New York: Gramercy Information Services. Monthly. $85. For the owner and investor. Financial reports on casinos in Nevada, Atlantic City, and abroad. Articles on casino management. News on laws and legislation.

1378. *Gambling Times.* Hollywood CA: Gambling Times. Monthly. $36.

For the professional gambler in all gaming fields. Articles on sports, games, systems, and betting procedures. Features stars of the game, gaming establishments, industry statistics, and book reviews.

1379. *Gaming and Wagering Business.* New York: BMT. Monthly. $36. News and developments in all gambling areas. Emphasis on management. Information on business strategy, marketing, finance, credit, government regulation, security, food service, and entertainment. Indexed in *Accountants Index.*

1380. Harness Tracks of America. *Track Topics.* Morristown NJ. Weekly. Membership. Official association publication. News and articles on track operations, track improvements, promotional ideas, pari-mutuel betting, and legislation and legal matters. Summaries of economic studies, financial reports, and position papers published by the association.

1381. *Lottery and Gaming.* Buffalo NY: Brent Ottaway. Monthly. $24.95. News and articles on gambling and the gambling industry. Emphasis on the games.

1382. *Lottery Players Magazine.* Cherry Hill NJ: Intergalatic. Monthly. $12. For the player more than the business community, but provides current news of state lotteries, winnings, and winners, background information, and features.

1383. National Association of State Racing Commissioners. *NASRC Weekly News Bulletin.* Lexington KY. Weekly. Membership. Official association publication. Emphasis on pari-mutuel aspects of racing industry. News of wagering law, legislation, and administrative rulings, conferences, reports, and meetings.

1384. *Public Gaming International.* Rockville MD: Public Gaming

Research Institute. Monthly. $65. Reports, articles, and news on state sponsored gambling worldwide. Emphasis on lottery, pari-mutuel, and off-track betting. Legislation, state control, statistics, and analysis featured.

1385. Thoroughbred Racing Associations of North America. *TRA Newsletter.* Lake Success NY. Monthly. Membership. Official association publication. News of tracks, management, and gambling and horse regulations. Racing statistics and calendar of events.

Bibliographies/Indexes

1386. Gardner, Jack. *Gambling: A Guide to Information.* Detroit MI: Gale Research, 1980. 286p. $62. Books, government and industry publications, periodicals, pamphlets, and articles on all aspects of gambling through the late 1970s. Emphasis on the games, but one of the few recreation and entertainment sourcebooks to contain an adequate listing of industry sources. Annotated with general index.

Associations

1387. American   Greyhound Track Operators Association. 1065 N.E. 125th St., Suite 219, North Miami FL 33161. (305) 893-2101. Association owners and operators of pari-mutuel racetracks in the United States. Compiles statistics. Maintains library. Publishes handbooks, statistics, directory.

1388. British Casino Association. 175 Piccadilly, London, England W1V 9DB. (01) 493-3033. Association of casinos in the United Kingdom. Compiles statistics. Conducts research.

1389. Harness Tracks of America. 35 Airport Rd., Morristown NJ 07960. (201) 285-9090. Association of pari-mutuel racetracks in the United States. Compiles statistics. Conducts research. Provides management counsel, seminars. Publishes standards, handbooks, statistics, directory, periodical.

1390. International Association of State Lotteries. 500 Sherbrooke St., W., Montreal, PQ, Canada H3A 3G6. (514) 854-5600. Federation of national and state public and non-profit lotteries throughout the world. Compiles statistics. Conducts research.

1391. Lotteries Council. 13 Dover St., London, England W1X 3PKH. (01) 499-3577. Association of state approved lottery organizations in the United Kingdom.

1392. National Association of Bookmakers. 2627 Cowcross St., London, England EC1M 6DQ. (01) 253-0044. Association of British off-track betting establishments. Compiles statistics.

1393. National Association of State Racing Commissioners. 535 W. Second St., Suite 300, Lexington KY 40508. (606) 254-4060. Federation of government regulatory agencies in the United States, Canada, the Bahamas, and Puerto Rico. Compiles statistics. Conducts research. Publishes statistics, periodical.

1394. North American Association of State and Provincial Lotteries. 401 Marina Blvd., Suite 220, South San Francsico CA 94080. (415) 742-9711. Association of government operated or approved lotteries in the United States and Canada. Compiles statistics. Provides management counsel, seminars. Publishes directory. Former name: National Association of State and Provincial Lotteries.

1395. Thoroughbred Racing Associations of North America. 3000 Marcus Ave., Suite 2W4, Lake Success NY 11040. (516) 328-2660. Association of racetracks. Compiles statistics. Publishes statistics, directory, periodical.

25. The Nightclub Industry

SIC Code: 5813.

Enterprises providing drinks and food, often with entertainment, usually in the afternoon and evening.

Directories

1396. National Alcoholic Beverage Control Association. *NABCA Contact.* Alexandria VA. Annual. $40. Lists state and local agencies involved in alcoholic beverage licensing giving name, address, and phone. Arrangement is geographical.

Management

1397. American Entrepreneurs Association. *Bar, Tavern/Nightclub.* Los Angeles, 1987. 192p. $60. Guide to establishing and operating a small business. Chapters on legal, management, marketing, operating, and financial procedures. Supplier addresses and a bibliography. Looseleaf format.

1398. _____. *No Alcohol Bar.* Los Angeles, 1981. 115p. $39.95. Guide to establishing and operating a small business. Chapters on legal, management, marketing, operating, and financial procedures. Supplier addresses and a bibliography. Looseleaf format.

1399. _____. *Starting a Restaurant.* Los Angeles, 1986. 173p. $55. Guide to establishing and ope-

rating a small business. Chapters on legal, management, marketing, operating, and financial procedures. Supplier addresses and a bibliography. Looseleaf format.

1400. Argiry, George P. *Catch the Sticky Fingers: A Guide to Bar Management and Mixed Drinks.* Canton OH: Beninda Enterprises, 1977. 143p. $5. Practical manual on supervision and control of bar operations so as to reduce losses resulting from poor management of pouring and other services. Separately titled supplement, *Bartender! Mixed Drinks for Everybody,* reflects the author's philosophy on the subject.

1401. Bank of America. *Bars and Cocktail Lounges.* San Francisco CA, 1981. 20p. $3. Procedures for operating an establishment. Includes "Sources for Further Information."

1402. Bank of America. *Restaurants.* San Francisco CA, 1981. 20p. $3. Procedures for operating an establishment. Includes "Sources for Further Information."

1403. Distilled Spirits Council of the United States. *Universal Numeric Code for Alcoholic Beverages.* Washington DC. Annual. Free. List of brand and vendor code numbers. Updated regularly. Looseleaf format.

1404. _____. *Summary of State Laws and Regulations Related to Distilled Spirits.* Washington DC. Biennial. $9. Laws and regulations state by state on control agencies, local option, on and off sale licenses, hours, markup, brand registration and wholesaling, credit, resale, and legal age.

1405. _____. *Tax Briefs.* Washington DC. Annual. Free. Current and historic data on federal excise taxes, United States import duties, and state and local revenues and tax rates.

1406. Fier, Bruce. *Starting and Running a Money-Making Bar.* Blue Ridge Summit PA: TAB, 1986. 240p. $14.95. Emphasizes succeeding by paying close attention to cost and management details.

1407. Green, Eric F.; Drake, Galen; and Sweeney, F. Jerome. *Profitable Food and Beverage Management: Operations.* Hasbrouck Heights NJ: Hayden, 1978. 429p. $21.95. Manual for daily operation of a restaurant including food, liquor, personnel, facilities, housekeeping, storage, sanitation, security, and safety.

1408. _____; _____; and _____. *Profitable Food and Beverage Management: Planning.* Hasbrouck Heights NJ: Hayden, 1978. 389p. $19.75. Manual for planning the operation and management of a restaurant (see **1407**).

1409. Horgan, Marvis M.; Sparrow, Margo Dewar; and Brazeau, Ron, comps. *Alcoholic Beverage Taxation and Control Policies: An International Survey.* Ottawa, Canada: Brewers Association of Canada, 1986. 563p. Controlled distribution. Alcoholic beverage laws and regulations for Europe, Canada, Japan, and the United States. Statistics on taxation, excise, and imports. Statistics on consumption of alcholic beverages by country.

1410. Johnson, R.H. *Running Your Own Restaurant,* 2nd ed. London: Hutchinson; Brookfield VT: Brookfield, 1982. 185p. $14.50.

British approach to pub and restaurant management.

1411. Katsigris, Costas, and Porter, Mary. *Pouring for Profit: A Guide to Bar and Beverage Management.* New York: Wiley, 1983. 433p. $18.95. Detailed examination of all facets of bar and beverage organization and management in a restaurant setting. Layout, equipment, personnel, procedures, forms, safety, and security.

1412. Mooney, Sean, and Green, George. *Sean Mooney's Practical Guide to Running a Pub.* Chicago: Nelson-Hall, 1979. 252p. $21.95. Tips from a successful pub owner.

1413. Moore, Philip. *Total Bar and Beverage Management.* New York: Lebhar-Friedman, 1981. 264p. $21.95. Emphasis on the bartender and that person's role in operating a successful operation.

1414. National Alcoholic Beverage Control Association. *Alcohol Server Liability,* 6th ed. Alexandria VA, 1987. 106p. $125. State dram shop laws and related statutes with cases and judicial rulings. Revised and updated every two or three years. Recent laws, cases, and rulings reported bimonthly in *Alcohol Beverage Legal Briefs* (see **1446**).

1415. _____. *NABCA Surveys.* Alexandria VA. Irregular. $50 each. Studies, directories, and compilations of laws related to alcoholic beverage control and nightclub management. Examples of the types of compilations published are: *Credit Extension Policies to On-Premise Licensees; Food Sales Requirements in On-Premise Establishments; Identification Card Requirements; On-Premise License Fees in Control Jurisdictions;* and *Sunday Sales.*

1416. National Restaurant Association. *Market Research for the Restaurateur: A Do-It-Yourself*

Handbook for Market Research. Washington DC, 1981. 118p. Controlled distribution. Procedural manual outlining the traditional survey approach to market research including sample questions and survey forms.

1417. Security World, Inc. *Restaurant and Bar Security.* Stoneham MA: Butterworth, 1980. 104p. $18.75. Manual for protecting your assets and property. Examined from two perspectives: guarding the cash and property and organizing against "the back door," hidden losses incurred through neglect and lack of employee supervision. Procedures and equipment.

1418. Stevenson, W.C. *Making and Managing a Pub.* Newton Abbot, England: David & Charles, 1986. 144p. $17.95. Part of a series of how-to-do-it manuals for the British entrepreneur.

1419. Van Kleek, Peter E. *Beverage Management and Bartending.* New York: Van Nostrand Reinhard, 1981. 164p. $14.95. Standard management text. Bartending emphasis.

1420. Ware, Richard, and Rudnick, James. *Restaurant Book: The Definitive Guide to Starting Your Own Restaurant.* New York: Facts on File, 1984. 198p. $17.95. Not all that definitive but a good manual with procedures and forms for getting started as a restaurateur.

Industry

1421. Brewers' Society. *International Statistical Handbook.* London. Biennial. Controlled distribution. Production and consumption of distilled spirits and beer worldwide. Excise and customs duties. Price and consumer expenditure data.

1422. _____. *United Kingdom Statistical Handbook.* London. Biennial. Controlled distribution. Production and consumption of distilled spirits and beer in the United Kingdom. Licensing statistics. Excise and customs duties. Price and consumer expenditure data. Beverage use comparisons and market analysis.

1423. Canada. Statistics Canada. *Restaurant, Caterer and Tavern Statistics.* Ottawa, Canada. Annual. $14. Establishments by category, total and net sales and receipts, and employment. Data nationwide and by province.

1424. Distilled Spirits Council of the United States. *Annual Statistical Review Distilled Spirits Industry.* Washington DC. Annual. Free. Production, inventory, sales, foreign trade, consumption, revenues, and consumer expenditures for alcoholic products. State by state statistics. Current and retrospective data. State and local regulations on drinking. Glossary, and selected bibliography of sources.

1425. _____. *Public Revenues from Alcoholic Beverages.* Washington DC. Annual. Free. Federal, state, and local revenue from on and off premise sale of beer, distilled spirits, and wine.

1426. Key Note Publications Ltd. *Public Houses,* 5th ed. London, 1987. 43p. $100. Survey of pubs and taverns in the United Kingdom. Examines industry organization, financial ratios, retail sales, and market. Bibliography.

1427. Laventhol and Horwath. *California Restaurant Operations.* Philadelphia PA. Annual. $50. Statistical compilation for full-service restaurants in California. Restaurants classified by type and location. Analysis of income and expenses per seat. Selected balance sheet ratios developed and analyzed. Composite data for performance, operations, and turnover.

1428. _____. *Restaurant Industry Operations Report*. Washington DC: National Restaurant Association. Annual. $38. Statistical compilation and analysis for food only and food and beverage restaurants based upon data supplied by approximately 1,000 establishments in the United States. Composite data for each of the two types of restaurants is provided for performance, operations, and finances. Industry ratios allow for local operational comparisons.

Market

1429. Distilled Spirits Council of the United States. *Apparent Consumption of Distilled Spirits by Class and by Type*. Washington DC. Annual. Free. Current and retrospective statistics.

1430. _____. *Apparent Consumption of Distilled Spirits by Months and by States*. Washington DC. Annual. Free. Statistics on license states, control states, and all states allowing sale of distilled spirits. Current and retrospective data.

1431. Gower, Wendy. *Drink in the U.K.* London: Economist Intelligence Unit, 1985. 172p. $150. Analysis of drinking habits by type of alcoholic beverage, producer and brand, and place consumed.

1432. *Liquor Handbook*. New York: Jobsen. Annual. $59.95. Specific brands of spirits, wine, and beer giving current and retrospective total and per capita sales by state, consumer preference and demographics, top markets, market share, pricing, and advertising expenditure.

1433. National Alcoholic Beverage Control Association. *NABCA Annual Summary*. Alexandria VA. Annual. Price varies each year. State control data, drinking age, number of state stores, sales, consumption, consumer preference, marketing trends, and summary of *NABCA Statistical Reports* (see **1434**).

1434. _____. *NABCA Statistical Reports*. Alexandria VA. Frequency and price vary. Brief statistical reports on sales by brand, class, and type. Examples of the types of reports published are: *Amaretto Analysis* (quarterly); *Brandy Ready Reference* (semiannually); *Distilled Spirits Brand Leaders* (monthly); *Monthly Summary for All States*; *Scotch and Canadian* (semiannually); *State Sales Report* (monthly); *Wine and Vermouth* (monthly); and monthly sales and inventory summaries for Michigan, North Carolina, Ohio, Pennsylvania, Vermont, and Montgomery County, Maryland.

1435. _____. *Revenue and Sales Effects of Higher Minimum Drinking Age*. Alexandria VA, 1984. 112p. $225. Study and analysis.

1436. Shanken, Marvin R., ed. *Impact American Beer Market Review and Forecast*. New York: M. Shanken Communications. Annual. $195. Statistics, charts, and analysis of United States beer consumption by type and brand. Market share, consumer and advertising expenditures, and consumer demographics. Forecasts future brand leaders and foreign and domestic competition.

1437. _____, ed. *Impact American Distilled Spirits Market Review and Forecast*. New York: M. Shanken Communications. Annual. $195. Statistics, charts, and analysis of United States liquor consumption by type and brand. Market share, consumer and advertising expenditures, and consumer demographics. Forecasts future brand leaders and foreign and domestic competition.

1438. _____, ed. *Impact American Wine Market Review and Forecast*. New York: M. Shanken Communications. Annual. $195. Statistics, charts, and analysis of United States wine consumption by type and brand. Market share, consumer and advertising expenditures, and consumer demographics. Forecasts future brand leaders and foreign and domestic competition.

Periodicals

1439. *Bar Products News*. Oxford MS: Opportunities. Monthly. Controlled distribution. News and articles on products used by on-premise establishments.

1440. *Bartender Magazine*. Liberty Corner NJ: Foley. Quarterly. $20. Articles on bartender of the month, greatest bar, and more original drink. Drink marketing tips. News of products, equipment, and services for the on-premise industry.

1441. *Beverage Profit Ideas*. Greenlawn NY: Beverage Profit Ideas. 3 issues. Free. For the bartender and club owner. Case histories of successful beverage and drink promotions and beverage recipes.

1442. *Bill of Fare*. Loudon TN: Images. Bimonthly. $12. Not to be confused with a Broadway theatre publication of the same name. This magazine is for the independent restaurant owner and top food chain executive. Focus is on equipment and services available to restaurateurs.

1443. *Briefing: The Restaurateur's News Digest*. New York: Walter Mathews. Monthly. $45. For the owner, operator, and manager. News briefs of events, actions, and

reports which influence the restaurant industry. Designed to alert management to trends. Looseleaf format.

1444. *Independent Restaurants*. Madison WI: EIP, Monthly. $30. For the non-franchise, non-chain restaurant. Articles on management, food buying and service, bar business, marketing, advertising and promotion, interior design, equipment and products, and food industry news. Special report: "Buyers Guide" in each May issue. Indexed in *Trade and Industry Index*.

1445. *Market Watch*. New York: M. Shanken Communications. Monthly. $60. For the alcoholic beverage retailer primarily but contains news and articles on consumer preference by type and label, consumption statistics, and marketing and promotion. Updates the "Impact" annuals.

1446. National Alcoholic Beverage Control Association. *Alcohol Beverage Legal Briefs*. Alexandria VA. Bimonthly. $150. Summaries of current alcoholic beverage control laws, cases, and judicial decisions. Began publication January 1987.

1447. National Licensed Beverage Association. *NLBA News*. Alexandria VA. 7 issues. Membership. Official association publication. News of legislations, laws, and cases, industry developments, state regulatory agencies, and the work of the association.

1448. National Restaurant Association. *Restaurant USA*. Washington DC. Monthly. $125. Articles on business, management, finance, operations, and marketing. Reports and forecasts on industry and market. Information and analysis of legislation, regulations, cases, decisions, and rulings on operations, safety, and personnel. Indexed in

Predicasts F&S Index: United States.

1449. *NightClub and Bar.* Oxford MS: Opportunities. Monthly. Controlled distribution. For owners, operators, and managers of nightclubs, discos, bars, and "fun" restaurants. Articles on successful owners, management and marketing programs, and product and service developments. News on legislation, regulations, trends, and the industry.

1450. *Restaurant Business.* New York: Restaurant Business. 18 issues. $63. For the executive in the food service industry but contains reports applicable to bars and nightclubs including menu planning, food and bar management, cost control, interior design, regulations, and liability. Indexed in *Business Periodicals Index, Predicasts F&S Index: United States, Trade and Industry Index.*

1451. *Restaurant Hospitality.* Cleveland OH: Penton. Monthly. $45. For the restaurant executive. Emphasis on management. Articles on operations management, merchandising, and decor. News of the industry, regulations, and trade shows. Indexed in *Accountants' Index, Predicasts F&S Index: United States, Real Estate Index, Trade and Industry Index.*

1452. *Restaurant Management.* Duluth MN: Harcourt Brace Jovanovich. Monthly. $24. For the independent restaurateur who owns and operates one or more establishments. Articles on the role of the independent restaurateur, management, labor, finance, marketing, advertising and promotion, design and decor, equipment, regulation, and liability.

General

Beverage industry magazines for the distributor, retailer, and on-premise bar, club, or tavern, containing state-oriented news on products, prices, and promotions are published in all 18 "Control States." Most of these publications are affiliated with Associated Beverage Publications, Inc., 161 Avenue of the Americas, New York NY 10013, (212) 620-0100.

Associations

1453. Brewers Association of Canada. 151 Sparks St., Suite 805, Ottawa, Ontario, Canada K1P 5E3. (613) 232-9601. Association of companies.

1454. Brewers' Society. 42 Portman Sq., London, England W1H 0BB. (01) 486-4831. Association of liquor and beer companies in the United Kingdom. Compiles statistics. Conducts research. Provides management counsel, seminars, trade shows. Maintains library. Publishes statistics.

1455. Canadian Restaurant and Foodservices Association. 80 Bloor St., W., Suite 1201, Toronto, Ontario, Canada M5S 2V1. (416) 923-8416. Association of food serving establishments and suppliers.

1456. Distilled Spirits Council of the United States. 1250 Eye St., N.W., Suite 900, Washington DC 20005. (202) 628-3544. Association of liquor producers and distributors. Compiles statistics. Conducts research. Provides seminars. Publishes handbooks, statistics.

1457. National Alcoholic Beverage Control Association. 4216 King St., Alexandria VA 22302. (703) 578-4200. Association of state agencies. Compiles statistics. Publishes statistics.

1458. National Licensed Beverage Association. 309 N. Washington St., Alexandria VA 22314. (703) 683-

6633. Association of bars, cocktail lounges, hotels, restaurants, taverns, and other licensed on-premise businesses in the United States. Publishes handbooks, directory, periodical.

1459. National Restaurant Association. 311 First St., N.W., Washington DC 20001. (202) 638-6100. Association of food serving establishments and suppliers. Compiles statistics. Conducts research. Provides management counsel, seminars, trade shows. Maintains library. Publishes standards, handbooks, statistics, periodicals.

26. The Tourist Lodging Industry

SIC Code: 7011.

Enterprises providing short-term accommodations for recreation travelers and vacationers.

Directories

1460. American Bed and Breakfast Association. *Treasury of Bed and Breakfast.* Washington DC. Annual. $12.95. Lists overnight accommodations in the United States giving name, address, phone, type of accommodation, cost, and host name. Also B and B reservation services giving name, address, phone, hours, and services. Arrangement is geographical.

1461. American Hotel and Motel Association. *Directory of Hotel and Motel Systems.* New York. Annual. $29.50. Hotel, motel, and resort chains operating at least three establishments. Each listing gives name of chain, address, phone, key executives, property locations, and room count. Arrangement is alphabetical.

1462. _____. *Hotel and Motel Red Book.* New York. Annual. $45. Lists hotels, motels, and resorts in the United States giving name, address, phone, toll free or TWX number, managers, room count, rates, and facilities. Arrangement is geographical with name index.

1463. American Resort and Residential Development Association.

Who's Who in Resort Development. Washington DC. Annual. Membership. Lists developers, industry professionals, and suppliers of products and services with addresses of developments in which involved. First edition, 1987.

1464. British Hotel, Restaurants and Caterers Association. *BHRCA Guide to Hotels and Restaurants.* London. Annual. Membership. Lists members of the association giving name, address, phone, key executives, and services. Arrangement is classified.

1465. Buzan, Norma Stephens. *Bed and Breakfast North America,* 4th ed. Bloomfield MI: Betsy Ross, 1986. 550p. $13.95. Lists reservation agencies for B and Bs in the United States, Canada, and Mexico giving name, address, phone, services, fees, and price range for accommodations. Also includes a selected list of inns "which have been owned and operated for years by the same family." Arrangement is geographical by state or province with city index.

1466. Carlson, Raymond, ed. *National Directory of Budget Motels.* Babylon NY: Pilot Industries. Annual. $3.95. Lists economy facilities part of motel chains in the United States and Canada giving name, address, and phone. Also list of chains giving name, address, phone, toll free number, credit cards accepted, and approximate rates for their facilities.

1467. Clark, Peter. *Bed and Break-*

159

fast in Britain. Seedhill, Scotland: Farm Holiday Guides. Annual. $4. Lists establishments in England, Scotland, and Wales giving name, address, host, rates, and facilities. Arrangement is geographical.

1468. *Hotel and Travel Index.* New York: Murdoch Magazines. Quarterly. $90. Primarily for the travel agency industry. Lists hotels, motels, inns, and resorts worldwide giving name, address, phone, toll free, and TWX numbers, key executives, room count, facilities, and travel agent access codes and commission. Also hotel and motel systems, chain representatives, and reservation services. Arrangement is geographical. Each quarterly issue is a complete listing.

1469. International Hotel Association. *International Hotel Guide.* Paris. Annual. $32. Lists hotel and restaurant members worldwide giving name, address, phone, telex, key executives, season, prices, facilities, and credit cards accepted. Arrangement is geographical.

1470. National TimeSharing Council. *Directory of Member Resorts.* Washington DC. Annual. Free. Lists name, address, phone, description of facilities, and airport location for each. Arrangement is geographical.

1471. *Official Hotel and Resort Guide.* New York: Murdoch Magazines. Annual. $225. Worldwide directory of hotels and resorts. Divided into 18 geographical segments. Arrangement is geographic and alphabetical. Descriptions of location, facilities, and rates. Looseleaf format.

1472. Taylor, Arlie L. *Directory of Hotel Lenders.* Dallas TX: Hospitality Media, 1986. 36p. $125. Lists institutional lenders, correspondents, and mortgage brokers engaged in hotel, motel, and resort financing.

Each listing gives name, address, phone, and services. Arrangement is geographical.

Note: Most state travel agencies and many state trade associations publish statewide directories, e.g., *Explore Minnesota Resorts; Florida Hotel and Motel Association Travel Directory; Vermont Four Season Vacation Rentals.*

Management

1473. American Entrepreneurs Association. *Bed and Breakfast Inn and Home.* Los Angeles, 1986. 118p. $55. Establishing and operating a small business. Chapters on legal, management, marketing, operations, and financial procedures. Sources to additional information. Looseleaf format.

1474. American Resort and Residential Development Association. *Timeshare Financial Manual.* Washington DC. 1982. 56p. $38.50. Procedures and forms.

1475. _____. *Timeshare Property Assessment and Taxation.* Washington DC. 1983. 48p. $31. Procedures and forms.

1476. Ballman, Gary, and Simonson, Larry. *Managing Small Resorts for Profit.* Saint Paul MN: University of Minnesota Agricultural Extension Service, 1985. 147p. Free. Policy, procedures, and forms. Looseleaf format.

1477. Blomstrom, Robert L., ed. *Strategic Marketing Planning in the Hospitality Industry: A Book of Readings.* East Lansing MI: Educational Institute of the American Hotel and Motel Association, 1982. 322p. $23.95. Basic concepts of marketing, strategic marketing, market research, target marketing, positioning, and advertising. "How-to" case studies.

1478. Conroy, Kathleen. *Valuing the Timeshare Property.* Chicago: American Institute of Real Estate Appraisers, 1981. 97p. Controlled distribution. Overview of the concept, types, characteristics, marketing, finance, and exchange of timeshare property. Major portion of book is devoted to the valuation process and an extensive case study with detailed charts and tables.

1479. Cournoyer, Norman G., and Marshall, Anthony G. *Hotel, Restaurant and Travel Law,* 2nd ed. Boston: Breton. 1983. 654p. $34.95. Analyzes the legal maze of rights and responsibilities in the hospitality industry in the United States. Case studies employed to explain the various facets of law and regulations.

1480. Davis, Mary E., et al. *So ... You Want to Be an Innkeeper: A Complete Guide to Operating a Successful Bed and Breakfast Inn.* San Francisco CA: 101 Productions, 1985. 218p. $14.95. Beginners guide to research, planning, starting, operating, and marketing. Used as a seminar text. Planning and management worksheets included. Bibliography and index.

1481. Edmonds, James. *International Timesharing,* 2d ed. London: Services to Lawyers, 1986. 591p. $75. International approach to the laws and legal aspects of timesharing. Regulation documents and forms. British and European emphasis.

1482. Etsell, Karen, and Brennan, Elaine C. *How to Open (and Successfully Operate) a Country Inn.* Stockbridge MA: Berkshire Traveller, 1983. 191p. $9.95. How-to-do-it guide with procedures and forms. Bibliography of sources and index.

1483. Eyster, James J. *Financing the Lodging Industry.* Philadelphia PA: Laventhol and Horwath, 1982. 39p. $45. Analysis based upon financial statements as to methods and sources for capital development. Statistics, charts, and graphs predominate.

1484. Gee, Chuck Y. *Resort Development and Management.* East Lansing MI: Educational Institute of America Hotel and Motel Association, 1981. 449p. $34.95. Probably the most respected resource book on this topic. Chapters on the concept and history, planning and development, human and public relations, management, marketing, finance, and the future of resorts.

1485. Glover, Fred, and Rogozinski, Jacques. *Resort Development: A Network-Related Model for Optimizing Sites and Visits.* Boulder CO: University of Colorado Business Research Division, 1980. 20p. $6. Mathematical model for locating resorts.

1486. Halm, Ann, ed. *Uniform System of Accounts and Expense Dictionary for Small Hotels, Motels, and Motor Hotels,* 3rd ed. East Lansing MI: Educational Institute of the American Hotel and Motel Association, 1986. 1v. $24.95. Textbook on accounting procedures and forms. Includes food and beverage accounting practices. Financial statements, balance sheets, forecasting, ratio analysis discussed.

1487. Henze, Mark E., and Schlaifer, Alan N. *Law and Business of Resort Development.* New York: Clark Boardman, 1986. 1v. $85. Legal, regulatory, financial, and management requirements of timesharing, resort development, and condominiums. Includes financial, management, and consumer-marketing forms. Looseleaf format.

1488. Hotton, Georgia. *Introduction to Resort Management.* Chicago:

Nelson-Hall, 1982. 206p. $21.95. Textbook on background, management, finance, personnel, and operations.

1489. Ingleby, Steven L., and Boyer, Ted. *Resort Timesharing Handbook.* Chicago: Real Estate Education, 1984. 245p. $39.95. Introduction to concept, planning, valuation, financing, marketing, and operation.

1490. Lynge, Richard J. *Real Estate Broker's Guide to Resort Timesharing.* Chicago: Real Estate Education, 1984. 262p. $24.95. Rules and regulations for dealing in timeshare properties. Sample real estate forms.

1491. Paananen, Donna M. *Condominiums and Timesharing in the Lodging Industry: A How-to Manual on Operation and Management.* East Lansing MI: Educational Institute of America Hotel and Motel Association, 1984. 52p. $12.95. "How-to-do-it" for owners and managers of resort condominiums and timesharing operations. Information on communications, marketing, reservations, services, housekeeping, maintenance, security, and legal problems.

1492. Pannell Kerr Foster, Inc. *Hotel Pricing Policies.* London: English Tourist Board, 1982. 92p. $5. Report commissioned by the English Tourist Board on the impact of development and operating costs on hotel pricing policies in Britain. Statistics, charts, and analysis.

1493. Powers, Thomas F. *Introduction to Management of the Hospitality Industry,* 2nd ed. New York: Wiley, 1984. 469p. $29.95. Overview of hotel, food service, restaurant, and tourism agency industries. Discusses management aspects of each. Statistical data on finances, operating ratios, labor, and market.

1494. Schnidman, Frank, ed. *Approval Process: Recreation and*

Resort Development Experiences. Washington DC: Urban Land Institute, 1983. 43p. Controlled distribution. Case studies in resort real estate and other recreational land development projects. Emphasis on planning and regulations.

1495. Stankus, Jan. *How to Open and Operate a Bed and Breakfast Home.* Chester CT: Globe Pequot, 1986. 290p. $10.95. First-hand experiences and personal observations are translated into a popular guide to getting started and managing a B and B. Appendix includes list of people willing to help a newcomer, B and B reservation agencies, state tourist offices, and an index to the publication.

1496. *Timesharing in Resort Properties.* S.L. (Minnesota), 1984. 87p. Free. Legal education training manual and forms for timesharing properties and condominiums. Minnesota-oriented but applies to law and regulations throughout the United States.

1497. U.S. Forest Service. *Development Planning: Winter Sports Resorts.* Washington DC, 1973. 53p. Out of print. Old, but still valuable, guide to planning winter resort development. Largely forms and diagrams. Developed in conjunction with the National Ski Areas Association.

1498. Vellacott, Audrey. *Doing Bed and Breakfast.* Newton Abbott, England: David & Charles, 1987. 96p. $11.95. Guide to opening and operating a B and B in the U.K. Bibliography of management resources and index to the contents.

Industry

1499. American Hotel and Motel Association. *Hotel/Motel Wage Rates* *and Other Payroll Costs for Major U.S. Cities.* New York. Annual. Controlled distribution. Comparative study of union wages in 17 job categories for approximately 20 U.S. cities. Statistics collected on hours per day, days per week, hourly wages, vacations, fringe benefits, and expenditures for other contract provisions.

1500. Canada. Statistics Canada. *Traveller Accommodation Statistics.* Ottawa, Canada. Annual. $6. Receipts, expenses, occupancy, and employment statistics for hotels, motels, campgrounds, and other types of traveler accommodations. Current and retrospective data.

1501. Gomes, Albert J. *Hospitality in Transition.* New York: American Hotel and Motel Association, 1987. 60p. $45. Report prepared by the staff of Pannell Kerr Foster, Inc., on the economic positioning of the lodging industry. Intended for the hotel/motel investor as a basis for evaluating his financial decisions.

1502. ICC Business Ratios. *Hotels.* London. Annual. $200. Compares individual and average performance of major companies in the United Kingdom. Provides three-year financial data and ratios.

1503. Key Note Publications Ltd. *Hotels,* 3rd ed. London, 1986. 41p. $100. Analyzes industry structure and trends over a five-year span and compares companies in the last three. Financial ratios and future development examined. Market structure and potential for overseas tourists reviewed. Bibliography.

1504. Laventhol and Horwath. *Canadian Lodging Industry.* Toronto, Canada. Annual. $35. Narrative and analysis based upon statistics provided by Canadian hotels. Composite statistics for the market, performance, occupancy, sales, payroll, and operating expenses. Balance sheet data and industry ratios. Narrative and statistical analysis is also produced for the *Western Canada Lodging Industry.*

1505. _____. *U.S. Economy Lodging Industry.* Philadelphia PA. Annual. $50. Narrative and analysis based upon statistics provided by over 1,000 economy hotels and motels. Composite statistics for the market, performance, occupancy, sales, payroll, and operating expenses. Balance sheet data and industry ratios. Former title: *U.S. Budget Lodging Industry.*

1506. _____. *U.S. Resort Lodging Industry.* Philadelphia PA. Annual. $35. Narrative and analysis based upon statistics provided by over 500 resorts. Composite statistics for the market, performance, occupancy, sales, payroll, and operating expenses. Balance sheet data and industry ratios.

In addition to the nationwide industry analyses, L&H produces state compilations for: *California Lodging Industry; Florida Lodging Industry;* and *Texas Lodging Industry.*

1507. National TimeSharing Council. *Timesharing Fact Sheet.* Washington DC, 1985. 12p. Free. Statistical abstract of general, company, financial, marketing, and other timesharing data for the United States with some worldwide statistics. Irregularly updated.

1508. Pannell Kerr Foster, Inc. *Outlook in the Hotel and Tourism Industries: Eurotrends.* London. Annual. Controlled distribution. Statistics on lodging and travel in Europe including domestic and international travel, sales, room and occupancy rates, salaries, operating costs, and revenues. Balance sheet analysis and industry ratios. Previous year comparisons.

1509. _____. *Trends in the*

Hotel Industry. Houston TX. Annual. Controlled ditribution. Statistics on operations in the United States including sales, room and occupancy rates, salaries, operating costs, and revenues. Balance sheet analysis and industry ratios. Previous year comparisons.

1510. _____. *Trends in the Hotel Industry International.* Toronto, Canada. Annual. Controlled distribution. Operational and financial data on hotels outside the United States. Statistics on operations including sales, room and occupancy rates, salaries, operating costs, and revenues. Balance sheet analysis and industry ratios. Previous year comparisons.

1511. Ragatz, Richard L. *Resort Timesharing Industry: A Socio-Economic Impact Analysis of Resort Timesharing.* Washington DC: American Land Development Association, 1980. 2v. Out of print. Indepth study and analysis of the current and potential impact of the timeshare industry on community social and economic development. Based upon specific community research. Numerous charts and tables.

1512. Urban Land Institute. *Recreation Development Handbook.* Washington DC, 1981. 272p. $46. Gives 30 case studies of dealing with recreational property planning, development, financing, marketing, and operations.

Market

1513. Euromonitor. *Hotel and Catering Industry.* London, 1982. 81p. $250. Study of five trends in demand for hotel accommodations and food catering in the United Kingdom. Includes both consumer and institu-

tional demand. Projects demand for next five years.

1514. Gallup Poll. *Study of Americans' Awareness and Attitudes Toward Vacation Timesharing.* Washington DC: National Time-Sharing Council, 1981. 1v. $65. Survey commissioned by and only available through the Council. Covers a variety of questions of importance to timeshare resort builders.

1515. Mill, Robert Christie, and Morrison, Alastair M. *Tourism System.* East Lansing MI: Educational Institute of the American Hotel and Motel Association, 1985. 457p. $27.95. Examines tourism from point of view of motivation, perception, selection, and personal bias. Seeks to formulate a plan based upon appeal to consumer perception of need and services provided by hotels, resorts, and other loading facilities. Discusses governmental positives and negatives in tourism.

1516. Ragatz, Richard L. *Overview of the Resort Timsharing Market: Consequences for the Local Community.* Washington DC: National TimeSharing Council, 1982. 26p. $10. Less detailed study than his 1980 analysis. Focuses on marketing implications and market potential of timesharing.

Periodicals

1517. American Bed and Breakfast Association. *Bed and Breakfast Shoptalk.* Washington DC. Monthly. Membership. Official association publication. Emphasis on operation of a B and B facility. News of seminars, book reviews and publication notices, editorials and letters to the editor with management tips, and information on regulations and laws.

1518. American Hotel and Motel Association. *Lodging.* New York. Monthly. $35. Official association publication. Management oriented articles on operations, employees, quality assurance, food, technology, and security. News of tourism trends, conventions, and government regulatory actions. Special report: "Buyers Guide for Hotels/Motels" in each April issue.

1519. American Resort and Residential Development Association. *Developments.* Washington DC. 11 issues. Membership. Official association publication. Articles on the industry, its market, management of resorts, timesharing facilities, resort development, and operation of specific facilities. Reports on laws and regulations and activities of time-share resort-park sub-councils. Former title: *Resort Timesharing Today.* Indexed in *Real Estate Index.*

1520. _____. *Timesharing Law Reporter Briefs.* Washington DC. Monthly. $62. Official association publication. News of federal, state, and local laws and regulations. Cases, administrative decisions, and court decisions. Analysis and interpretation. Indexed in *Real Estate Index.*

1521. British Hotels, Restaurants and Caterers Association. *British Hotelier and Restauranteur.* Sircup, England. Monthly. Membership. Official association publication. Former name: *BHRCA Journal.*

1522. *Canadian Hotel and Restaurant.* Toronto, Canada: Maclean Hunter. Monthly. $49. Articles on operations, cost control, marketing, and staff efficiency. Features about top hotels and restaurant service. News of equipment, regulations, and events.

1523. *Cornell Hotel and Restaurant Administration Quarterly.* Ithaca NY: Cornell University School of Hotel Administration. Quarterly. $25. Research articles on administration and management of hospitality institutions. Information on research, studies, and statistical reports. Book reviews. Indexed in *Business Periodicals Index, PAIS, Real Estate Index, Trade and Industry Index.*

1524. *Hospitality Scene.* Minneapolis MN: Medcom. 10 issues. $18. Emphasis on profitable management of lodging and food. Articles on cost control, efficient use of personnel, and management procedures. News of equipment, innovative ideas, quality service and performance, and educational opportunities.

1525. Hotel and Motel Brokers of America. *Innside Issues.* Kansas City MO. Bimonthly. Controlled distribution. Official association publication. News and articles on the market, investment, and the hotel, motel, and resort trade. Financial and legislative issues summarized.

1526. *Hotel and Motel Management.* Cleveland OH: Harcourt Brace Jovanovich. 18 issues. $25. Articles on developments and trends in finance, management, and marketing of hotels and motels. News of technology, food service, government, and security. Tips and features on promotions and sales. Special report: "Buyer's Guide" in each December issue. Absorbed *Motel and Motor Inn, Motor Inn Journal.* Indexed in *Business Periodicals Index, Real Estate Index, Trade and Industry Index.*

1527. *Hotel and Resort Industry.* New York: Coastal Communications. Monthly. Controlled distribution. For managers and suppliers in the hotel, motel, and resort industry. Articles on design, operations, security, equipment and supplies.

Columns on management and marketing.

1528. *Inn Business.* Unionville, Canada: Zanny. 6 issues. $25. Emphasis on efficiency, effectivity, and profitability. Articles and ideas for management, operations, marketing, and accounting. News of the Canadian hospitality industry, products, and legislation. Features on how to improve, upgrade, and maintain your facilities.

1529. *Innkeeping: The Innkeeper's Newsletter.* Inverness CA: Mary Davis. Monthly. $48. Tips by a practicing innkeeper. News of other B and B activities particularly on the West Coast. Calendar of seminars and other events.

1530. Laventhol and Horwath. *Canadian Trend of Business: Hotels.* Toronto, Canada. Quarterly. Controlled distribution. Financial and operating statistics compiled from hotels and motels. Largely graphs and tables.

1531. _____. *National Trend of Business: Economy/Limited Service Lodging.* Philadelphia PA. Monthly. Controlled distribution. Financial and operating statistics compiled from United States economy hotels and motels. Largely graphs and tables.

1532. *Lodging Hospitality.* Cleveland OH: Penton. Monthly. $40. For hotel, motel, and resort managers, and public relations. Information on individual and chain finance and management, as well as industry-wide statistics. Special reports: "Buyer's Guide" in each March issue and "Lodging's 300" in each August issue. Former title: *Hospitality Lodging.* Indexed in *Real Estate Index, Trade and Industry Index.*

1533. *Marketing and Sales Promotion Update.* Mountain View CA: Newsletter Group. Monthly. $48.

Articles on successful techniques for increasing hotel, motel, and resort occupancy. International in scope.

1534. *Monthly Resort Real Estate Property Index.* Marina Del Rey CA: MDR Telecom. Monthly. Controlled distribution. List of resort timeshares and condominums for rent. Gives name of resort, address, type of rental, management, and details about the unit, e.g., size, cost, amenities.

1535. *Motel/Hotel Insider Newsletter.* New York. Atcom. Weekly. $88. Newsmagazine for the industry. Commentary on trends in tourism, changes in the industry, and legislation. Management and marketing tips. Statistical tables and data. Features on specific hotels, chains, and hotel development.

1536. Preferred Hotels Association. *PHA President's Newsletter.* Oakbrook Terrace IL. Monthly. Membership. Official association publication. Emphasis on marketing. Statistical and management data. Inside tips on promoting the "preferred" market. News of members, the association, and activities and events.

1537. *Resort and Hotel Management.* Del Mar CA: Source Communication. 8 issues. $25. For owners and operating executives of resort hotels, vacation resorts, and resort complexes. Articles on management, finance, marketing, and all major aspects of resort operations. Case studies of "successful resorts." Indexed in *Real Estate Index.*

1538. *Resort Development.* Bellingham WA: CHB. 8 issues. $35. News and articles on projects, finance, marketing, regulation, and trends. Information on timesharing, resort condominiums, and RV campgrounds.

1539. *Southern Golf — Landscape*

and Resort Management. Clearwater FL: Brantwood. Bimonthly. $9. For owners and managers of courses and resorts in the Sunbelt. Emphasis on course and turf maintenance. Articles on course and resort operations, management, pro shop, and equipment.

Databases

1540. MDR Telecom. *RELS.* Marina Del Ray CA. Updated monthly. $100. Text. Description of resort properties for rent or sale. Access via The Source.

Bibliographies/Indexes

1541. Clatanoff, Robert M. *Valuation of Resort and Recreational Property: A Classified Annotated Bibliography.* Chicago: International Association of Assessing Officers, 1984. 29p. $10. Books and articles.

1542. Cornell University School of Hotel Administration. *Bibliography of Hotel and Restaurant Administration.* Annual. $15. Record of new materials received by the SHA Library. Arrangement is by subject with author and titles indexes.

1543. _____. *Subject Catalog of the Library.* Boston MA: G.K. Hall, 1981. 2v. $210. Special library collection.

1544. Kruel, Lee M.; Dennington, Lloyd J.; and Lohr, Judi. *Digest of Current Lodging Industry Market Research Studies.* New York: American Hotel and Motel Association, 1985. 92p. $30. Summarizes 35 reports on selection, reservations, length of stay, promotions, and security as factors in marketing the lodging industry.

Associations

1545. American Bed and Breakfast Association. P.O. Box 23294, Washington DC 20026. (703) 237-9777. Association of innkeepers. Compiles statistics. Provides seminars. Publishes handbooks, directory, periodical.

1546. American Hotel and Motel Association. 888 7th Ave., New York NY 10106. (212) 265-4506. Federation of state and regional hotel associations. Compiles statistics. Conducts research. Publishes statistics, directories, periodical.

1547. American Resort and Residential Development Association. 1220 L St., N.W., Washington DC 20005. (202) 371-6700. Association of developers of resorts and recreational timesharing resorts along with other types of recreational residential development. Compiles statistics. Conducts research. Provides management counsel, seminars. Maintains database. Publishes handbooks, statistics, periodical. Formerly: American Land Development Association.

1548. British Federation of Hotel, Guest House, and Self-Catering Associations. 23 Abingdon St., Blackpool, Lancastershire, England FY1 4PD. (02) 532-4241. Federation of local associations, small hotels and guest houses, and individuals involved in management.

1549. British Hotels, Restaurants and Caterers Association. 42 Priestlands Park Rd., Sidcup, Kent, England DA1S 7HJ. Association of large hospitality establishments. Compiles statistics. Conducts research. Provides seminars. Publishes directory, periodical.

1550. Caribbean Hotel Association. 18 Marseilles St., Suite 1A, Santurce, Puerto Rico 00907. (809) 725-

9139. Federation of regional hotel associations and tourist hotels. Compiles statistics. Provides management counsel, seminars, trade shows.

1551. Hotel and Motel Brokers of America. 10920 Ambassador Dr., Suite 520, Kansas City MO 64153. (816) 891-7070; (800) 821-5191. Association of real estate brokers specializing in sale of or investment in hotel and motel properties. Publishes handbooks, periodical.

1552. Hotel Association of Canada. 900 W. Georgia St., Vancouver, BC, Canada V6C 2W6. (604) 681-7164. Federation of provincial hotel associations.

1553. International Hotel Association (Association Internationale d'Hotellerie). 89 Rue de la Roquette. Paris, France 75008. Federation of national associations. Publishes directory.

1554. National Bed and Breakfast Association. P.O. Box 332, Norwalk CT 06852. (203) 847-6196. Association of small, family-owned inns in the United States. Provides management counsel.

1555. National TimeSharing Council. 1220 L St., N.W., Suite 510, Washington DC 20005. (202) 371-6700. Association of developers of timesharing resorts in the U.S. Division of American Resort and Residential Development Association. Compiles statistics. Conducts research. Provides seminars.

1556. Preferred Hotels Association. 1901 S. Meyers Rd., Suite 220, Oakbrook Terrace IL 60148. (312) 953-0404. Association of independent, luxury hotels and resorts in the United States. Compiles statistics. Provides management counsel, seminars. Publishes periodical.

1557. Resort Timesharing Council of Canada. 48 Hayden St., Toronto, Ontario, Canada M4Y 1V8. (416) 960-4930. Association of resort development corporations.

1558. Tourist House Association of America. Rt. 2, Box 355A, Greentown PA 18426. (717) 857-0856. Association of innkeepers in the United States and Canada. Provides management counsel. Publishes handbooks.

27. The Campgrounds Industry

SIC Code: 7033.

Enterprises providing overnight or short-term sites for hikers, recreational vehicles, or tents. For enterprises whose primary emphasis is organized camping see Chapter 28, The Camping Industry.

Directories

1559. American Youth Hostels, Inc. *AYH Handbook.* Washington DC. Annual. $5. Lists AYH establishments in the United States giving name, address, phone, host, capacity, facilities, location, directions, and map for each site. Arrangement is geographical.

1560. Canadian Hostelling Association. *Youth Hotel Handbook.* Vanier, Canada. Annual. $5. Lists AYH establishments in Canada giving name, address, phone, host, capacity, facilities, location, directions, and map for each site. Arrangement is geographical.

1561. International Youth Hostel Federation. *International Youth Hostel Handbook.* Weywyn Garden City, England. Annual. $5 each. Lists AYH establishments worldwide giving name, address, phone, host, capacity, facilities, location, directions, and map for each site. Includes hosteling rules for each country before the listing. Arrangement is geographical. Published in two volumes: *Europe and the Mediter-*

ranean, Youth Hostels Outside Europe (except United States).

1562. Kampgrounds of America, Inc. *KOA Directory.* Billings MT. Annual. $2. Lists KOA franchised facilities giving name, address, phone, rates, facilities, and services. Arrangement is geographical.

1563. National Federation of Site Operators. *Chalet Sites Guide.* Gloucester, England. Annual. $2.50. Touring and tent sites and other types of self-service, overnight accommodations in the United Kingdom.

1564. *Rand McNally Campground and Trailer Park Directory.* Skokie IL: Rand McNally. Annual. $12.95. Campgrounds for tent and RV campers in the United States, Canada, and Mexico. Generally recognized as the most comprehensive listing of such facilities, giving name, address, phone, season, capacity, and facilities. Arrangement is geographical with name index. Includes map for each state, province, and district giving location of private and public campgrounds.

1565. *Trailer Life RV Campground and Services Directory.* Agoura CA: Trailer Life. Annual. $13.95. Lists campgrounds, RV parks, and RV services in the United States, Canada, Mexico, and Central America giving name, address, phone, location, cost, and facilities. Arrangement is geographical.

1566. *Wheeler's Recreational Vehicle Resort and Campground*

Guide. Elk Grove IL: Print Media Services. Annual. $10.95. Lists private and public campgrounds and resorts in the United States, Canada, and Mexico. Each listing gives name, address, phone, CB call numbers, location, season, facilities, and if the camp is public or private. Arrangement is geographical.

1567. *Woodall's Campground Directory*. Lake Bluff IL: Woodall. Annual. $12.95. Lists campgrounds in the United States, Canada, and Mexico giving name, address, phone, location, rates, and rating of camp and facilities. Arrangement is geographical. Includes service locations for RV, sightseeing information, and special events. Also published in regional editions.

Note: Most state travel agencies and many state trade associations publish statewide directories, e.g., *Explore Minnesota Campgrounds; Illinois Camping Guide; Vermont Private Campgrounds.*

Management

1568. American Youth Hostels, Inc. *Help Hosteling Grow*. Washington DC, 1986. 16p. Free. Introduction to hostel operations. Background information, steps to becoming an operator, glossary of terms, sample forms and diagram, and list of regional AYH councils.

1569. _____. *Marketing Plan*. Washington DC. Annual. Membership. AYH plan for national promotion of hosteling including media development, assistance to regional and state councils, grants, publication, "budget adventure travel" program for hostelers, membership marketing, travel stores, and programs for the local hostel.

Industry

1570. Canada. Statistics Canada. *Traveller Accommodation Statistics*. Ottawa, Canada. Annual. $6. Receipts, expenses, occupancy, and employment statistics for hotels, motels, campgrounds, and other types of traveler accommodations. Current and retrospective data.

1571. National Campground Owners Association. *American Campground Industry Economic Analysis and Occupancy Data*. Washington DC. Annual. $40. Two part statistics: Part 1 gives number of business, volume, revenue, expenses, and profitability: Part 2 details occupancy by type, time, and region.

1572. Wood, Thomas J. *Minnesota Private Campground 1985 Assessment*. Duluth MN: University of Minnesota, Duluth, Bureau of Business and Economic Research, 1986. 19p. Free. Study of ownership, employment, facilities, revenue, and operating and capital costs of the state's campgrounds. Statistics and financial data. Sample survey forms.

1573. _____. *Trends in the Camping Industry*. Duluth MN: University of Minnesota, Duluth, Bureau of Business and Economic Research, 1985. 33p. Free. Operating and revenue statistics for 1979 through 1982, development projects through 1990, and an analysis of the Indian Point Campground, Duluth, Minnesota.

Periodicals

1574. American Youth Hostels, Inc. *Hosteler's Knapsack*. Washington DC. Quarterly. Membership. For the hosteler rather than the owner or operator of the hostel but includes articles of hostel operations, services needed by hostelers, and what to look for in a good hostel.

1575. *Caravan Business.* Epson, England: A.E. Morgan. Monthly. $25. News of British campgrounds, caravaning, and equipment and supplies. Special report: "Directory" in each March issue.

1576. Kampground Owners Association. *KOA News.* Phoenix AZ. 6 issues. Membership. Official association publication. News of KOAS, management, services, products, and the industry. Features on specific KOA facilities. Calendar of events.

1577. National Campground Owners Association. *NCOA News.* Washington DC. Monthly. Membership. Official association publication. News of trends, regulations, and products. Reports on association activities and shows, state association activities, and training courses and seminars.

1578. National Federation of Site Operators. *Site Operator Journal.* Gloucester, England. 6 issues. Membership. Official association publication.

1579. *Woodall's Campground Management.* Lake Bluff IL. Monthly. $10. Articles on trends, successful operations, and tourism. News of products, regulations, and park happenings. Special reports: "Guide to Products and Services" in March issue and "National Campground Owners Association Convention" in each December issue. Former title:*Campground Management.*

Bibliographies/Indexes

1580. Clotfelter, Cecil F. *Camping and Backpacking: A Guide to Information Resources.* Detroit MI: Gale Research, 1979. 327p. $65. Annotated bibliography of books, pamphlets, and AV materials on organized and unorganized (backpacking, hiking, mountaineering, orienteering, outdoor life, etc.) camping. Emphasis is on participation, not business. Importance of the resource lies in its general reading references and, even though dated, appendixed lists of manufacturers and distributors, state agencies, and organization in the United States and Canada. Author-Title index.

Associations

1581. American Youth Hostels, Inc. P.O. Box 37613, Washington DC 20013. (202) 783-6161. Association of travelers, hikers, and campers. State and regional affiliated association. Maintains system of low-cost overnight accommodations, 40 percent privately owned, in the United States. Compiles statistics. Conducts research. Provides management counsel, seminars. Publishes standards, handbooks, directory, periodicals.

1582. Canadian Hostelling Association. 333 River Rd., Vanier, Ontario, Canada K1L 8H9. (613) 748-5638. Association of travelers, hikers, and campers. Maintains system of low-cost overnight accommodations in Canada. Publishes directory.

1583. International Youth Hostel Federation. Howardsgate, Welwyn Garden City, Herts, England AL8 6BT. (07) 962-4710. Federation of national associations. Compiles statistics. Conducts research. Provides seminars. Publishes directory.

1584. Kampground Owners Association. 6103 N. 35th Ave., Phoenix AZ 85017. (202) 973-0160. Association of KOA franchises. Compiles statistics. Provides management counsel, seminars. Publishes periodical.

1585. National Campground Owners Association. 804 D St., N.E., Washington DC 2002. (202) 543-6260. Association of commercial campgrounds and suppliers as associate members. State affiliated associations. Compiles statistics. Conducts research. Provides management counsel, seminars, trade shows. Publishes standards, handbooks, statistics, periodical.

1586. National Federation of Site Operators. 31 Park Rd., Gloucester, England GL1 1LH. (04) 522-6911. Association of overnight accommodations for campers. Compiles statistics. Conducts research. Provides seminars, trade shows. Publishes handbooks, directory periodical.

1587. Ontario Private Campground Association. 55 Nugget Ave., Suite 224, Scarborough, Ontario, Canada M1S 3L1. (416) 293-2090. Association of establishments in the province.

1588. RV Park and CampResort Council. 1220 L St., N.W., Washington DC 20005. (202) 371-6700. Association of owners and managers in the camp park industry. Focus is on development of campgrounds with or in association with a recreational facility. Division of the American Resort and Residential Development Association (see Tourist Lodging Industry).

1589. Scottish Youth Hostels Association. 7 Glebe Crescent, Stirling, Scotland FR8 2JA. (07) 862-2821. Association of travelers, hikers, and campers. Maintains system of low-cost overnight accommodations in Scotland. Local affiliated associations.

1590. Youth Hostels Association. Trevelyan House, Saint Albans, Herts, England AL1 2DY. (07) 635-5215. Association of travelers, hikers, and campers. Maintains system of low-cost overnight accommodations in England and Wales. Local affiliated associations.

28. The Camping Industry

SIC Code: 7032.

Enterprises providing organized recreation activity outdoors. For enterprises whose primary emphasis is lodging see Chapter 27, The Campgrounds Industry, or Chapter 26, The Tourist Lodging Industry.

Directories

1591. American Camping Association. *Parent's Guide to Accredited Camps.* Martinsville IN. Annual. $9.95. Lists camps accredited by the American Camping Association, Discusses choosing a camp. Camps listed alphabetically by state under two categories: day camps and resident camps. Each listing gives name, address, phone, directors, fee, capacity, and comments. Indexes chart specific programs, special clientele served, on-site directors (alphabetical arrangement), camps (alphabetical arrangement by name), and certified camp directors.

1592. Association of Independent Camps. *Guide to Selecting a Private Camp.* New York. Annual. Free. Lists AIC member camps, largely in the eastern United States, giving name, address, phone, sex and age level, capacity, location, facilities and activities, cost, and names of directors.

1593. Bast, Carol J. *Master Guide to Sports Camps.* Grand Rapids MI: Masters, 1987. 4v in 1. $24.95. Lists

regional summer camps for four areas of the United States for elementary, and high school students giving name, address, phone, location, programs, staff, facilities, equipment needed, and costs. Arrangement is geographical.

1594. Christian Camping International/USA. *Guide to Christian Camps and Conference Centers.* Wheaton IL. Annual. $10.95. Each listing gives name, address, phone, location, capacity, and facilities. Arrangement is geographical.

1595. Dude Ranchers' Association. *Dude Ranch Vacation Directory.* LaPorte CO. Annual. Free. Lists member ranches in nine western states giving name, address, location, name of owner or manager, season, description of area, size, and cost. Arrangement is geographical.

1596. Farm and Ranch Vacations, Inc. *Farm, Ranch, and Country Vacations.* New York. Biennial. $10. Working farms, ranches, and other country hosts offering "down-home" opportunities to get back to the land. "What," "where," and "how much" information included. Arrangement is geographical. Former title: *Country Vacations USA.*

1597. *Guide to Summer Camps and Summer Schools.* Boston: Porter Sargent. Biennial. $10. Camps and schools in the United States and Canada giving name, address, phone, capacity, sex, age or grade level, cost, and season. Special programs identified. Arrangement is geographical with name and program index.

1598. Midwest Association of Private Camps. *Midwest Private Camps.* Chicago. Annual. Free. Lists members, giving name, address, phone, capacity, sex and/or age factors, season, description of activities, cost, and names of directors.

1599. North American Gamebird Association. *Directory of Hunting Resorts.* Cayce-West, Columbia SC. Biennial. Free. Lists hunting preserves and game farms open to the general public. Each listing gives name, address, phone, availability to non-members, and species of birds stocked. Arrangement is geographical.

Management

1600. American Camping Association. *Camp Staff Job Descriptions.* Martinsville IN, 1981. 18p. $1.25. Descriptions for camp positions from director to cook. Sample staff organization chart.

1601. _____. *Dealing with Government.* Martinsville IN, 1982. 111p. $7.50. Federal and state laws and regulations on camps. Updated by a periodical, *A.C.A. Legislative Pipeline.* Covers the legislative scene. Looseleaf format.

1602. _____. *Standards with Interpretations for the Accreditation of Organized Camps.* Martinsville IN, 1984. 116p. $10.50. Guidelines for A.C.A. accreditation of resident and day camps. Core standards and standards for selected programs, e.g. aquatics, horse, travel. Briefer *Standards Without Interpretations* also published.

1603. Ball, Armand B., and Ball, Beverly H. *Basic Camp Management.* Martinsville IN: American Camping Association, 1982. 156p. $9. Designed for the new director. Classroom textbook.

1604. _____, and _____, eds. *Business and Finance: A Resource Book for Camps.* Martinsville IN: American Camping Association, 1986. 240p. $9.95. Legal aspects, management, marketing, personnel management, and use of computers in camp administration.

1605. _____, ed. *Cost Study of Resident Camps, 1985.* Martinsville IN: American Camping Association, 1985. 55p. $15. Cost-ratio study of camp operations. Practical tool for financial planning and management. Also guidelines for planning other than financial. Separate charts for private, religious, and agency camp operations.

1606. Farley, Elizabeth, ed. *Prospectives on Camp Administration.* Martinsville IN: American Camping Association, 1982. 125p. $12.50. Essential book for camp organizers and directors. Philosophy, organization, administration, programming, and future of camping.

1607. Goodrich, Lois. *Decentralized Camping.* Martinsville IN: American Camping Association, 1982. 183p. $14. Administration of an outdoor camp, staffing, operations, activities, buildings, budget, and maintenance.

1608. Hammett, Catherine T. *Camp Director Trains His Own Staff.* Martinsville IN: American Camping Association, 1982. 32p. $2. "How-to-do-it" for precamp and in-camp training.

1609. Jones, Daniel Frederick. *Critical Issues Camp Directors Face in the United States in the 1980's.* DEd Thesis, Indiana University, 1983. 280p. 319 camp directors were asked to evaluate 101 issues identified as problems by a jury of recreation experts. Directors could not agree completely that any one issue was critical. Large majority identified financial survival, emotional conflicts in youth, growth in legislation and regulation, and need for qualified personnel as crucial. Study valuable as a guide for new camp managers.

1610. Mitchell, Grace. *Fundamentals of Day Camping*. Martinsville IN: American Camping Association, 1982. 249p. $14.50. Presents data on day camp administration along with most aspects of program organization development.

Industry

1611. Levine, Frank M. *Economic Impact of Organized Camping*. Martinsville IN: American Camping Association, 1984. 54p. $8.75. Impact on the local and U.S. economy. For resident and day camps, both for-profit and non-profit. Camp statistics by type, expenditures, and various economic impact aspects.

Market

1612. National Family Opinion Research, Inc. *Hunting Frequency and Participation Study*. Riverside CT: National Shooting Sports Foundation, 1986. 70p. $70. Hunting activity, hunting attitudes, and firearms ownership.

Periodicals

1613. American Camping Association. *Camping Magazine*. Martinsville IN. 7 issues. $15. Official association publication. Articles directed at managers and directors of camps. Special reports: "Buying Guide" in each March issue and "American Camping Association" in each September/October issue. Indexed in *Magazine Index, Readers' Guide*.

1614. Association of Independent Camps. *AIC Newsletter*. New York. Monthly. Membership. Official association publication. News of industry, specific camps, and the association.

1615. Camp Horsemanship Association. *CHA Newsletter*. Lawrence MI. Semiannual. Membership. Official association publication. Articles on instruction methods, safety, and dealing with youth. News of certified programs, seminars, and association events.

1616. Christian Camping International/USA. *Journal of Christian Camping*. Wheaton IL. Bimonthly. $14.95. Official association publication. Articles on organization, standards, and camp programs. Profiles of camps and centers. News of the association, people, events and conferences, and government laws and regulations. Former title: *Camps and Conferences Magazine*.

1617. Dude Ranchers' Association. *Dude Rancher*. LaPorte CO. Semiannual. Membership. Official association publication. Articles on association activities, individual ranches, and equipment.

1618. North American Gamebird Association. *Wildlife Harvest*. Cayce-West Columbia SC. Monthly. $15. Official association publication. News and information on commercial club operations as well as data on gamebirds and the association.

Bibliographies/Indexes

1619. Clotfelter, Cecil F. *Camping and Backpacking: A Guide to Information Resources.* Detroit MI: Gale Research, 1979. 327p. $65. Annotated bibliography of books, pamphlets, and AV materials on organized and unorganized (backpacking, hiking, mountaineering, orienteering, outdoor life, etc.) camping. Emphasis is on participation, not business. Importance of the resource lies in its general reading inferences and, even though dated, appendixed lists of manufacturers and distributors, state agencies, and organization in the United States and Canada. Author-Title index.

1620. Van de Smissen, Betty, and Brookhiser, Judy. *Bibliography of Research: Organized Camping, Environmental Education, and Interpretive Services.* Martinsville IN: American Camping Association, 1982. 300p. $8.75. Research through 1980. Indexed by subject and author/institution.

Associations

1621. American Camping Association. 5000 State Rd. 67 N., Martinsville IN 46151. (317) 342-8456. Association of camp owners, directors, and others interested in organized camping. Compiles statistics. Conducts research. Provides management counsel, seminars. Maintains library. Publishes standards, handbooks, directory, periodical.

1622. Association of Independent Camps. 60 Madison Ave., New York NY 10010. (212) 679-3230. Association of private residential camps for children on the east coast of the United States. Provides seminar, trade shows. Publishes standards, directory, periodical.

1623. Camp Horsemanship Association. P.O. Box 188, Lawrence MI 49064. (616) 674-8074. Association of certified camps, schools with horsemanship programs, and certified instructors. Compiles statistics. Provides seminars. Publishes standards, handbooks, periodical. Certifies institution, instructors.

1624. Christian Camping International/USA. P.O. Box 646, Wheaton IL 60189. (312) 462-0300. Association of camps, sponsoring organizations, and related individuals. Purpose is to interchange information. Publishes standards, directory periodical.

1625. Dude Ranchers' Association. P.O. Box 471, LaPorte CO 80535. (303) 493-7623. Association of ranches in nine western states and others interested in ranching. Publishes directory, periodical.

1626. Midwest Association of Private Camps. 36 S. State St., Chicago IL 60603. (312) 332-0833. Association of camps. Purpose is to coordinate camp promotion and interchange information. Publishes directory.

1627. North American Gamebird Association. P.O. Box 2105, Cayce-West Columbia SC 29171. (803) 796-8163. Association of commercial game breeders and operators of shooting preserves. Conducts research. Provides management counsel, seminars. Publishes directory, periodical.

29. The Tour Industry

SIC Codes: 4489, 4725.

Enterprises providing recreation and entertainment excursions and travel.

Directories

1628. Alpine, Andy, and Hansen, Steve, eds. *Specialty Travel Index: The Directory to Special Interest Travel.* Fairfax CA: Alpine Hansen. 2 issues. $5. Paid listing of tour operators giving name, address, phone, description of tours offered, destination, length, and cost. Arrangement is alphabetical with activity and destination indexes.

1629. Calder, Simon. *Adventure Holidays,* 10th ed. Oxford, England: Adventure Work; Cincinnati OH: Writer's Digest, 1987. 160p. $8.95. Lists commercial and nonprofit tour organizations in the activity adventure vacation business giving name, address, phone, contact, description of activity, dates and length, itinerary, instruction provisions, specialized equipment needed, and costs.

1630. *Consolidated Tour Manual.* Miami FL: Travel Concepts. 3 issues. $45. Lists package tours in the United States giving organizer, address, phone, description, rates for adults and children, deposit and cancellation requirements, and general information and instructions for tourism agents. Arrangement is alphabetical.

1631. *Cruise Calendar.* Woodland Hills CA. 4 issues. Controlled distribution. Lists tourist cruises worldwide giving name of cruise line and ship, address, phone, length of voyage, itinerary, and minimum and maximum fares. Arrangement is alphabetical. Port of departure and destination indexes. Picture and profile of ships.

1632. DeLand, Antoinette. *Fielding's Worldwide Cruises,* 3rd ed. New York: Morrow, 1987. 469p. $12.95. Lists cruise lines sailing from and to ports throughout the world giving name of cruise, operator, address, phone, itinerary, description of ships, and prices. Arrangement is alphabetical.

1633. Dickerman, Pat. *Adventure Travel North America.* New York: Holt, 1986. 256p. $12.95. Lists guides, outfitters, tours, and associations offering adventure tours in the United States, Canada, and Mexico, giving name, address, type of tour, itinerary, and cost. Arrangement is alphabetical.

1634. *Ford's International Cruise Guide.* Woodland Hills CA: Ford's Travel Guides. 4 issues. $30. Lists cruises worldwide giving name of cruise line, address, phone, and branches; ships used with name registry, date built, description, and photo; cruise dates, itinerary, and fares. Arrangement is geographical by port of departure with cruise line, ship, port of call, and departure date indexes.

1635. Kallen, Christian, ed.

Sobek's Adventure Vacations, 4th ed. Philadelphia PA: Running, 1986. 1v. $24.80. Lists outdoor adventure trips worldwide sponsored by the Sobek's International Explorer's Society. Gives name of trip, level experience needed, itinerary, method of travel, season, length, cost, and tour operator. Arrangement is geographical by continent then by country with type and date indexes.

1636. Pratson, Frederick, ed. *Consumer Guide to Package Travel Around the World.* Chester CT: Globe Pequot, 1984. 272p. $10.95. Selected list of tour operators worldwide giving name, address, phone, and descriptions of over 1,000 tours. Arrangement is alphabetical with destination and activity indexes.

1637. *Travel Weekly's World Travel Directory.* New York: Murdoch Magazines. Annual. $85. Lists travel agencies, tour operators, sightseeing services, and transportation companies giving name, address, phone, and services provided. Arrangement is classified by type of service then geographical for travel agencies and tour operators and alphabetical for most others.

Management

1638. National Tour Association. *Partners in Profit: An Introduction to Group Travel Marketing.* Lexington KY, 1984. 87p. Membership. Outlines marketing concepts and procedures. Identifies and discusses working elements, e.g. hotels, airlines, sightseeing attractions, which are an integral part of the tour. Reference sources and a glossary of tourism terms.

1639. Reilly, Robert T. *Handbook of Professional Tour Management.* Wheaton IL: Merton House,

1982. 138p. $19.95. Textbook used for course to prepare tour operators. Outlines elements and their roll in the tour industry. Examines cooperative interrelationships which must exist. Describes and presents procedures for organizing, operating, managing, marketing, and surviving. Bibliography and index.

Industry

1640. Centaur Associates, Inc. *Analysis of the North American Cruise Industry.* Washington, U.S. Maritime Administration, 1980. 145p. $5. Industry statistics on ships, passengers, income and expenditures, employment, and assets. General analysis and data by port of call. Bibliography.

1641. ICC Business Ratios. *Travel Agents and Tour Operators.* London. Annual. $250. Compares individual and average performance of major companies in the United Kingdom. Provides three-year financial data and ratios.

1642. Key Note Publications Ltd. *Travel Agents/Overseas Tour Operators.* London. Annual. $70. Analyzes industry and market structure in the United Kingdom for overseas tours, trends and tourism developments, financial reports of major tour and package holiday operators, and industry ratios over the past three years.

Market

1643. U.S. Travel Data Center. *U.S. Market for Package Tours.* Washington DC, 1983. 88p. $60. Analysis of characteristics of package tour. Compares actual and potential market, foreign and domestic market, escorted and unescorted tours, air and bus tours, and regional patterns. Based on 1981–82 survey.

Periodicals

1644. American Tour Managers Association. *ATMA/AGA Newsletter.* West Hollywood CA. Monthly. Membership. Official association publication.

1645. Association of Travel Marketing Executives. *Travel and Tourism Executive Newsletter.* Washington DC. Monthly. Membership. Official association publication.

1646. *Cruise Travel.* Evanston IL: World. Bimonthly. $12. News and schedules on ships, ports, and prices. Features on cruise lines, ship, and destinations. Special report: "Cruise Calendar" in each April, August, and December issue.

1647. International Association of Tour Managers—North American Region. *Tour Manager.* New Haven CT. Quarterly. Membership. Official association publication.

1648. National Tour Association. *NTA Courier.* Lexington KY. Monthly. $36. Official association publication. Primarily articles on tour sites but includes information and discussions on tour organization and management, news of tourism, and activities of the association.

1649. _____. *Tuesday.* Lexington KY. Biweekly. $18. Official association publication. News of association and industry happenings, events, reports, and publications. Resume of news important to tour professionals.

1650. *Tour and Travel News.* Manhasset NY: CMP. 30 issues. Controlled distribution. Newspaper of

the tour industry. Emphasizes sales, marketing, and tour promotion information. Data on tours, cruises, group travel, and suppliers. Special reports: "Cruise Report" in each January issue "Cruise Industry Report" in each December issue.

Associations

1651. American Guides Association. 8909 Dorrington Ave., West Hollywood CA 90048. (213) 550-7660. Association of professional guides in the United States. Affiliated with American Tour Managers Association (see **1653**).

1562. American Sightseeing International. 309 Fifth Ave., New York NY 10016. (212) 689-7744. Association of independent sightseeing companies worldwide. Provides seminars.

1653. American Tour Managers Association. 8909 Dorrington Ave., West Hollywood CA 90048. (213) 550-7660. Association of companies, agencies, and individuals involved in the tour industry. Provides management counsel, seminars. Publishes periodical.

1654. Association of Travel Marketing Executives. P.O. Box 43563, Washington DC 20010. (202) 232-7107. Association of individuals engaged in the marketing of travel and tour products and services. Conducts research. Provides seminars. Publishes periodical.

1655. Cruise Lines International Association. 17 Battery Pl., New York NY 10004. (212) 425-2700. Association of tourist passenger ship companies. Provides seminars. Former names: International Passenger Ship Association; Pacific Cruise Conference.

1656. International Association

of Tour Managers — North American Region. 1646 Chapel St., New Haven CT 06511. (203) 777-5994. Association of professional tour managers with tour operators as associated members. Compiles statistics. Conducts research. Provides seminars. Publishes periodical. Certifies professionals. Affiliated with American Society of Travel Agents and Universal Federation of. Travel Agents' Associations.

1657. National Tour Association. P.O. Box 3071, 546 E. Main St., Lexington KY 40596. (606) 253-1036. Association of group travel operators and tour industry associates in the United States. Compiles statistics. Conducts research. Provides management counsel, seminars, trade shows. Publishes handbooks, periodicals. Certifies professionals.

1658. Sobek's International Explorer's Society. One Sobek Tower, Angels Camp CA 95222. (209) 736-4524. Association of adventure tour organizers. Provides management counsel, seminars. Maintains library. Publishes directory.

1659. United States Tour Operators Association. 211 E. 51st St., Suite 12B, New York NY 10022. (212) 944-5727. Association of wholesale tour operators in the United States with travel and tour industry organizations as associate and allied members. Provides seminars.

30. The Tourism Agency Industry

SIC Codes: 4724, 4729.

Enterprises providing information and reservations for recreation and entertainment travel.

Directories

1660. American Society of Travel Agents. *ASTA Membership Roster.* Washington DC. Annual. $125. Separate lists for agency, allied, and associate members. Agency listing gives name, address, phone, contact, description of business, and business mix code numbers. Arrangement under categories is geographical with personal and company name indexes.

1661. Institute of Certified Travel Agents. *ICTA Directory.* Wellesley MA. Annual. Membership. Certified agents, candidates, and fellows of the institute in separate listings. Each listing gives name, address, and phone. Arrangement is geographical. Name index.

1662. International Federation of Popular Travel Organizations. *IFPTO Member Organizations.* Paris, France. Annual. Membership. Lists nongovernment organizations engaged in and promoting international travel giving name, address, phone, cable address, telex, membership, key executives, and organization. Arrangement is geographical.

1663. *Personnel Guide to Canada's Travel Industry.* Toronto, Canada: Baxter. Semiannual. $50.

Lists travel agents, tour operators, and other tourism related enterprises giving name, address, key personnel, and number of employees. Arrangement is by line of business then alphabetical.

1664. Society of Incentive Travel Executives. *SITE Directory.* New York. Annual. Membership. Lists individuals involved in the development, marketing, and administration of travel and tours as incentives, giving name, address, phone, and specialization or position.

1665. Travel and Tourism Research Association. *TTRA Directory of Members.* Salt Lake City UT. Annual. $25. Lists federal, state and local tourism bureaus and other member tourism and travel organizations giving name, address, and phone. Arrangement is alphabetical with personal name and geographical indexes.

1666. Travel Industry Association of America. *TIA Directory of Membership and Services.* Washington DC. Annual. Membership. Listing of members by organization of which they are a part, giving name, address, phone, and title. Arrangement is alphabetical by corporate name with individual name and industry classification name index.

1667. _____. *TIA International Travel News Directory.* Washington DC. Biennial. Membership. Lists media worldwide involved in publicizing tourism. Arrangement is by categories. United States state governmental tourism agency directory included.

1668. *Travel Industry Personnel Directory.* New York: American Traveler. Annual. $20. Lists tourism agencies in the United States and Canada giving name, address, phone, and key personnel. Arrangement is by line of business then alphabetical.

1669. *Travel Weekly's World Travel Directory.* New York: Murdoch Magazines. Annual. $85. Lists travel agencies, tour operators, sightseeing services, and transportation companies giving name, address, phone, and services provided. Arrangement is classified by type of service then geographical for travel agencies and tour operators and alphabetical for most others.

1670. U.S. Travel Data Center. *Survey of State Travel Offices.* Washington DC. Annual. $60. Lists state agencies responsible for promotion of tourism giving name, address, phone, key executives, number of employees, and number directly involved in tourism promotion. Data and statistics on each state's financial and operational involvement in tourism promotion. Arrangement is classified by activity then geographical.

1671. _____. *USTDC Membership Directory.* Washington DC. Annual. Free. Lists member organizations and individuals giving name, address, and phone. Arrangement is alphabetical.

1672. Universal Federation of Travel Agents' Associations. *UFTAA Directory.* Brussels, Belgium, 1986. 300p. Membership. Lists member national associations, registered agencies, and registered tourism-related enterprises giving name, address, phone, cable address, telex, owner or contact, and, for some, services. Arrangement is by categories of activity or line of business.

Management

1673. American Entrepreneurs Association. *Travel Agency.* Los Angeles, 1986. 130p. $45. Guide to establishing and operating a small business. Legal, management, marketing, operations, and financial procedures. Supplier addresses and a bibliography. Looseleaf format.

1674. Anolik, Alexander. *Law and the Travel Industry,* 2nd ed. San Francisco CA: Alchemy, 1984– . $40 per issue. Discusses legal status, laws, and regulations controlling tourism agency activities. Documents, cases, and interpretations. Looseleaf format. Updated periodically.

1675. Davidoff, Phillip D., and Davidoff, Doris. *Financial Management for Travel Agencies.* Wheaton IL: Merton House, 1986. 320p. $25.95. Textbook on financial management, procedures, forms, and case studies. Questions and reading sources.

1676. Dervaes, Claudine. *Travel Agent Training Workbook.* Tampa FL: Solitaire, 1985. 6v. $125. Manuals for preparing the agent to handle scheduling and accounting of airline, hotel, car, cruise, and international reservations. Industry overview, sales techniques, and computerization of services also reviewed. For class and correspondence study. Looseleaf format.

1677. DeSouto, Martha S. *Group Travel Operations Manual.* Wheaton IL: Merton House, 1984. 386p. $25.95. Textbook on concept, organization, procedures, forms, and case studies. Questions and reading sources.

1678. Fremont, Pamela. *How to Open and Run a Money-Making Travel Agency.* New York NY: Wiley, 1983. 224p. $8.95. Introduction to planning, opening, and operating a travel agency. Economic organization emphasized. Useful addresses and an index.

1679. Gee, Chuck Y.; Choy, Dexter J.L.; and Makens, James C. *Travel Industry.* Westport CT: AVI, 1984. 253p. $27.50. Textbook discussing elements of the tourism industry. Includes information on development of tourism, selling and servicing, and specific transportation as hospitality organization. Extensive use of diagrams, charts, and statistics. Outlines, questions, and readings reinforce the text. List of industry organizations and index.

1680. Godwin, Nadine. *Complete Guide to Travel Agency Automation,* 2nd ed. Wheaton IL: Merton House, 1987. 201p. $19.95. Manual featuring hardware, software, discussion of applications, and case studies.

1681. Institute of Certified Travel Agents. *ICTA CTC Certification Text Series.* Wellesley MA, 1980–1986. 5v. $150. Five manuals which are the textbook basis of the curriculum leading to a Certified Travel Consultant designation. Authors and titles are: Hiett, Grace, ed., *Risk Management;* Kelley, Edward M., ed., *Business Management;* Starr, Nona S., ed., *Marketing;* _____, ed., *Tourism;* and _____, ed., *Travel Industry Business.*

1682. Krygel, Barbara A. *Ticketing Series.* Detroit MI: Travel Text, 1983. 3v. $24.95. Manual of instructions, procedures, and forms for ordering, reserving, and accounting for airline tickets in an airline, independent ticketing office, or travel agency. Largely forms.

1683. Lehmann, Armin D. *Travel and Tourism: An Introduction to Travel Agency Operations.* New York: Bobbs-Merrill, 1978. 358p. $27. Textbook emphasizing types of services offered by an agency with reference to agency information resources. Discusses travel areas throughout the world from the tourist perspective. Chapter on travel industry and agencies in Canada. Glossary, airlines and airport codes, government and state tourism offices, major cruise ships, major hotel chains, major charter operators trade journals. Of introductory value to the novice but not as much as would have been the case with a bibliography and index.

1684. Lerner, Elaine, and Abbott, C.B. *Way to Go: A Woman's Guide to Careers in Travel.* New York: Warner, 1982. 192p. $6.95. Discusses what goes into operating a travel agency and the relationships with the tourism industry. Outlines educational and experience qualifications. Lists government and state tourism offices, travel periodicals, and travel industry textbooks.

1685. Lundberg, Donald E. *Tourist Business,* 5th ed. New York; Wokingham, England: Van Nostrand Reinhold, 1985. 252p. $25.95. Covers all facets of the tourism-travel industry worldwide. Definitions, viewpoints and quotations, tables, statistics, businesses, government agencies, abbreviations, and an index.

1686. Miller, Jeffrey R. *Legal Aspects of Travel Agency Operation,* 2nd ed. Wheaton IL: Merton House, 1986. 215p. $25.95. Textbook on law, cases, decisions, and implications. Questions and readings.

1687. _____. *Legal Forms for Travel Agents.* Wheaton IL: Merton House, 1985. 122p. $29.95. Examples and procedures. Questions and readings.

1688. Stevens, Laurence. *Guide to Starting and Operating a Successful Travel Agency,* 2nd ed. Wheaton IL: Merton House, 1985. 403p. $29.95. Textbook of background information, procedures, forms, instructions, and addresses. Bibliography and index.

1689. _____. *Guide to Travel Agency Security.* Wheaton IL: Merton House, 1982. 36p. $6. Procedures, policies, equipment, and problems.

1690. _____. *Travel Agency Personnel Manual.* Wheaton IL: Merton House, 1979. 90p. $21.95. Textbook on concepts, organization, procedures, forms, and case studies. Questions and reading sources.

Industry

1691. ICC Business Ratios. *Travel Agents and Tour Operators.* London. Annual. $250. Compares individual and average performance of major companies in the United Kingdom. Provides three-year financial data and ratios.

1692. Key Note Publications Ltd. *Tourism in the U.K.* London, 1984. 39p. $100. Analyzes industry structure and trends over a five-year span and compares companies in the last three. Financial ratios and future development examined. Market structure and potential for overseas tourists reviewed. Bibliography.

1693. _____. *Travel Agents/ Overseas Tour Operators.* London. Annual. $70. Analyzes industry and market structure in the United Kingdom for overseas tours, trends and tourism developments, financial reports of major tour and package holiday operators, and industry ratios over the past three years.

1694. Organization for Economic Cooperation and Development. *Tourism Policy and International Tourism in OECD Member Countries.* Brussels, Belgium. Annual. $19. Documents policies by country and presents statistics on international tourism flow, receipts, expenditures, air traffic, occupancy rates, accommodations, employment, and price trends.

1695. *Travel Industry World Yearbook.* New York: Child & Waters. Annual. $56. Reports on world travel industry and trends in tourism by region and industry segment. Numerous tables and charts.

1696. U.S. Travel Data Center. *Economic Review of Travel in America.* Washington DC. Annual. $50. Summary and projections of tourism receipts, prices, spending, traffic, payrolls and employment, tax revenue, and regional and international travel presented in tables, charts, and analysis. Former title: *Travel in America.*

Market

1697. Canada. Statistics Canada. *Travel Between Canada and Other Countries.* Ottawa, Canada. Annual. $26. Statistics on trips, duration, and spending by domestic and foreign travelers.

1698. Cleverdon, Robert. *USA and UK on Holiday: Patterns, Determinants, Trends, and Implications.* London: Economist, 1983. 149p. $150. Identifies and examines factors influencing holiday travel and projects future demand. Documents dramatic increase in tourism growth through 1990s barring major economic or political upheaval.

1699. Edwards, Anthony. *International Tourism Forecasts to 1995.*

London: Economist, 1985. 314p. $230. International and individual country projections on spending for travel, trips, overnights, and exchange rates with analysis and statistical tables and charts. Based upon Economist Intelligence Unit studies. Discusses anticipated changes in the development of tourism services and agencies.

1700. Euromonitor. *U.K. Holidays and Tourism Report.* London: 1985. 150p. $150. Study of holiday patterns as to type, destination, transportation, accommodations, and duration.

1701. Goeldner, Charles R., and Duea, Karen. *Travel Trends in the United States and Canada.* Boulder CO: University of Colorado Business Research Div., 1984. 262p. $45. Tourism data for family, vacation, international travel, length and cost of stay, and party size. Indicators of economic impact. Bibliography of travel research statistical sources.

1702. Pearce, Philip L. *Social Psychology of Tourist Behavior.* Oxford, England; New York; and Toronto, Canada: Pergamon, 1982. 155p. $21. Examination of social research on tourists from standpoints of psychological patterns, role in society, motivations, visitor and host, environment, and the perspective and direction of future study. Size and author's approach to reporting research make this book essential reading for tourist agents.

1703. Senior, Robert. *World Travel Market.* London: Euromonitor; New York: Facts on File, 1983. 250p. $60. Examines the growth and development of international travel market over a decade. Provides statistical data on tourism consumption on a regional and country by country basis throughout the world. Largely statistical tables.

1704. *Travel Market Yearbook.* New York: Murdoch Magazines. Annual. $58. Statistics and analysis on the tourism market, the consumer, transportation, and travel agencies. Industry highlights and selected special markets. Glossary, bibliography, and index.

1705. U.S. Travel Data Center. *National Travel Survey.* Washington DC. Quarterly. $75 each. Sampling of United States adults as to transportation modes, lodging, purpose, distance, and duration of vacation travel. Demographic characteristics of sample. Comparison with previous year.

1706. U.S. Travel Service. *Summary and Analysis of International Travel to the U.S.* Washington DC: U.S. Government Printing Office. Monthly with quarterly and annual cumulations. Free. Statistics on visitor arrivals and market analysis of international travel by residents of foreign countries. Data on country of origin, purpose, destination, and demographic profiles.

1707. World Tourism Organization. *Traveller Departures and Main Destination.* Madrid, Spain. Annual. $30. Statistics worldwide on travel abroad by country, county or region of destination, and purpose.

1708. _____. *Yearbook of Tourism Statistics.* Madrid, Spain. Annual. $50. Statistical data on supply and demand for national and international travel. Part 1 lists data on arrivals, receipts, accommodations, employment at the international and regional level. Part 2 provides a country by country profile with data on arrivals, capacity and usage, and economic overview of tourism. Part 3 is a list of tourism agencies. Former titles: *Compendium of Tourism Statistics; Tourism Compendium.*

Periodicals

1709. American Society of Travel Agents. *ASTA Notes.* Washington DC. Weekly. Membership. Official association publication. Newsletter of brief resumes and announcements on current issues affecting the way agents conduct their business, current developments in the industry, and the association.

1710. American Society of Travel Agents. *ASTA Agency Management.* Washington DC. 21 issues. $10. Official association publication. Emphasis on travel agency operations. Features on destinations. Reports on ASTA events. Former title: *ASTA Travel News.*

1711. *Annals of Travel Research.* Elmsford NY: Pergamon. Quarterly. $75. Emphasis is on the nature and impact of tourism on the state, national, and international economy but includes studies on tourism agencies and the management of tourism industries. Indexed in *Leisure, Recreation and Tourism Abstracts, PAIS.*

1712. Association of Group Travel Executives. *AGTE Topics.* New York. Bimonthly. Membership. Official association publication.

1713. Association of Retail Travel Agents. *ARTAfacts.* Croton-on-Hudson NY. Monthly. Membership. Official association publication. Emphasis on retail marketing of travel services to the general public. News important to agents and agency management, information on hotels, resorts, tours, and the tourist trade, and data on credit and finance.

1714. Association of Travel Marketing Executives. *Travel and Tourism Executive Newsletter.* Washington DC. Monthly. Membership. Official association publication.

1715. *Canadian Travel Courier.* Toronto, Canada: Maclean Hunter. Biweekly. $38.25. Articles on market conditions, automations, and promotions. Features each issue on a specific area of the world, destinations, hospitality, and transportation. News of travel, tourism, tariffs, and national and international regulations. Canadian emphasis but worldwide perspective. Special report: "Appointment Diary/Industry Directory" in each November issue. Incorporating: *Canadian Travel News.*

1716. *Canadian Travel Press Weekly.* Toronto, Canada: Baxter. Weekly. $20. Emphasis is on how-to articles for agent and tour organizers and operators on management, marketing, and tourism pricing. News of industry trends, rates and fares, and travellers and expenditures. Features on destinations. Special reports: "Marketing and Media" in each October issue and "Industry Forecast" in each December issue.

1717. *From the State Capitals: Tourist Business Promotion.* New Haven CT: Wakeman/Walworth. 12 issues. $75. Newsletter analyzing state and municipal actions affecting recreation, entertainment, and tourism businesses. Emphasizes state promotion, tourism legislation, and regulation. Discusses finance, support, and construction of recreation and entertainment facilities with state and local funds.

1718. *International Tourism Reports.* London: Economist. Quarterly. $200. Each issue features four or five country or regional analyses with current and retrospective statistical data on tourism for each. Details the history of tourism in the country or region, foreign investment, generalized and statistical profile of visitors, accommodations and tourism features, and industry financial data. Special "Short Industry Reports" examine segments of the tourism industry, e.g. cruise lines, package tours, travel agencies, tourism marketing, recessions and travel. Indexed in *Leisure, Recreation and Tourism Abstracts*.

1719. Society of Incentive Travel Executives. *In-Site*. New York. Quarterly. Membership. Official association publication. News of the association, its activities and members. Information useful to executives responsible for incentive travel programs.

1720. Tourism Industry Association of Canada. *TIAC Newsletter*. Ottawa, Canada. Monthly. Membership. Official association publication.

1721. *Travel Agency*. London: Maclean Hunter. Monthly. $65. For tourism agencies in the United Kingdom. Articles on management, marketing, and sales. Industry trends and news of travel organizations. Features destination profiles.

1722. *Travel Agent*. New York: American Traveler. Semiweekly. $12. Newsletter for the travel agent. Information on market research, travel marketing, trends and forecasts from domestic and foreign scene, and national and international regulations. Data on tour offerings, tariffs, and agent training. Many issues devoted to single topic. Indexed on *PAIS, Trade and Industry Index*.

1723. Travel Agents Computer Society. *TACS Update*. Cambridge MA. Bimonthly. Membership. Official association publication. Information on computer applications, software innovations, computer technology, and the travel industry.

1724. *Travel and Tourism Executive Report*. Washington DC: Leisure Industry/Recreation News. 24 issues. $65. For managers and policymakers. Newsletter providing resumes of news articles and reports of trends, developments, and prospects in the tourism agency and travel fields. Emphasizes brevity and extensive use of statistics.

1725. Travel and Tourism Research Association. *Journal of Travel Research*. Boulder CO: University of Colorado Business Research Div. Quarterly. $65. Scholarly articles on tourism topics, reports on latest research, analysis of studies and surveys, and proposals for innovative management and marketing techiques for the industry. Book reviews and bibliography of new publications. Cumulative index. Indexed in *Leisure, Recreation and Tourism Abstracts*.

1726. _____. *TTRA Members Newsletter*. Boulder CO: University of Colorado Business Research Div. Monthly. Membership. Official association publication. Reports news, surveys, market research, and new publications. Features meetings and seminars, association activities, and achievements of members.

1727. *Travel Business Report*. New York: Walter Mathews. Monthly. $48. News digest of trends, industry activities, and company actions in tourism. Emphasis on profit decision making information and ideas.

1728. *Travel Digest: U.S. Travel Industry Monthly*. New York: Transatlantic. Monthly. $9. For the tourism agent. Reports on development of tourist worldwide. Emphasis on travel marketing in nine categories: air, sea, land, tours, hotels, government, events, sights, and sports. Features on destinations.

1729. Travel Industry Association of America. *TIA Newsline*. Washington DC. Monthly. Membership.

Official association publication. News of tourism trends and projections, tourism marketing, and governmental actions in support of tourism. Reports on laws and legislation.

1730. *Travel Management Daily.* New York: Official Airline Guides. Daily. $425. For the tourism agency owner and the passenger transportation industry executive. An alerting medium: brief reports on happenings today and tomorrow in tourism. News of governmental, industry, and tourism agency activities and actions.

1731. *Travel Marketing and Agency Management Guidelines.* Culver City CA: Travel Marketing. Bimonthly. $35. Leading advisory newsletter for the tourism agent industry. Reports trends and suggests management solutions.

1732. *Travel Trade: The Business Paper of the Travel Industry.* New York: Travel Trade. Weekly. $8. Analyzes current industry trends and marketing potential. News of agency development and operations. Separate "newspaper" sections focus on specific tourism groups and destinations.

1733. *Travel Weekly.* New York: Murdoch Magazines. Semiweekly. $16. Emphasizes analysis and interpretation of industry trends. Features economic and market statistics. Special reports: "Economic Survey" in each January issue; "Spring/Summer Tour Directory" in each February issue; "Telephone Directory of the Travel Industry" in each March issue; "Guide to Business and Group Travel" in each April and October issue; "Fall/Winter Tour Guide" in each July issue; and "Profit Guide" in each August issue.

1734. U.S. Travel Data Center. *Travel Printout.* Washington DC. Monthly. $65. Reports and news of research on the U.S. travel industry. Regular features: travel price index, national travel survey, and current travel indicators.

1735. World Tourism Organization. *World Travel/Tourisme Mondial.* Madrid, Spain. Bimonthly. $14. Official association publication. News of research, publications, industry events, and organization activities. Indexed in *Leisure, Recreation and Tourism Abstracts.*

Bibliographies/Indexes

1736. Corley, Nora Teresa. *Travel in Canada: A Guide to Information Resources.* Detroit MI: Gale Research, 1983. 294p. $62. Annotated books, periodicals, and guides. For the tourism agent, only the list of travel associations gives value to this publication. Index.

1737. Forman, Stephen. *Travel and Tourism Research: A Guide to Information Sources in the Washington D.C. Area.* Boulder CO: University of Colorado Business Research Div., 1982. 107p. $10. This publication reflects a business person's approach to industry intelligence. Librarians will probably find it less useful since it emphasizes periodical data and services, organizations, and directory information more than reference tools. The reference list is too general to pinpoint specific tourism and travel data. Organization and title index but no subject index continues the author's agency rather than library information source theme.

1738. Goeldner, Charles R., and Dicke, Karen. *Bibliography of Tourism and Travel Research Studies, Reports and Articles.* Boulder CO: University of Colorado Business Research Div., 1980. 9v. $60.

Annotated listing of United States and Canadian studies from January 1, 1960 to January 1, 1980. Several volumes cover a specific aspect of tourism, e.g., international, lodging, statistics. Volume one contains a list of general sourcebooks. Volume nine is an author-title index. Significant business references included.

1739. _____. *Data Sources for Tourism Research.* Boulder CO: University of Colorado Business Research Div., 1985. 16p. $5. Annotated listing of reports, documents, and articles. Former title: *Where to Find Travel Research Facts.*

1740. Green, Susan, and Nichols, Jan L. *Forecasting Travel and Tourism: An Annotated Bibliography.* Washington, U.S. Travel Data Center, 1979. 53p. $12. Listing of studies, research, and reference books, pamphlets, and articles. Arrangement is by subject with author and title indexes. Items located in USTDC and University of Colorado Travel Reference Center.

1741. Heise, Jon O., and O'Reilly, Dennis. *Travel Book: Guide to the Travel Guides.* New York and London: Bowker, 1981. 319p. $26.95. Selective, annotated, evaluated list of guides predominately for North America but does include, even more selectively, the remainder of the world. Large number of lists are of organizations rather than historic and cultural attractions making the publication of limited value to business people seeking information on tourism businesses. Evaluative annotations are another plus for the information searcher. Basically, this is an excellent sourcebook for guides but not the tourism-travel business. Directory of publishers and index.

1742. Post, Joyce A., and Post, Jeremiah B. *Travel in the United States: A Guide to Information Sources.* Detroit MI: Gale Research, 1981. 578p. $62. For business research in the chapter on "The United States Travel Industry" which includes source materials, magazines, publishers, and tourist trade organizations, much of it is out of date. Travel industry sources in the remainder of the book divided between general works and organization references. All citations annotated. Limited to the United States. Arrangement is by state. Author, title, subject, geographic, organization, and publisher indexes.

1743. University of Colorado Business Research Division. *Forecasting Travel and Tourism Activity: An Annotated Bibliography.* Boulder CO, 1979. 53p. $12. Summaries of over 100 forecasting publications in the Travel Reference Center Library. Includes books, pamphlets, and articles in the collection with annotations. Arrangement is by subject.

1744. World Tourism Organization. *Tourism Bibliography.* Madrid, Spain. 3 issues. $15. Listing of new publications in tourism and travel. Emphasis on reports, studies, and statistical compilations. Though far from ideal, this periodic list is probably the most useful bibliographic source for keeping up to date with business oriented publications for tourism agencies available.

Associations

1745. American Society of Travel Agents. 4400 MacArthur Blvd., Washington DC 20007. (202) 965-7520. Association of travel agencies worldwide and allied and associate members from travel related fields. Local affiliated associations. Compiles statistics. Conducts research. Provides management counsel, seminars, trade shows. Publishes handbooks, directory, periodicals.

1746. Association of British Travel Agents. 55/57 Newman St., London, England W1P 4AH. (01) 637-2444. Association of agencies in the United Kingdom and Ireland. Provides seminars. Publishes standards.

1747. Association of Group Travel Executives. 424 Madison Ave., Suite 707, New York NY 10017. (212) 486-4300. Association of individuals primarily concerned with promotion of group travel. Publishes periodical. Affiliated with Travel Industry Association of America.

1748. Association of Retail Travel Agents. 25 S. Riverside Ave., Croton-on-Hudson NY 10520. (914) 271-4357. Association of agencies and agents in the United States who deal directly with the non-business traveling public. Provides management counsel, seminars. Publishes periodical.

1749. Association of Travel Marketing Executives. P.O. Box 43563, Washington DC 20010. (202) 232-7107. Association of individuals engaged in the marketing of travel and tourism products and services. Conducts research. Provides seminars. Publishes periodical.

1750. Incentive Travel Association of Canada. 2 Carlton St., Suite 1711, Toronto, Ontario, Canada M5B 1J3. (416) 598-0444. Association of agencies in Canada.

1751. Institute of Certified Travel Agents. P.O. Box 56, 148 Linden St., Wellesley MA 02181. (617) 237-0280. Association of certified travel agents in the United States. Purpose is to provide a program of education, examination, and certification of agents as Certified Travel Counsel-

ors. Maintains library. Publishes directory.

1752. International Federation of Popular Travel Organizations (Federation Internationale des Organisateurs de Tourisme Social). 38 Blvd. Edgar Quinet, Paris, France 75014. Association of non-government organizations engaged in and promoting international travel. Provides seminars. Publishes directory.

1753. Metropolitan Travel Agents. 227 Utica Ave., Brooklyn NY 11213. (718) 771-8400. Association of black travel agencies in the United States.

1754. Society of Incentive Travel Executives. 271 Madison Ave., New York NY 10016. (212) 889-9340; (Canada Office) 716 Gordon Baker Rd., Suite 200, Willowdale, Ontario, Canada M2H 3B4. (416) 494-4695. Association of individuals worldwide involved in the development, marketing, and administration of travel and tours as company incentives to employees, university extracurricular activities for students, association opportunities for members, or product promotion. Purpose is primarily information exchange. Provides seminars. Publishes directory, periodical. Certifies professionals.

1755. Tourism Industry Association of Canada. 130 Albert St., Suite 1016, Ottawa, Ontario, Canada K1P 5G4. (613) 238-3883. Association of provincial and local associations. Publishes periodical.

1756. Travel Agents Computer Society. 238 Main St., Suite 302, Cambridge MA 02142. (617) 491-6001. Association of travel agents dedicated to the advancement of automation within the travel industry. Compiles statistics. Provides seminars. Publishes periodical.

1757. Travel and Tourism Research Association. P.O. Box 8066,

Foothill Station, Salt Lake City UT 84108. (801) 581-3351. Association of private, public, and university organizations involved in tourism promotion and marketing in the United States. Regional affiliated associations. Compiles statistics. Conducts research. Provides management counsel, seminars. Publishes statistics, directory, periodicals.

1758. Travel Industry Association of America. 1899 L St., N.W., Washington DC 20036. (202) 293-1433. Association of private, public, and local travel and tourism executives in the United States. Purpose is information exchange and coordination of the diverse elements of the travel and tourism industry in a united promotional effort. Compiles statistics. Conducts research. Provides seminars. Publishes directories, periodical. Former name: Discover America Travel Organizations.

1759. U.S. Travel Data Center. 1899 L St., N.W., Washington DC 20036. (202) 293-1040. Service organization for the travel industry. Purpose is to conduct statistical, economic, and market research concerning the tourist and travel trade. Provides seminars. Publishes directory, periodical.

1760. Universal Federation of Travel Agents' Associations (Federation Universalles des Associations d'Agences de Voyages). 1 Rue Defacqz, Brussels, Belgium 1050. 2 2303763. Federation of national associations. Purpose is to formulate and seek legislation through international and national governments worldwide for uniform regulation of tourism agency reservations and accounts. Publishes directory. Former name: International Federation of Travel Agencies.

1761. World Tourism Organization (Organisation Mondiale du Tourisme). 42 Calle Capitan Haya, Madrid, Spain 28020. 1 2792804. Service organization for the international tourism industry. Compiles statistics. Conducts research. Publishes statistics, periodical.

Appendix A:
Basic Reference Sources

Guides

A1. Epperson, Alvin F. *Private and Commercial Recreation,* 2nd ed. State College PA: Venture, 1982. 463p. $23.95. Not a guidebook in the usual sense; nevertheless, one of the best guides to the U.S. recreation and entertainment industries individually and collectively that has ever been assembled. Examines the various definitions and parameters of the trades, studies the background and growth of the commercial recreation and entertainment and tourism, and then defines each industry's scope and references its major resources. Significant portions of the publication are devoted to a textbook presentation of planning and development, management, marketing, and implications for the future. Charts, statistics, sic definitions, glossary, bibliographies, and a subject index to the work. The publication is actually intended as a text for a course in recreation management, but it represents much more.

A2. Gratch, Bonnie; Chan, Betty; and Lingenfelter, Judith, comps. *Sports and Physical Education: A Guide to Reference Resources.* Westport CT: Greenwood, 1983. 198p. $35. Annotated guide to over 600 sources. Divided into three sections: individual sports, general resources, and special services including databases. Personal author, corporate author, title, and subject indexes. Though not its primary purpose, this publication is probably the closest to a business sourcebook in the recreation and entertainment industries that has been published.

Dictionaries

A3. Cuddon, J.A. *International Dictionary of Sports and Games.* New York: Schocken, 1980. 869p. $25. Definitions from a worldwide perspective with identification of the sport, game, or country with which associated. Some major dates and events. Short on business terms but has a comprehensive list of sports and games words.

A4. Slide, Anthony. *American Film Industry: A Historical Dictionary.* Westport CT: Greenwood, 1986. 441p. $49.95. Film business definitions and brief histories of over 100 motion picture companies. Name index.

A5. Trapido, Joel, et al., eds. *International Dictionary of Theatre Language.* Westport CT: Greenwood, 1985. 1,032p. $95. Definitions with language if not English and source reference. Both drama and production words give this publication a scope not found in other theatre dictionaries. Bibliography.

A6. Wilmeth, Don B. *Language of American Popular Entertainment:*

A Glossary of Argot, Slang, and Terminology. Westport CT: Greenwood, 1981. 305p. $35. Definitions with cross references to the nonclassical forms of popular theatre, i.e., burlesque, circus, magic, shows, vaudeville. Though the author refers to these terms as part of a "dead" language, they still reflect a small but "lively" segment of the entertainment industries. Selected bibliography.

Yearbooks

A7. *International Motion Picture Almanac.* New York: Quigley. Annual. $55. Classified yearbook-directory of the motion picture business. Short on details but excellent for the business user seeking companies and agencies. Contains motion picture "Who's Who." United States, Canada, Great Britain, and some worldwide data. Most directory listings give name, address, and phone. Many statistical and award charts.

A8. *International Television and Video Almanac.* New York: Quigley. Annual. $55. Classified yearbook-directory similar to "International Motion Picture Almanac" (see **A7**). Includes same "Who's Who" sections.

A9. *Kemps International Film and Television Yearbook.* London: Kemps Group. Annual. $50. Similar in approach to other annuals above. Production companies, supplier, professionals, and agents in Great Britain and worldwide giving name and address. British emphasis. Arrangement is geographical, then classified by subject under each country.

A10. *Kemps International Music and Recording Industry Yearbook.* London: Kemps Group; New York: Bowker. Annual. $30. Lists servicers of the music industry in Great Britain and worldwide giving name, address, and phone. Arrangement is geographical then classified by activity.

Directories

A11. *American Business Directory Series.* Omaha NE: American Business Directories. Annual. $60–$500 each. A set of individual volumes for industries and geographical areas in the United States compiled from telephone Yellow Pages. Each listing gives name, address, and phone. Arrangement is geographical. Also available online via "Instant Yellow Page Service." Individual directories for recreation and entertainment industries.

A12. *AVMP/Audio Video Market Place, A Multimedia Guide.* New York: Bowker. Annual. $49.95. Lists 4,500 producers, distributors, and servicers of the audio, motion picture, and video industries in the United States, giving name, address, key executives, and list of products or services. Arrangements is geographical by state with classified products and services and names and numbers indexes. Should be among the first motion picture/music directories purchased.

A13. Bension, Shmuel, ed. *Producer's Masterguide.* New York: New York Production Manual. Annual. $69.95. Lists 50,000 production companies and service organizations in film and video in the United States, Canada, and Great Britain, giving name, address, phone, and services. Arrangement is classified by activity then geographical. No name index.

A14. *Camping Caravan and Sports Equipment Trades Directory.* London: Camping and Sports Equipment. Annual. $80. Lists British manufacturers, wholesalers, distributors, and servicers of camping and sports equipment giving name, address, phone, contact, and products or services. Arrangement is classified, suppliers by products and manufacturers by trade names.

A15. *Canadian Sporting Goods and Playthings Directory.* West Hill, Canada: Lloyd. Annual. $35. Lists Canadian manufacturers, exporters, importers, agents, wholesalers, distributors, and servicers, giving name, address, phone, contacts, and products or services. Arrangement is classified by product and trade name.

A16. *Music and Booking Source Directory.* Santa Monica CA: Music & Booking, Inc. Annual. $65. Lists locations where live music is booked, agents, promoters plus artists, recording companies, and record and equipment manufacturers giving name, address, and contact and brief data for agencies and companies. Arrangement is classified by activity or product with alphabetical name and geographical indexes.

A17. *Music Industry Directory,* 7th ed. Chicago: Marquis Who's Who, 1983. 678p. $67.50. Lists United States and Canadian associations, agencies, unions, professional companies, competitions, festivals, schools, publications, and industry firms giving name, address, phone, key executives, and, for many, description of activities. The most massive assemblage of music industry referrals published.

A18. *Sporting Goods Directory.* St. Louis MO: Sporting News. Annual. $30. Lists manufacturers, wholesalers, agents, and industry associations giving name, address, phone, and products or services. Arrangement is alphabetical with product/service index.

A19. *Sports Market Place.* Princeton NJ: Sportsguide. Annual with midyear supplement. $105. Lists manufacturers, agents, professional clubs, associations, and related organizations serving the sports industry, giving name, address, phone, contact, and products or services. Arrangement is by broad type of activity category and alphabetical with name, organization name, and product or trade name index.

A20. *Studio Blu-Book Directory.* Hollywood CA: Hollywood Reporter. Annual. $45. Hollywood's most comprehensive directory to companies, services, and people in the motion picture industry or related to it, e.g. hotels, restaurants, clubs. Serves as almanac, telephone directory, and index. Arrangement is classified by activity then alphabetically by name.

A21. *Travel Weekly's World Travel Directory.* New York: Murdoch Magazines. Annual. $85. Lists travel agencies, tour operators, sightseeing services, and transportation companies giving name, address, phone, and services provided. Arrangement is classified by type of service then geographical for travel agencies and tour operators and alphabetical for most others.

A22. *Variety International Motion Picture Market Place.* New York and London: Garland. Annual. $50. Lists worldwide motion picture companies and agencies, giving name, address, telephone/cable/telex numbers, key executive, and activities. Arrangement is geographical with classified activity and name and number indexes.

A23. Wasserman, Paul, and Applebaum, Edmond. *Festivals Sourcebook.* Detroit MI: Gale Research, 1984. 725p. $130. Lists festivals and fairs giving location, name, dates, contact, address, and description. Arrangement is classified by theme then subarranged geographically by state. Chronological, event name, geographical, and subject indexes.

A24. Wasserman, Steven R., ed. *Lively Arts Information Directory,* 2nd ed. Detroit MI: Gale Research, 1985. 1,040p. $165. Compendium of addresses of agencies, schools, programs, publications, and awards in the performing arts giving name, address, date, and specialty. Arrangement varies, is alphabetical for some, classified for others, and geographical with alphabetical name index.

A25. _____, ed. *Recreation and Outdoor Life Directory,* 2nd ed. Detroit MI: Gale Research, 1983. 1,020p. $150. Compendium of addresses of agencies, schools, programs, publications, and awards in recreation giving name, address, date, and specialty. Arrangement varies — is alphabetical for some, classified for others, and geographical with alphabetical name index. Though the format of this publication duplicates the preceding guide, the contents are very different.

Industry

A26. *Art Murray's Box Office Register.* Hollywood CA. Annual. $70. Compilation of financial data from film distributors on box office activities. For each motion picture listed gives distribution information, box office income, and screen week total. Arrangement is alphabetical by title and by order of gross income and weekly totals. Based upon similar data published weekly in *Variety.*

A27. Canada. Statistics Canada. *Traveller Accommodation Statistics.*

Ottawa, Canada. Annual. $6. Receipts, expenses, occupancy, and employment statistics for hotels, motels, campgrounds, and other types of traveller accommodations. Current and retrospective data.

A28. U.S. Bureau of the Census. *Census of Manufacturers: Industry Series (SIC 2000–3999).* Washington DC: U.S. Government Printing Office. Every five years on 2nd and 7th year of decade. Industry statistics from the current and previous three censuses and the *U.S. Annual Survey of Manufacturers* and statistics for selected states from the current and previous census. Each table gives data for establishments, employees, production workers, payroll, value added by manufacture, cost of materials, value of shipments, and new capital expenditures. Additional tables give quantity and value of products produced by product subclasses and the quantity and cost of materials consumed by the industry and its components. Statistical compilations for individual recreation and entertainment industries are listed in the appropriate chapter of this publication under title.

A29. _____. *Census of Retail Trade.* Washington DC: U.S. Government Printing Office. Every five years on 2nd and 7th year of decade. Industry statistics for establishments, employees, payroll, and sales from the current and previous three censuses, sales by major merchandise lines as a percent of total sales from the current and previous census, comparative industry statistics for establishments, employees, payroll, and sale by state from the current and previous census, and selected industry ratios by state from the current and previous census. Statistical compilations for individual recreation and entertainment industries are listed in the appropriate chapter of this publication under title.

A30. _____. *Census of Service Industries.* Washington DC: U.S. Government Printing Office. Every five years on 2nd and 7th year of decade. Industry statistics for establishments, employees, payroll, and sales from the current and previous three censuses, comparative industry statistics by state from the current and previous census, and selected industry ratios by state from the current and previous census. Statistical compilations for individual recreation and entertainment industries are listed in the appropriate chapter of this publication under title.

A31. _____. *Census of Wholesale Trade.* Washington DC: U.S. Government Printing Office. Every five years on 2nd and 7th year of decade. Industry statistics for establishments, employees, payroll, and sales from the current and previous two censuses, sales by major commodity lines as percent of total sales from the current and previous census, comparative industry statistics for establishments, employees, payroll, and sales by state from the current and previous census, and selected industry ratios by state from the current and previous census.

A32. _____. *County Business Patterns.* Washington DC: U.S. Government Printing Office. Annual. For each SIC industry in the United States including recreation and entertainment gives data on number of employees, payroll first quarter and annual, and number of business establishments total and by size class for counties and states in the United States. Arrangement under states and counties is by SIC number.

A33. U.S. Travel Data Center.

Impact of Foreign Visitors on State Economices. Washington DC, 1985. 50p. $30. Estimates of foreign visitor spending by state and region in the United States, by purpose of trip, and by spending categories. Includes estimates of payroll, employment, and tax revenue generated by this spending.

A34. _____. *Impact of Travel on State Economies.* Washington DC, 1986. 1v. $55. Statistical analysis and estimates from the Travel Economy Impact Model of travel spending, employment and payroll income, and tax revenues generated by six tourism industry segments.

A35. _____. *Survey of State Travel Offices.* Washington DC. Annual. $65. State by state analysis of budgets, advertising programs, promotional efforts, public relations activities, and economic development of tourism.

A36. University of Colorado Business Research Division. *Tourism's Top Twenty.* Boulder CO, 1984. 110p. $25. Tables of domestic and international tourism information. Statistics on state tourism expenditures, number of tourism agencies, number of recreation facilities, etc.

Market

A37. American Fishing Tackle Manufacturers Association. *Outdoor Indexes at a Glance 1977–1985.* Arlington Heights IL. 1986. 29p. Free. Statistical charts on various aspects of fishing, boating, and hunting. Data is national and by U.S. regions. Number or dollar expenditure for such subjects as fishing licenses, shipment of sporting goods, firearm tax collections. Statistic indexed with 1977 as the base year.

A38. Goeldner, Charles R., and

Duea, Karen. *Travel Trends in the United States and Canada*. Boulder CO: University of Colorado Business Research Div., 1984. 262p. $45. Tourism data for family, vacation, international travel, length and cost of stay, and party size. Indicators of economic impact. Bibliography of travel research statistical sources.

A39. Hope Reports, Inc. *Hope Reports 1986 Market Trends: A Special Report and General Forecast on AV Media Potential*. Rochester NY, 1986. 19p. $55. Charting audio-video production, growth, and sales potential. Based upon the *Hope Reports Industry Quarterly* market letter.

A40. *Travel Market Yearbook*. New York: Murdoch Magazines. Annual. $58. Statistics and analysis on the tourism market, the consumer, transportation, and travel agencies. Industry highlights and selected special markets, e.g. gambling. Glossary, bibliography, and index.

A41. U.S. Travel Data Center. *National Travel Survey*. Washington DC. Quarterly. $75 each. Sampling of U.S. adults as to transportation modes, lodging, purpose, distance, and duration of vacation travel. Demographic characteristics of sample. Comparison with previous year.

A42. U.S. Travel Service. *Summary and Analysis of International Travel to the U.S.* Washington DC: U.S. Government Printing Office. Monthly with quarterly and annual cumulations. Free. Statistics on visitor arrivals and market analysis of international travel by residents of foreign countries. Data on country of origin, purpose, destination, demographic profiles, and country of origin studies.

A43. Van Horne, Merle J., et al. *National Recreation Survey 1982–83*.

Washington DC: U.S. Government Printing Office, 1986. 95p. $6. U.S. National Park Service study of U.S. citizen participation during 1982–83 in outdoor activities, levels of enjoyment, expenditures, influence of distance, length of stay, recreation decision factors, and senior citizen recreation. Not limited to national parks but includes sampling from all types of recreation areas.

A44. World Tourism Organization. *Traveller Departures and Main Destination*. Madrid, Spain. Annual. $30. Statistics worldwide on travel abroad by country, county or region of destination, and purpose.

A45. _____. *Yearbook of Tourism Statistics*. Madrid, Spain. Annual. $50. Statistical data on supply and demand for national and international travel. Part 1 lists data on arrivals, receipts, accommodations, employment at the international and regional level. Part 2 provides a country by country profile with data on arrivals, capacity and usage, and economic overview of tourism. Part 3 is a list of tourism agencies. Former titles: *Compendium of Tourism Statistics; Tourism Compendium*.

Periodicals

A46. American Camping Association. *Camping Magazine*. Martinsville IN. 7 issues. $15. Official association publication. Articles directed at managers and directors of camps. Special reports: "Buying Guide" in each March issue and "American Camping Association" in each September/October issue. Indexed in *Magazine Index, Readers' Guide*.

A47. American Resort and Residential Development Association. *Developments*. Washington

DC. 11 issues. Membership. Official association publication. Articles on the industry, its market, management of resorts, timesharing facilities, resort development, and operation of specific facilities. Reports on laws and regulations and activities of timeshare resort-park sub-councils. Former title: *Resort Timesharing Today.* Indexed in *Real Estate Index.*

A48. _____. *Timesharing Law Reporter Briefs.* Washington DC. Monthly. $62. Official association publication. News of federal, state, and local laws and regulations. Cases, administrative decisions, and court decisions. Analysis and interpretation. Indexed in *Real Estate Index.*

A49. American Society of Composers, Authors, and Publishers. *ASCAP in Action.* New York. 3 issues. Membership. News and articles on music copyright legislation, cases, and licensing. Indexed in *Music Index.*

A50. American Symphony Orchestra League. *Symphony Magazine.* Washington DC. Bimonthly. $25. Official association publication. For orchestra managers, board members, conductors, and the symphony community. Profiles, programming, fund raising, management tips, industry trends, and technological developments featured. Special report: "North American Orchestra Directory" in December issue. Calendar of symphonic events each issue. Indexed in *Music Index.*

A51. *Amusement Business.* Nashville TN: Billboard. Weekly. $60. News from the entire spectrum of mass entertainment and public amusements industry. Numerous special directories. Special reports: "Managing the Leisure Facility" in each February, May, August, and December issue. Indexed in *Trade and Industry Index.*

A52. *Annals of Travel Research.* Elmsford NY: Pergamon. Quarterly. $75. Emphasis is on the nature and impact of tourism on the state, national, and international economy but includes studies on tourism agencies and the management of tourism industries. Indexed in *Leisure, Recreation and Tourism Abstracts, PAIS.*

A53. Association of Independent Video and Filmmakers. *Independent.* New York. Monthly. Membership. Official association publication. Information on business and legal questions, fundraising, distribution. News of productions, festivals, grants, equipment, and services. Indexed in *Film Literature Index.*

A54. *Back Stage.* New York: Back Stage. Weekly. $45. Service news magazine for the communications and entertainment industry, especially film, television and stage. Film and television news dominate. *Business Screen* section provides management and statistical data. Information on industry, government involvement, productions, labor, and equipment and services. Special issue: *Back Stage Television, Film, Tape, and Production Directory* (each March, $20). Indexed in *Predicasts F&S Index: United States, Trade and Industry Index.*

A55. *Billboard.* New York: Billboard. Weekly. $148. News magazine of the music of the music business. News of people, events, recordings, companies, and the economic condition of the industry. Indexed in *Music Index, Predicasts F&S Index: United States, Trade and Industry Index.*

A56. *Bluegrass Unlimited.* Broad Run VA: Bluegrass Unlimited. Monthly. $15. News and articles on bluegrass groups, performers, and clubs, appearance calendar, and discographies. Special reports: "Festival Guide" in each March issue and "Bluegrass Talent Directory" in each December issue. Indexed in *Music Index.*

A57. *Boating Business.* London: Ravenshead Marine. Monthly. $15. Provides coverage of the British boat industry. Articles on the market, products, and the industry. Indexes in *Predicast F&S Index: United States.*

A58. *Boating Industry.* New York: Whitney Communications. Monthly. $20 (includes *Boating Product News*). Articles and data on consumer trends and market, information on the industry and news of firms and individuals. Special issue: *Boating Industry Marine Buyers' Guide* (each December, $25). Indexed in *Trade and Industry Index.*

A59. *Box Office: The National Film Monthly.* Chicago: RLD Communication. Monthly. $35. World, national, and local industry news, management and operations features, production and distribution statistics and trends. Special section each month on theater facilities and operations. Special reports: "Snack Bar" in each July issue; "Automation and Computerization" in each August issue; "Buyers' Guide" in each September issue; "Merchandising and Concessions" in each November issue; and "Trade Shows" in each December issue. Indexed in *Film Literature Index, Predicasts F&S Index: United States.*

A60. *Canadian Musician.* Toronto, Canada: Norris. Bimonthly. $15. News and articles on groups, professional performances, and the Canadian music scene. Information on equipment, products, and instruction. *Canadian Music Trade* is a more important source of music and record industry statistics. Special reports: "Songwriter's Market Guide" in each June issue and "Canadian Recording Studio Guide" in each October issue. Indexed in *Music Index.*

A61. *Cash Box: The International Music-Record Weekly.* New York: Cash Box. Weekly. $125. Primary industry source for record reviews, ratings, and lists. Information on the music video and music amusements fields. Current news, information on the economic state of the industry, and record marketing tips. Industry statistics. Special issue: *Cash Box Directory* (each July, $15). Indexed in *Music Index.*

A62. *Cornell Hotel and Restaurant Administration Quarterly.* Ithaca NY: Cornell University School of Hotel Administration. Quarterly. $25. Research articles on administration and management of hospitality institutions. Information on research, studies, and statistical reports. Book reviews. Indexed in *Business Periodicals Index, PAIS, Real Estate Index, Trade and Industry Index.*

A63. *DealerNews.* Santa Ana CA: Harcourt Brace Jovanovich. Monthly. Controlled distribution. Retailing and servicing cycles and information on new products. Special issue: *Dealer New Buyers Guide* (each November, $20). Former title: *Motorcycle DealerNews.* Indexed in *Trade and Industry Index.*

A64. *Drama: The Quarterly Theatre Review.* London: British Theatre Association. Quarterly. $15. Primary emphasis is drama, but contains articles on theatre, stage, and production management and theater operations. Index in *British Humanities Index, Humanities Index.*

A65. *From the State Capitals: Tourist Business Promotion.* New

Haven CT: Wakeman/Walworth. 12 issues. $75. Newsletter analyzing state and municipal actions affecting recreation, entertainment, and tourism businesses. Emphasizes state promotion, tourism legislation, and regulation. Discusses finance, support, and construction of recreation and entertainment facilities with state and local funds.

A66. *Gaming and Wagering Business.* New York: BMT. Monthly. $36. News and developments in all gambling areas. Emphasis on management. Information on business strategy, marketing, finance, credit, government regulation, security, food service, and entertainment. Indexed in *Accountants Index.*

A67. *Gifts and Decorative Accessories.* New York: Geyer-McAllister. Monthly. $28. For retail store buyers. National and international industry news, market data, and product information. Profiles of retailers and their merchandising methods. Display and promotion tips. Special issue: *Gifts and Decorative Accessories Buyers Directory* (each September, free with subscription). Indexed in *Trade and Industry Index.*

A68. *Hotel and Motel Management.* Cleveland OH: Harcourt Brace Jovanovich. 18 issues. $25. Articles on developments and trends in finance, management, and marketing of hotels and motels. News of technology, food service, government, and security. Tips and features on promotions and sales. Special report: "Buyer's Guide" in each December issue. Absorbed *Motel and Motor Inn, Motor Inn Journal.* Indexed in *Business Periodicals Index, Real Estate Index, Trade and Industry Index.*

A69. *Independent Film Journal: Trade Paper for Exhibitors of Motion Pictures.* New York: Pubsun.

Monthly. $25. Buying and booking data, production news, articles on theater facilities and operations, information on film ratings and censorship issues. Special reports: "Adult Films" in each March issue; "Distribution Guide" in each August issue; and "Equipment, Concessions and Services Buyer's Guide" in each September issue. Former name: *Film Journal.* Indexed in *Film Literature Index.*

A70. Imperial Society of Teachers of Dancing. *Dance.* London. Bimonthly. $10. Official association publication. Articles on all forms of dance, competitions, technique, and the dance world. Indexed in *Magazine Index.*

A71. Institute of Leisure and Amenity Management. *Leisure Manager.* Cambridge, England: John S. Turner. Monthly. $60. Official association publication. For the park and recreation executive. Emphasis on management concerns. Indexed in *Leisure, Recreation and Tourism Index.*

A72. *International Tourism Reports.* London: Economist. Quarterly. $200. Each issue features four or five country or regional analyses with current and retrospective statistical data on tourism for each. Details the history of tourism in the country or region, foreign investment, generalized and statistical profile of visitors, accommodations and tourism features, and industry financial data. Special "Short Industry Reports" examine segments of the tourism industry, e.g. cruise lines, package tours, travel agencies, tourism marketing, recessions and travel. Indexed in *Leisure, Recreation and Tourism Abstracts.*

A73. *Journal of Arts Management and Law.* Washington DC: Helref. Quarterly. $55. Articles and decisions on management, contract, corporate, labor, and legal aspects of the performing arts. Indexed in *Index to Legal Periodicals, Music Index.*

A74. *Leisure Industry Digest.* Washington DC: Leisure Industry/ Recreation News. 24 issues. $65. For managers and policy makers who want recreation and entertainment industries news in capsule form. Provides resumes of news articles and reports of trends, developments, and prospects. Emphasizes brevity and extensive use of statistics.

A75. *Lodging Hospitality.* Cleveland OH: Penton. Monthly. $40. For hotel, motel, and resort managers. Articles on operations, maintenance, personnel, marketing, and public relations. Information on individual and chain finance and management, as well as industry-wide statistics. Special reports: "Buyer's Guide" in each March issue and "Lodging's 300" in each August issue. Former title: *Hospitality Lodging.* Indexed in *Accountants' Index, Real Estate Index, Trade and Industry Index.*

A76. *Music Trades Magazine.* Englewood NJ: Music Trades. Monthly. $12. For retailers of musical instruments. Articles on products, merchandising, and store operations. Data on industry trends and production. Special issue: *Music Trades Magazine Purchaser's Guide to the Music Industry* (each October, included in subscription). Indexed in *Music Index,* Predicasts F&S Index: United States.

A77. *National Racquetball.* Clearwater FL. Monthly. $18. For club owners, managers, professionals, and amateurs. Emphasis on play and tournaments but includes extensive information on new clubs, play and fitness organization, and the industry. Indexed in *Real Estate Index.*

A78. National Recreation and Park Association. *Journal of Leisure Research.* Alexandria VA. Quarterly. $20. Of the two major research journals in leisure recreation, this is the most business oriented. Research articles on psychology and sociology of consumer involvement in leisure, perceptions of leisure satisfaction, and cost-benefit analyses are regularly reported. Well documented and referenced. Indexed in *CIJE, Social Science Index.*

A79. National Recreation and Park Association. *Parks and Recreation.* Alexandria VA. Monthly. $18. Official association publication. For the executive, public officials, and community leaders responsible for park and recreation development and management. Articles on trends in recreation, park management policy, planning, financing, legislation, regulations, and liability. Regular columns include "Washington Report," "Product Report," and "Coming Events." Indexed in *CIJE, PAIS, Reader's Guide, Real Estate Index.*

A80. *On Location Magazine.* Los Angeles: On Location. Monthly. $44. "The film and videotape production magazine." Articles on preproduction, postproduction, special effects, animation, and commercials. Features on shooting locations and layouts. News of films in production, companies, and management. Heavily illustration. Indexed on *Film Literature Index.*

A81. Photo Marketing Association International. *Photo Marketing.* Jackson MI. Monthly. $12. Official association publication. Studies and reports on marketing trends. Management information for finishers and retailers. Merchandising tips. Indexed in *Predicasts F&S Index: United States.*

A82. *Playthings.* New York: Geyer-McAllister. Monthly. $18. Primary industry information magazine for the merchandiser of toys, hobbies, and crafts. Sales and promotional techniques, sales and earnings of toy companies, and new products. Special reports: "Hobby Show" in each January issue; "Toy Fair" in each February issue; and "Who's Who in Importing" in each November issue. Special issue: *Playthings Directory* (May, $18). Indexed in *Business Periodicals Index, Predicast F&S Index: United States, Trade and Industry Index.*

A83. *Record Research.* Brooklyn NY. Bimonthly. $10 for 10 issues. Individual and collective statistics on phonorecord sales. Market information and analysis. Indexed in *Music Index.*

A84. *Resort and Hotel Management.* Del Mar CA: Source Communication. 8 issues. $25. For owners and operating executives of resort hotels, vacation resorts, and resort complexes. Articles on management, finance, marketing, and all major aspects of resort operations. Case studies of "successful resorts." Indexed in *Real Estate Index.*

A85. *Restaurant Business.* New York: Restaurant Business. 18 issues. $63. For the executive in the food service industry but contains reports applicable to bars and nightclubs including menu planning, food and bar management, cost control, interior design, regulations, and liability. Indexed in *Business Periodicals Index, Predicasts F&S Index: United States, Real Estate Index, Trade and Industry Index.*

A86. *Restaurant Hospitality.* Cleveland OH: Penton. Monthly. $45. For the restaurant executive. Emphasis on management. Articles on operations management, merchandising, and decor. News of the industry, regulations, and trade shows. Indexed in *Accountants' Index, Predicasts F&S Index: United States, Real Estate Index, Trade and Industry Index.*

A87. *Shooting Industry.* San Diego CA: Publishers' Development. Monthly. $25. For manufacturers, distributors, retailers, and commercial users of shooting goods and equipment. Articles on the industry, its products, and government. Statistics and regulations. Special reports: "National Sporting Goods Association Show" in each January issue and "Buyer's Guide" in each July issue. Indexed in *Trade and Industry Index.*

A88. *Skiing Trade News.* New York: CBS Magazines. 7 issues. Controlled distribution. Articles on products, merchandising, and management of ski shops. Special report: "Buyers Guide" in September issue. Indexed in *Trade and Industry Index.*

A89. *Sporting Goods Business.* New York: Gralla. Monthly. $9. "National news magazine of the sporting goods industry." Emphasis on retailing. News and articles on products, operation of stores, and industry developments. Special report: "National Sporting Goods Association Report" in each January issue. Indexed in *Trade and Industry Index.*

A90. *Sports Business.* Downsview, Canada: Page Publications. 12 issues. $65. Endorsed by the Canadian Sporting Goods Association for the sporting goods retailer. Articles on retail management, store operations, merchandising, marketing, and new products. Special issues: *Sports Business Directory and Buying Guide* (each September/October, $25). Former titles: *Sporting Goods*

Trade, Sporting Trade Canada, Sports Trade Canada. Indexed in *Canadian Business Index.*

A91. *Sports Industry News.* Camden ME: Game Point. Weekly. $227. Professional and major amateur sports. News and articles on leagues, sales, television and player contracts, labor relations, concessions, endorsements, and legal problems and solutions. Statistics on attendance, salaries, income, and expenditures. Indexed in *Predicasts F&S Index: United States.*

A92. *Theatre Crafts.* New York: Theatre Crafts. 10 issues. $24. Emphasis on production and equipment for theatre and television. Features on set design, costuming, and technical theatre. Profiles of theatre productions. News of scenery, lighting, and sound equipment. Special issue: *Theatre Crafts Directory of Manufacturers, Distributors, and Suppliers of Products for the Performing Arts* (each June/July, $10). Indexed in *Education Index, Magazine Index, Readers' Guide.*

A93. *Travel Agent.* New York: American Traveler. Semiweekly. $12. Newsletter for the travel agent. Information on market research, travel marketing, trends and forecasts from domestic and foreign scene, and national and international regulations. Data on tour offerings, tariffs, and agent training. Many issues devoted to single topic. Indexed in PAIS, *Trade and Industry Index.*

A94. Travel and Tourism Research Association. *Journal of Travel Research.* Boulder CO: University of Colorado Business Research Div. Quarterly. $65. Scholarly articles on tourism topics, reports on latest research, analysis of studies and surveys, and proposals for innovative management and marketing techniques for the industry. Book reviews and bibliography of new publications. Cumulative index. Indexed in *Leisure, Recreation and Tourism Abstracts.*

A95. United States Tennis Association. *World Tennis.* New York: Family Media. Monthly. $16. For the tennis player but contains some business information. Special reports: "Tennis Camp Directory Yearbook," "Equipment Directory," "Tennis Shoe Guide," "Racquet Review," "World Tennis's Vacation Guide." Indexed in *Magazine Index, Readers' Guide.*

A96. *Variety.* New York: Variety. Weekly. $75. The entertainment world's official newspaper. News articles are supplemented with extensive management, industry, and market statistics. Special reports: "Anniversary," "Show Business" in January issue, "NAPTE Convention" in February issue, "American Film Market" in March issue, "International Television" in April issue, "International Film (Cannes)" in May issue, "Auditorium-Arena" in July issue, "Home Video" in September issue, "MIFED (Milan)" in October issue, and "Canadian" in November issue. Indexed in *Film Literature Index, Music Index, Predicasts F&S Index: United States, Trade and Industry Index.*

A97. *Video Marketing Newsletter.* Hollywood CA: Video Marketing. Bimonthly. $347. For the executive. News service monitoring the home video market. Industry news, statistics, and calendar of events. Indexed in *Predicasts F&S Index: United States.*

A98. World Tourism Organization. *World Travel/Tourisme Mondial.* Madrid, Spain. Bimonthly. $14. Official association publication. News of research, publications, industry events, and organization activities. Indexed in *Leisure, Recreation and Tourism Abstracts.*

Databases

A99. American Business Directories, Inc. *Instant Yellow Page Service.* Omaha NE. Updated monthly. $95 annual/$60 per contact hour. Directory. One of a number of similar services giving name, address, phone, and product or service for companies listed in the telephone Yellow Pages. Access direct. Also available in print format with separate volumes by type of product or occupation.

A100. Baseline, Inc. *Baseline.* New York. Updated annually. $93 base/$75 annual/$45 per contact hour. Directory, news, statistics. Information directory to the U.S. entertainment industry. News of productions, producers, contracts, and the trade. Statistics on box office grosses. Access direct.

A101. Billboard Publications, Inc. *Billboard Information Network.* New York. Updated daily. $200. Text. Music chart and paylist statistics from 600 broadcasting and entertainment outlets. Record, video, video game, and computer software sales and rental statistics from 600 outlets. Online 24 hours per day via Tymeshare.

A102. CAB International. *Leisure, Recreation and Tourism Abstracts.* Farnham Royal, England. Updated quarterly. Costs vary with vendor. Bibliography. Citations with abstracts to books, articles, reports, and proceedings in the English language worldwide. Access via vendors. Also available in print format. Former title: *Rural Recreation and Tourism Abstracts.*

A103. *Hollywood Hotline.* Burbank CA. Updated daily. $48 per contact hour. News. Daily news happenings in the entertainment industries. Some business information and market data but mainly people, productions, and prizes. Access via vendors.

Indexes

A104. *Film Literature Index.* Albany NY: Film and Television Documentation Center. Quarterly with annual cumulation. $225. Citations to articles in over 225 international film and television periodicals. Alphabetical author/subject arrangement. Television added in recent years. Emphasis on film and television programming, but covers all aspects of motion picture industry, companies, production, management, and marketing. Essential.

A105. *Leisure, Recreation and Tourism Abstracts.* Farnham Royal, England: CAB International. Quarterly. $102. Citations with abstracts to books, articles, reports, and proceedings in English worldwide. Alphabetical author/subject arrangement. Though not specifically directed towards recreation and entertainment management, provides the best international resource available. Also available online. Former title: *Rural Recreation and Tourism Abstracts.*

A106. *Music Index.* Detroit MI: Information Coordinators. Monthly with biennial cumulation. $840. Citations to articles in over 350 music periodicals by author and subject. Extensive coverage of music industry information and reports. A must for any entertainment library or information center even though publication is still five years behind.

Bibliographies

A107. Cornell University School of Hotel Administration. *Bibliography of Hotel and Restaurant Administration*. Ithaca NY. Annual. $15. Record of new materials received by the SHA Library. Arrangement is by subject with author and titles indexes.

A108. Goeldner, Charles R., and Dicke, Karen. *Bibliography of Tourism and Travel Research Studies, Reports and Articles*. Boulder CO: University of Colorado Business Research Div., 1980. 9v. $60. Annotated listing of U.S. and Canadian studies from January 1, 1960 to January 1, 1980. Several volumes cover a specific aspect of tourism, e.g. international, lodging, statistics. Volume one contains a list of general sourcebooks. Volume nine is an author-title index. Significant business references included.

A109. Kruel, Lee M., Dennington, Lloyd J., and Lohr, Judi. *Digest of Current Lodging Industry Market Research Studies*. New York: American Hotel and Motel Association, 1985. 92p. $30. Summarizes 35 reports on selection, reservations, length of stay, promotions, and security as factors in marketing the lodging industry.

A110. Ontario Research Council on Leisure. *Catalogue of Canadian Recreation and Leisure Research*. Toronto, Canada. 2 to 3 issues. $25. Citations with abstracts to published studies. Emphasis on recreation and leisure activities but includes tourism statistical reports and some industry analysis.

A111. World Tourism Organization. *Tourism Bibliography*. Madrid, Spain. 3 issues. $15. Reports, studies, and statistical compilations on tourism and travel worldwide. Though far from complete, this periodic list is probably the most useful bibliographic source for keeping up to date with business-related publications in tourism industries.

Appendix B:
Publisher Directory

ABC Leisure Magazines, Inc.
State Rd.
Great Barrington MA 01230
(413) 637-2978

Ablex Publishing Corp.
355 Chestnut St.
Norwood NJ 07648
(201) 767-8450

Abrams, Harry N., Inc.
110 E. 59th St.
New York NY 10022
(212) 758-8600

Alchemy Books
717 Market, Suite 514
San Francisco CA 94103
(415) 777-2197

Allen, J.A., and Co. Ltd.
One Lower Grosvenor Pl.
London, England SW1W 0EL
(01) 834-5606

Allen, J.A., and Co. Ltd.
Sporting Book Center
Canaan NY 12029
(518) 794-8998

Alpine Hansen, Publishers
Nine Moro Ave.
Fairfax CA 94930
(415) 459-4900

American Business Directories, Inc.
P.O. Box 27347
Omaha NE 68127
(402) 593-4600

American Council for the Arts
570 Seventh Ave.
New York NY 10018
(212) 354-6655

American Entrepreneurs Association
2311 Pontius Ave.
Los Angeles CA 90064
(213) 479-3987; (800) 421-2300

American Institute of Certified
    Public Accountants
1211 Ave. of the Americas
New York NY 10036
(212) 575-6200

American Institute of Real Estate
    Appraisers
430 N. Michigan Ave.
Chicago IL 60611
(312) 329-8521

American Land Development
    Association
1220 L St., N.W., Fifth Floor
Washington DC 20005
(202) 371-6700

American Music Conference
1000 Skokie Blvd.
Wilmette IL 60091
(312) 251-1600

American National Standards
    Institute
1430 Broadway
New York NY 10018
(212) 354-3300

American Traveler
Two W. 46th St.
New York NY 10036
(212) 575-9000

Archibald Press, Ltd.
6405 Atlantic Blvd.
Norcross GA 30071
(404) 441-9003

Architectural Press Ltd.
Nine Queen Anne's Gate
London, England SW1H 9BY
(01) 222-4333

Arch-Way Publishers, Ltd.
7560 Lawrence Dr.
Burnaby, Canada V5A 1T6
(604) 420-6115

Arco Publishing Co.
One Gulf Western Bldg.
New York NY 10023
(212) 373-8931

Art Murphy's Box Office Register
P.O. Box 3786
Hollywood CA 90078

Arthurs Publications Ltd.
520 Dixie Rd., Suite 204
Mississauga, Canada L4W 1E4
(416) 625-5277

Arts Administration Research
  Institute
75 Spark St.
Cambridge MA 02138

Associates International, Inc.
700 Orange St.
Wilmington DE 19801
(307) 656-2209

Atcom, Inc.
2315 Broadway
New York NY 10024
(212) 873-5900

Atheneum Publishers
597 Fifth Ave.
New York NY 10017
(212) 486-2700

Auburn House Publishing Co., Inc.
14 Dedham
Dover MA 02030
(617) 785-2220

Audits and Surveys, Inc.
One Park Ave.
New York NY 10016

Automobile Association
Farnum House
Basingstroke, HAMP, England
  RG21 2EA
(02) 562-0123

AVI Publishing Co., Inc.
250 Post Rd. E., P.O. Box 831
Westport CT 06881
(203) 226-0738

Avon Books
1790 Broadway
New York NY 10019
(212) 399-4500

BackStage Publications, Inc.
330 W. 42nd St.
New York NY 10036
(212) 947-0020

Balding and Mansell, Ltd.
Park Works, Weisbech
Cambridge, England PE13 2AX

Bank of America
P.O. Box 3700, 555 California St.
San Francisco CA 94137
(415) 622-3456

Baseline Inc.
80 E. 11 St., Suite 516
New York NY 10003
(212) 254-8325; (800) CHAPLIN

BASS Communications
One Bell Rd.
Montgomery AL 36117
(205) 272-9530

Batiste Publications Ltd.
Pembroke House, Campsbourne
   Rd., Hornsley
London, England N8

Batsford, B.T., Ltd.
Four Fitzhardinge St.
London, England W1H 0AH
(01) 486-8484

Baxter Publishing
310 Dupont St.
Toronto, Ontario, Canada M5R 1V9
(416) 968-7252

Beardsley Publishing Corp.
P.O. Box 644, 45 Main St.
North Woodbury CT 06798
(203) 263-0888

Beninda Enterprises
P.O. Box 9251
Canton OH 44711

Benn, Ernest, Ltd.
35 Bedford Row
London, England WC1R 4JH
(01) 242-0946

Berkely, Price, Publishing Group
200 Madison Ave.
New York NY 10016
(212) 686-9820; (800) 223-0510

Berkshire Traveller Press
Pine St.
Stockbridge MA 01262
(413) 298-3636

Betsy Ross Publications
3057 Betsy Ross Dr.
Bloomfield MI 48013
(313) 646-5357

Beverage Marketing Corp.
850 Third Ave.
New York NY 10022
(212) 688-7640

Beverage Profit Ideas, Inc.
67 Broadway
Greenlawn NY 11740
(516) 754-8007

BFI Publishing
127 Charing Cross Rd.
London, England WC2H 0EA

Billboard Publication
P.O. Box 24970
Nashville TN 37202
(615) 748-8120

Billboard Publications, Inc.
1515 Broadway, 39th Fl.
Nwe York NY 10036
(212) 764-7300

Billboard Publications, Inc.
9107 Wilshire Blvd. 700
Beverly Hills CA 90210
(213) 273-7040

Bingley, Clive, Ltd.
16 Pembridge Rd.
London, England W11

Bingo Science, Inc.
8340 Delmar Blvd.
Saint Louis MO 63124
(314) 432-0010

Bloodstock Research Information
   Services Inc.
P.O. Box 4097, 801 Corporate Dr.
Lexington KY 40544
(606) 223-4444

Bluegrass Unlimited, Inc.
P.O. Box 111
Broad Run VA 22014
(703) 361-8992

BMT Publications, Inc.
254 W. 31st St.
New York NY 10001
(212) 594-4120

Boardman, Clark, Co.
435 Hudson St.
New York NY 10014
(212) 929-7500

Boating Almanac Co., Inc.
203 McKinsey Rd.
Severna Park MD 21146
(301) 647-0084

Bobbs-Merrill Company, Inc.
630 Third Ave.
New York NY 10017
(212) 697-7050

Bolger Publications
3301 Como Ave. S.E.
Minneapolis MN 55414
(612) 645-6311

Borowsky, Ben
2416 Laurel Dr.
Cinnaminson NJ 08077
(609) 829-8680

Bowker, R.R., Co.
205 E. 42nd St.
New York NY 10017
(212) 916-1600

Boynton and Associates, Inc.
Clifton House
Clifton VA 22024
(703) 830-1000

Brantwood Publications, Inc.
Northwood Plaza Sta.
Clearwater FL 33519
(813) 796-8150

Brave Beaver Pressworks, Ltd.
290 Jarvis St.
Toronto, Ontario, Canada M5E 2C5
(416) 977-6318

Brent Ottaway
367 Linwood Ave.
Buffalo NY 14209

Breton Publications
20 Park Plaza
Boston MA 02116
(617) 482-2344

British Council
11 Portand Place
London, England W1N 4EJ
(01) 499-8011

Brooks, Stanley J., Co.
1416 Westwood Blvd., Suite 201
Los Angeles CA 90024
(213) 470-2849

Brown, Wm. C., Publishers
2460 Kerper Blvd.
Dubuque IA 52001
(319) 589-2822

Bureau of Business
University of Nevada
Reno NV 89557
(702) 784-6877

Burgess Publications
7108 Ohms Ln.
Minneapolis MN 55435
(612) 831-1344

Business Press International, Ltd.
Quadrant House
Sutton, Surrey, England SM2 5AS

Butterworth Legal Publishers
80 Montvale Ave.
Stoneham MA 02180-2471
(617) 438-8464

CAB International
Farnham House, Farnham Royal
Slough, Great Britain SL2 3BN
(02) 814-2281; (800) 528-4841

CACI, Inc.
8260 Willow Oakes Corp. Dr.
Fairfax VA 22031
(703) 876-2332; (800) 292-2224

Cahners Publishing Co.
1350 E. Touhy
Des Plaines IL 60018
(312) 635-8800

Cambridge University Press
The Edinburgh Bldg., Shaftesbury
 Rd.
Cambridge, England CB2 2RU

Cambridge University Press
32 E. 57th St.
New York NY 10022
(212) 688-8888; (800) 872-7423

Camping and Sport Equipment Ltd.
Four Spring St.
London, England W2 3RA

Canada Publishing Centre
Ottawa, Ontario, Canada K1A 0S9
(819) 997-2560

Canada Systems Group
955 Green Valley Crescent
Ottawa, Ontario, Canada K2C 3V4
(613) 727-5445

Canadian Library Association
151 Sparks St.
Ottawa, Ontario, Canada K1P 5E3
(613) 232-9625

Cash Box
330 W. 58th St.
New York NY 10019
(212) 586-2640

Cato Institute
224 Second St., S.E.
Washington DC 20003
(202) 546-0200

CBD Research Ltd.
154 High St.
Beckenham, Kent, England BR3
 1EA
(01) 650-7745

CBI Publishing Co.
51 Slee Per St.
Boston MA 02210
(617) 426-2224

CBS Magazines
1515 Broadway, 11th Fl.
New York NY 10036
(212) 973-4321

Center for Arts Administration
1155 Observatory Dr., University of
 Wisconsin
Madison WI 53706

CHB Co., Inc.
P.O. Box 5627
Bellingham WA 98227
(206) 676-4146

Child and Waters, Inc.
516 Fifth Ave.
New York NY 10036
(212) 840-1935

Chilton Book Co.
Chilton Way
Radnor PA 19089
(215) 964-4000

Cinc-Communications
Two College St., Suite 203
Toronto, Ontario, Canada M5G
 1K3
(416) 920-2558

Circle Publications
P.O. Box 34
Lyndhurst NJ 07071

CMP Publications, Inc.
600 Community Dr.
Manhasset NY 11030
(516) 365-4600

Coastal Communications Corp.
488 Madison Ave.
New York NY 10022
(212) 888-1500

Collier Macmillan International Inc.
866 Third Ave.
New York NY 10022
(212) 935-2000

Columbia Books, Inc.
1350 New York Ave., N.W.
Washington DC 20005
(202) 737-3777

Comedia Publishing Ltd.
Nine Poland St.
London, England W1V 2DG
(01) 439-2059

Commerce Clearing House, Inc.
4025 W. Peterson Ave.
Chicago IL 60646
(312) 583-8500

Communication Channels
6255 Barfield Rd.
Atlanta GA 30328
(404) 256-9800

Conference Board of Canada
255 Smyth Rd.
Ottawa, Ontario, Canada K1H
   8M7
(613) 526-3280

Conference Board, Inc.
Avenue Louise, 207 — Bte 5
B-1050 Brussels, Belgium

Conference Board, Inc.
845 Third Ave.
New York NY 10022
(212) 759-0900

Congressional Information Service
   Inc.
4520 East-West Hwy., Suite 800
Bethesda MD 20814
(301) 654-1550; (800) 638-8380

Cottage Communications, Inc.
P.O. Box 484
Lake Forest IL 60045
(312) 234-5052

Council of Planning Librarians
1313 E. 60th St.
Chicago IL 60637-2897
(312) 947-2007

Council of State Governments
P.O. Box 11910
Lexington KY 40578
(606) 252-2291

Council on Hotel, Restaurant and
   Institutional Education, Inc.
HRIM Henderon Bldg.
University Park PA 16802
(814) 863-0586

Creative Age Publications, Inc.
7628 Densmore Ave.
Van Nuys CA 91406
(818) 782-7328

Creative Media, Inc.
10244 Best Dr.
Dallas TX 75229
(214) 351-6208

Crowell, Thomas Y., Co.
Ten E. 53rd St.
New York NY 10022
(212) 593-3900

Crown Publishers, Inc.
225 Park Ave. S.
New York NY 10003
(212) 254-1600

Cruise Calendar
P.O. Box 505, 22859 Hatteras St.
Woodland Hill CA 91365
(818) 347-1693

CRV Publications Canada Ltd.
3414 Park Ave., Suite 221
Montreal, PQ, Canada H2X 2H5
(514) 282-0191

csi Press
1923 Bacharach Blvd.
Atlantic NJ 08401

Cycle News, Inc.
2201 Cherry Ave.
Long Beach CA 90806
(213) 595-4753

Cycling Press, Inc.
80 Eighth Ave.
New York NY 10011
(212) 206-7230

Daily Variety Ltd.
1400 N. Cahuenga Blvd.
Hollywood CA 90028
(213) 469-1141

Danad Publishing Co., Inc.
33 W. 60th St.
New York NY 10023
(212) 245-9050

David and Charles, Inc.
P.O. Box 57
North Pomfret VT 05053
(802) 457-1911

David and Charles Ltd.
Brunel House, Forde Rd.
Newton Abbot, Devon, England
  TQ12 4PU

Davis, Mary
P.O. Box 267
Inverness CA 94937
(415) 669-7304

dbi Books, Inc.
One Northfield Plaza
Northfield IL 60093
(312) 441-7010

Disclosure Information Group
5161 River Rd.
Bethesda MD 20816
(301) 951-1300; (800) 638-8076

Dorset Theatre Festival and Colony
  House, Inc.
P.O. Box 519
Dorset VT 05251
(802) 867-2223

Doubleday and Co., Inc.
245 Park Ave.
New York NY 10017
(212) 984-7561; (800) 645-6156

Dow Jones and Co.
200 Liberty St.
New York NY 10281
(413) 592-7761

Dow Jones and Co., Inc.
P.O. Box 300
Princeton NJ 08543
(800) 257-5114

Dow Jones–Irwin, Inc
1818 Ridge Rd.
Homewood IL 60430
(312) 798-6000

Drama Book Publishers
821 Broadway
New York NY 10003
(212) 228-3400

Duke University Press
6697 College Sta.
Durham NC 27708
(919) 684-2173

Dun and Bradstreet Canada
365 Bloor St., E., 14th Fl.
Toronto, Ontario, Canada M4W 364
(416) 963-6694

Dun and Bradstreet Ltd.
26-32 Clifton St., Box 17
London, England EC2P 2LY
(01) 377-4377

Duns Marketing Services
Three Century Dr.
Parsippany NJ 07054
(201) 455-0900; (800) 526-0651

Dutton, E.P.
Two Park Ave.
New York NY 10016
(212) 725-1818

EBSCO Publishing
P.O. Box 1943
Birmingham AL 35201
(205) 991-6660; (800) 633-6088

Economist Publications Ltd.
40 Duke St.
London, England W1A 1DW
(01) 493-6711

Edgell Communications, Inc.
545 Fifth Ave.
New York NY 10017
(212) 503-2990

Educational Film Library Association, Inc.
45 John St., Suite 301
New York NY 10038
(212) 227-5599

Educational Institute of the American Hotel & Motel Association
1407 S. Harrison Rd.
East Lansing MI 48823
(517) 353-5500

EIP, Inc.
2132 Fordem Ave.
Madison WI 53704
(608) 244-3528

EMAP National Publications, Ltd.
Bretton Court, Bretton
Peterborough, England PE3 8DZ

Entertainment Law Reporter Publishing Co.
2210 Wilshire Blvd., Suite 311
Santa Monica CA 90403
(213) 736-1089

Euromonitor Publications, Ltd.
18 Doughty St.

London, England WC1N 2PA
(01) 242-0042

Facts on File, Inc.
460 Park Ave. S.
New York NY 10016
(212) 683-2244

Fairchild Books and Visuals
Seven E. 12th St.
New York NY 10003
(212) 741-4280

Fairleigh Dickinson University Press
440 Forsgate Dr.
Cranbury NJ 08512
(609) 655-4770

Family Media, Inc.
149 Fifth Ave.
New York NY 10010

Farm and Ranch Vacations, Inc.
36 E. 57th St.
New York NY 10022
(212) 355-6334

Film and Television Documentation Center
State University of New York at Albany
Albany NY 12222
(518) 442-5745

Film Publications of Canada Ltd.
175 E. Bloor St.
Toronto, Ontario, Canada M4W 1E1

Fink, Wendy, Associates, Inc.
9 Hampden St.
Wellesley MA 02181
(617) 235-1769

Fleet Street Corp.
656 Quince Orchard Rd.
Gaithersburg MD 20878
(301) 977-3900

Florida Trades Publications
P.O. Box 6126
Clearwater FL 33518
(813) 736-5616

Flyer Publication, Inc.
P.O. Box 189
Oregon WI 53575

Fodor's Modern Guides, Inc.
Two Park Ave.
New York NY 10016
(212) 340-9800

Foley Publishing Corp.
P.O. Box 150
Liberty Corner NJ 07938
(201) 580-1887

Ford's Travel Guides
22151 Clarendon St.
Woodland Hills CA 91365
(818) 347-1677

Four Ward Corp.
500 Summit St., Suite 300
Stamford CT 06901
(203) 964-0900

Freed-Crown-Lee Publishing Co.,
    Inc.
6630 Odessa Ave.
Van Nuys CA 91406
(818) 997-0644

Gale Research Co.
Book Tower
Detroit MI 48226
(333) 961-2242

Gambling Times, Inc.
1018 N. Cole Ave.
Hollywood CA 90038
(213) 466-5261

Game Point Publishing, Inc.
P.O. Box 946
Camden ME 04843
(207) 236-8346

Garland Publications, Ltd.
32 Devonshire Rd.
Chiswick, London, England W4
    2HD
(01) 994-6783

Garland Publishing, Inc.
136 Madison Ave., 2nd Floor
New York NY 10016
(212) 686-7492

G.B. Her Majesty's Stationery Office
Saint Crispins, Duke St.
Norwich, England NR3 1PO
(060) 362-2211

Geyer-McAllister Publications, Inc.
51 Madison Ave.
New York NY 10010
(212) 689-4411

Glasco Associates
33 S. Presbyterian Ave.
Atlantic City NJ 08404
(609) 347-1225

Glenn, Peter, Publications, Inc.
17 E. 48th St.
New York NY 10017
(212) 668-7940

Globe Pequot Press
Old Chester Rd.
Chester CT 06412
(203) 526-9572

Golf Digest—Tennis Inc.
P.O. Box 395
Trumbill CT 06611
(203) 373-7119

Good Ideas Co.
P.O. Box 296
Berea OH 44017
(216) 234-5411

Gordon Press, Publishers
P.O. Box 459, Bowling Green Sta.
New York NY 10004
(718) 668-8819

Gralla Publications
1515 Broadway
New York NY 10036
(212) 869-1300

Gramercy Information Services, Inc.
Box 2003, Madison Square Sta.
New York NY 10159
(212) 228-4769

Granada (now Grafton Books)
Eight Grafton St.
London, England W1X 3LA
(01) 493-7070

Greenwood Press
P.O. Box 5007
Westport CT 06880
(203) 226-3571

Grosset and Dunlap, Inc.
51 Madison Ave.
New York NY 10010
(212) 689-9200

H.P. Books
P.O. Box 5367
Tucson AZ 85703
(602) 888-2150

Harcourt Brace Jovanovich, Inc.
111 Fifth Ave.
New York NY 10022
(212) 614-3000

Harcourt Brace Jovanovich, Inc.
1700 E. Dyer Rd., Suite 250
Santa Ana CA 93705
(714) 250-8060

Harcourt, Brace, Jovanovich, Inc.
120 W. Second St.
Duluth MN 55802
(218) 723-9238

Harper and Row, Publishers, Inc.
Ten E. 53rd St.
New York NY 10022

Harris Publications
79 Madison Ave.
New York NY 10016
(212) 686-4121

Harvard Common Press
535 Albany St.
Boston MA 02118
(617) 423-5803

Harvard University Press
79 Garden St.
Cambridge MA 02138
(617) 495-2600

Hastings House Publishers, Inc.
Ten E. 40th St.
New York NY 10016
(212) 689-5400

Hayden Book Co.
Ten Mulholland Dr.
Hasbrouck Heights NJ 07604
(201) 393-6300

Haynes Publishing Group
Sparkford, Nr. Yeovil
Somerset, England BA22 7JJ
(0963) 40635

Heinemann, William, Ltd.
Ten Upper Grosvenor St.
London, England W1X 9PA
(01) 493-4141

Heldref Publications
4000 Albemarle St. N.W.
Washington DC 20016
(202) 362-6445

Hippocrene Books, Inc.
171 Madison Ave.
New York NY 10016
(212) 685-4371

Hobby Publications, Inc.
Rt. 9, Rd. 3, Box 490
Englishtown NJ 07726
(201) 972-1022

Hollywood Hotling
P.O. Box 1945
Burbank CA 91507
(818) 843-2837

Hollywood Reporter
6715 Sunset Blvd.
Hollywood CA 90028
(213) 464-7411

Holmes and Meyers Publishers, Inc.
30 Irving Pl.
New York NY 10003
(212) 254-4100

Holmes and Meyers Publishers Ltd.
131 Trafalgar Rd., Greenwich
London, England SE10 9TX

Holt, Rinehart & Winston
383 Madison Ave.
New York NY 10017
(212) 872-2000

Home Viewer
11 N. Second St.
Philadelphia PA 19106
(215) 629-1588

Hope Reports, Inc.
1600 Lyell Ave.
Rochester NY 14606
(716) 244-6630

Hospitality Media
15912 Windy Meadow Dr.
Dallas TX 75248
(214) 934-6520

House of Collectibles, Inc.
1904 Premier Row
Orlando FL 32809
(305) 857-9095

Human Kinetics Publishers
P.O. Box 5076
Champaign IL 61820
(217) 351-5076

Hutchinson Educational Ltd.
Brookmount House, 62-65 Chandos Place
London, England WC2N 4NW
(01) 240-3411

Icarus Press, Inc.
120 W. LaSalle St., Suite 906
South Bend IN 46601
(219) 291-3006

ICC Information Grove Ltd.
81 City Rd.
London, England EC1Y 1GO
(01) 250-3922

ILR Press
Cornell University
Ithaca NY 14851
(607) 255-3061

Image Publications
P.O. Box 474
Loudon TN 37774
(615) 458-3560

Industry Publishers, Inc.
915 N.E. 125th St.
North Miami FL 33164
(305) 893-8771; (800) 327-3736

Industry Shopper Publishing, Inc.
P.O. Box 2087 C.V.S.
Thousand Oaks CA 91362
(805) 496-1979

Information Access Co.
11 Davis Dr.
Belmont CA 94002
(415) 591-2333; (800) 277-8431;
    (800) 227-8432

Information Coordinators, Inc.
1435 Randolph St.
Detroit MI 48226
(313) 962-9720

Institute for Studies in American
    Music

Brooklyn College Conservatory of
   Music
Brooklyn NY 11210
(718) 780-5655

Institute of Social Research
P.O. Box 1248
Ann Arbor MI 48106
(313) 764-8378

Intergalactic Publishing Co.
P.O. Box 5013
Cherry Hill NJ 08034

Inter-Ski Services, Inc.
P.O. Box 3635, Georgetown Sta.
Washington DC 20007
(202) 342-0886

International Association of
   Assessing Officers
1313 E. 60th St.
Chicago IL 60637
(312) 947-206

International Thompson Retail
   Press, Inc.
345 Park Ave., S.
New York NY 10010
(212) 682-7744

International Trade Center,
   UNCTAD/GATT
P.O. Box 30, CH-1211
Geneva, Switzerland 21-Mf

Interstate Printers and Publishers,
   Inc.
19 N. Jackson St.
Danville IL 61832
(217) 446-0500

J.A. Micropublishing, Inc.
P.O. Box 218
Eastchester NY 10700
(800) 227-CIRR

Jobsen Publishing Co.
352 Park Ave., S.

New York NY 10010
(212) 685-4848

Kagan, Paul, Associates, Inc.
26386 Carmel Rancho Ln.
Carmel CA 93923
(408) 624-1536

Kampgrounds of America, Inc.
P.O. Box 30550
Billings MT 59114
(402) 690-7200

Kane Communications, Inc.
401 N. Broad St., Suite 226-27
Philadelphia PA 19108
(215) 925-9744

Kelthorne, Ltd.
26 Commercial Blvd.
Dunston, Tyne and Ward, England
   NE11 9AA

Kemps Group, Ltd.
1-5 Bath St.
London, England EC1V 9QA
(01) 253-4761

Key Note Publications, Ltd.
28-42 Banner St.
London, England EC1Y 8QE
(01) 253-3006

King Publications Ltd.
6/7 Great Chapel St.
London, England W1

Kingman and Ford Consulting
   Group
P.O. Box 16029
Saint Paul MN 55116
(612) 646-6558

Knowledge Industry Publications
Two Corporate Dr.
White Plains NY 10604
(914) 694-8686

Kraus International Publications
Rt. 100
Millwood NY 10546
(914) 762-2200

La Costa Music Business Consul-
tants
P.O. Box 147
Cardiff by the Sea CA 92007

Lakewood Publications, Inc.
50 S. Ninth St.
Minneapolis MN 55402
(612) 333-0471

Lance, Stephen and Jean, Publications
Brook House, Mint St.
Godalming, Surry, England GU7
1HE

Larkin Publications, Inc.
210 Boylston St.
Chestnut Hill MA 02167
(617) 964 5100

Laventhol and Horwath
1845 Walnut St.
Philadelphia PA 19103
(215) 491-1700

Law-Arts Publications
159 W. 53rd St. N. 14F
New York NY 10019
(212) 586-6380

Lawyers for the Creative Arts
220 S. State, Suite 1404
Chicago IL 60604

Lebhar-Friedman Books
425 Park Ave.
New York NY 10022
(212) 371-9400

Leicester University Press
Fielding Johnson Bldg., University
Rd.
Leicester, England LE1 7RH

Leisure Industry/Recreation News
P.O. Box 43563
Washington DC 20010
(202) 232-7107

Leisure Publications, Inc.
3923 W. Sixth St.
Los Angeles CA 90020
(213) 385-3926

Lexington Books
125 Spring St.
Lexington MA 02173
(617) 862-6650; (800) 235-3565

Lexington Publishers Ltd.
1910 Harrodsburg Rd., Suite 202
Lexington KY 40503
(606) 276-4465

Libraries Unlimited, Inc.
P.O. Box 263
Littleton CO 80160
(303) 770-1220

Limelight Editions
118 E. 30th St.
New York NY 10016
(212) 532-5525

Little, Arthur C., Inc.
25 Acorn Park
Cambridge MA 02140
(617) 864-5770

Little, George, Management, Inc.
Two Park Ave., Suite 1100
New York NY 10016
(212) 532-0251

Lloyd Publications of Canada
P.O. Box 262
West Hill, Ontario, Canada M1E
4R5
(416) 986-4875

Lone Eagle Publishing
9903 Santa Monica Blvd., Suite 204
Beverly Hills CA 90212
(213) 471-8066

Luebbers, David J.
78 S. Jackson
Denver CO 80209
(303) 388-8534

McFarland & Co., Inc., Publishers
P.O. Box 611
Jefferson NC 28640
(919) 246-4460

McGraw-Hill, Inc.
1221 Avenue of the Americas
New York NY 10020
(212) 997-4321

Mackay Publishing Corp.
309 Fifth Ave.
New York NY 10016
(212) 679-6677

Maclean Hunter Ltd.
76 Oxford St.
London, England W1N 9FD

Maclean Hunter Ltd.
777 Bay St.
Toronto, Ontario, Canada M5W
  1A7
(416) 596-5782

Macmillan London Ltd.
Four Little Essex St.
London, England WC2R 3LF
(01) 836-6633

McMillan Martin, Ltd.
Charles Roe House, Chestergate
Macclesfield, England SK11 6DZ
(0625) 613000

Madison Publishing Co.
P.O. Box 1936
Appleton WI 54913
(414) 733-2301

Maher Publications
222 W. Adams St.
Chicago IL 60606
(312) 580-7790

Maltby, Ralph, Enterprises, Inc.
4820 Jacksontown Rd.
Neward OH 43055
(614) 323-4193

Management Learning Laboratories
3337 Stoneybrook
Champaign IL 61821
(217) 359-3769

Mariah Publications Corp.
1165 N. Clark St.
Chicago IL 60610
(312) 951-0990

Marina News, Inc.
27601 Little Mack
Saint Clair Shores MI 48081
(313) 777-8866

Market Data Retrieval Inc.
16 Progress Dr.
Shelton CT 06484
(203) 926-4800; (800) 243-5538

Market Place Publications
P.O. Box 58421
Dallas TX 75258
(214) 747-4274

Marlor Press
4304 Brigadoon Dr.
Saint Paul MN 55126
(612) 483-1588

Marquis Who's Who
3002 Glenview Rd.
Wilmette IL 60091
(312) 441-2307; (800) 621-9669

Maryland Department of Economic
  and Community Development
2525 Riva Rd.
Annapolis MD 21401

Masters Press
5460 33rd St., N.E.
Grand Rapids MI 49508
(616) 947-4704; (800) 722-2677

Mathews, Walter, Associates, Inc.
28 W. 38th St.
New York NY 10018
(212) 869-4680

MDR Telcom
13464 Washington Blvd.
Marina Del Ray CA 90292
(213) 823-1200; (800) 423-6377

Means, Robert Snow, Company,
    Inc.
100 Construction Plaza
Kingston MA 02364

Medcom, Inc.
3301 Como Ave., S.E.
Minncapolis MN 55414
(612) 645-6311

Media Records, Inc.
370 Seventh Ave.
New York NY 10001

Mediac Press
P.O. Box 3315
Van Nuys CA 91407
(818) 904-0515

Mediamark Research, Inc.
341 Madison Ave.
New York NY 10017
(212) 599-0444

Merton House Travel and Tourism
    Pubs., Inc.
2100 Manchester Rd., Suite 507
Wheaton IL 60187
(312) 668-7410

Micromedia Ltd.
158 Pearl St.
Toronto, Ontario, Canada M5H 1L3
(416) 593-5211; (800) 387-2689

Miller Publishing Co.
2501 Wayzata Blvd.
Minneapolis MN 55440
(612) 374-5200

Minnesota Office of Tourism
150 E. Kellogg Blvd.
Saint Paul MN 55101
(612) 296-2755

Miramar Publishing Co.
2048 Cutner Ave.
Los Angeles CA 90025
(213) 477-1033

Morgan, A.E. Publications Ltd.
Nine West St.
Epson, Surry, England KT 187
    RL

Morris, Robert, Associates
P.O. Box 8500
Philadelphia PA 19178
(215) 665-2850

Morrow, William, & Co., Inc.
105 Madison Ave.
New York NY 10016
(212) 889-3050

Motorbooks International
729 Prospect Ave.
Oscela WI 54020
(715) 294-3345

Murdoch Magazines
One Park Avenue
New York NY 10016
(212) 503-5600

Music and Booking, Inc.
2210 Wilshire Blvd., Suite 206
Santa Monica CA 90403
(213) 281-1817

Music Trades Corp.
P.O. Box 432
Englewood NJ 07631
(201) 871-1965

N P D Special Industry Services
900 West Shore Rd.
Port Washington NY 11050
(516) 625-0700

National Association of Realtors
430 N. Michigan Ave.
Chicago IL 60611
(312) 329-8292

National Register Publishing Co.
3004 Glenview Rd.
Wilmette IL 60091
(312) 256-6067; (800) 323-6772

National Standards Assn.
5161 River Rd.
Bethesda MD 20816

Neal-Schuman Publishers, Inc.
23 Leonard St.
New York NY 10013
(212) 925-8650

Nelson-Hill, Inc.
111 N. Canal St.
Chicago IL 60606
(312) 922-0856

New York Graphic Society Books
34 Beacon St.
Boston MA 02106
(617) 227-0730

New York Production Manual, Inc.
611 Broadway, Suite 807
New York NY 10012
(212) 777-4002

New York School of Hotel
  Administration
Cornell University, Statler Hall
Ithaca NY 14853
(607) 256-5093

Newsletter Group, Inc.
1552 Gilmore St.
Mountain View CA 94040
(415) 941-7525

Nichols Publishing Co.
P.O. Box 96
New York NY 10024
(212) 580-8079

Nick Hock Associates
537 Post Rd.
Darien CT 06820
(203) 655-3216

Norris Publications
832 Mount Pleasant Rd.
Toronto, Ontario, Canada M4P 2L3
(416) 485-8284

North American Publishing Co.
401 N. Broad St.
Philadelphia PA 19108
(215) 574-9600

Northwood Institute Press
110 W. Signet
Midland MI 48640
(517) 631-1600

Official Arline Guides, Inc.
888 Seventh Ave.
New York NY 10106
(212) 977-8312

Offord, John, Publications, Ltd.
12 The Avenue
Eastbourne, East Sussex, England
  37841

O'Hara, J. Philip, Inc.
Valerie St.
Merrick NY 11566
(516) 379-4283

On Location Publishing Co.
6777 Hollywood Blvd., Suite 600
Los Angeles CA 90028
(213) 467-1268

One Hundred and One Productions
834 Mission St.
San Francisco CA 94103
(415) 495-6040

Ontario Crafts Council
Craft Resource Centre, 346 W.
  Dundas St.
Toronto, Ontario, Canada M5T 1G5

Opportunities Publishing
305 W. Jackson Ave.
Oxford MS 38655
(601) 236-5510

Organization for Economic
   Cooperation and Development
Two, rue Andre-Pascal
Paris, France 75775
(1) 45248200

Organization for Economic
   Cooperation and Development
1750 Pennsylvania Ave.
Washington DC 20006
(202) 724-1657

Oryx Press
2214 N. Central Ave.
Phoenix AZ 85004
(602) 254-6156

Owen Sound Public Library
824 First Ave. W.
Owen Sound, Ontario, Canada
   N4K 4K4

Pacifica Publishing
1732 LeBec Ct.
Lodi CA 95240
(209) 369-2368

Page Publishing Co., Ltd.
501 Oakdale Rd.
Downsview, Ontario, Canada M3N
   1W7
(416) 746-7360

Pannell Kerr Foster, Inc.
55 University Ave., Suite 800
Toronto, Ontario, Canada M53 2L4
(416) 863-1234

Penton Publishing Co.
1100 Superior St.
Cleveland OH 44114
(216) 696-7000

Pergamon of Canada, Ltd.
104-150 Consumers Rd.
Willowdale, Ontario, Canada M2J
   1P9

Pergamon Press
Headington Hill Hall
Oxford, England OX3 0BW
0865-64881

Pergamon Press, Inc.
Maxwell House, Fairview Park
Elmsford NY 10523
(914) 592-7700

Peterson Publishing Co., Ltd.
Peterson House, Northbank, Berry-
   hill Industrial Estate
Droitwich, England WR(9BL

Pilot Industries, Inc.
103 Cooper St.
Babylon NY 11702
(516) 422-2225

PJS Publications, Inc.
P.O. Box 1790
Peoria IL 61656
(309) 682-6626

Plays, Inc.
Eight Arlington St.
Boston MA 02116
(617) 536-7420

PLM Publishing Co., Inc.
P.O. Box 1700
Santa Monica CA 90406
(213) 451-1344

Porter Sargent Publishers, Inc.
11 Beacon St.
Boston MA 02108
(617) 523-1670

Practicing Law Institute
810 Seventh Ave.
New York NY 10019
(212) 765-5700

Predicasts
11001 Cedar Ave.
Cleveland OH 44106
(216) 795-3000; (800) 321-6388

Prentice Hall, Inc.
Rt. 9W
Englewood Cliffs NJ 07632
(201) 592-2000

Print Media Services, Ltd.
1310 Jarvis Ave.
Elk Grove Village IL
(312) 981-0100

Printwheel Press
2674 E. Main St., Suite C-124
Ventura CA 93003
(805) 643-0965

PTN Publishing Corp.
210 Crossways Park Dr.
Woodbury NY 11797
(516) 496-8000

Public Affairs Information Service,
   Inc.
11 W. 40th Sst.
New York NY 10018
(212) 736-6629; (800) 841-1416

Public Gaming Research Inst.
15828 Shady Grove, Suite 130
Rockville MD 20850

Publishers Development Corp.
591 Camino De la Reina
San Diego CA 92108
(619) 297-5350

Publishing Horizons, Inc.
P.O. Box 02190
Columbus OH 43202

Pubsun Corp.
244 W. 49th St., Suite 305
New York NY 10019
(212) 246-6460

Quigley Publishing Co., Inc.
159 W. 53rd St.
New York NY 10019
(212) 247-3100

Quinn Publications
612 Cougar Loop, N.E.
Albuquerque NM 87122
(818) 358-1846

Radius Group Inc.
408 W. 57th St.
New York NY 10019
(212) 496-ARTS

Rand McNally and Co.
8255 Central Park Ave.
Skokie IL 60076
(312) 267-6868

Random House, Inc.
201 E. 50th St.
New York NY 10022
(212) 751-2600

Ravenshead Marine Press Ltd.
44 Hatton Garden
London, England EC1N 8ER

Real Estate Education Co.
500 N. Dearborn St.
Chicago IL 60610
(312) 836-0466

Record Research
65 Grand Ave.
Brooklyn NY 11205
(212) UL7-7003

Restaurant Business, Inc.
633 Third Ave.
New York NY 10017
(212) 986-4800

Reston Publishing Co.
P.O. Box 500
Englewood Cliffs NJ 07632
(201) 592-2427

Retailer Publishing, Inc.
25 Willowdale Ave.
Port Washington NY 11050
(516) 767-2500

Riling Arms Books Co.
P.O. Box 18925
Philadelphia PA 19119
(215) 438-2456

RL Publishing, Inc.
5000 Dufferin St., Suite 203
Downsville, Ontario, Canada M3H
575
(416) 736-0865

RLD Communications, Inc.
P.O. Box 25485
Chicago IL 60625
(312) 271-0425

Rodale Press, Inc.
33 E. Minor St.
Emmaus PA 18049
(215) 967-5171

Roper Organization
205 E. 42nd St.
New York NY 10017
(212) 599-0700

Rutledge Books, Inc.
300 Mercer St., Suite 32M
New York NY 10003
(212) 460-8000

Saint Martin's Press, Inc.
175 Fifth Ave.
New York NY 10010
(212) 674-5151

Salesmans' Guide, Inc.
1140 Broadway
New York NY 10001
(718) 684-2985

Scarecrow Press, Inc.
P.O. Box 656
Metuchen NJ 08840
(201) 548-8600

Schirmer Books
866 Third Ave.
New York NY 10022
(212) 935-2000

Schocken Books, Inc.
62 Cooper Square
New York NY 10003
(212) 475-4900

Scribner's, Charles, Sons
597 Fifth Ave.
New York NY 10017
(212) 486-2700

Services to Lawyers, Ltd.
Standard House, 16-22 Epworth St.
London, England EC2A 4DR
(01) 628-8441

Seven Arts Press, Inc.
6253 Hollywood Blvd., Suite 1100
Hollywood CA 90028
(213) 469-1095

Shanken, M., Co., Inc.
400 E. 51st St.
New York NY 10022
(212) 751-6500

Sherwood Co.
P.O. Box 21645
Denver CO 80221
(303) 423-6481

Shoe String Press, Inc.
P.O. Box 4327
Hamden CT 06514
(203) 248-6307

Shore Communication, Inc.
180 Allen Rd., Suite 300
Atlanta GA 30328
(404) 252-8831; (800) 241-9034

Shull, Leo, Publications
136 W. 44th St.
New York NY 10036
(212) 586-6900

Simon and Schuster, Inc.
1230 Avenue of the Americas
New York NY 10017
(212) 245-6400

Simon Archery Foundation
Manchester Museum, The University
Manchester, England M13 9PL

Slideways Publications
P.O. Box 188
Marne MI 494-35
(616) 361-6229

Smith, W.R.C., Publishing Co.
1760 N.W. Peachtree Rd.
Atlanta GA 30357
(404) 874-4462

Society of Craft Designers
247 Centre St.
New York NY 10013
(212) 925-7320

Solitaire Publishers
216 S. Bungalow, P.O. Box 14508
Tampa FL 33690
(813) 876-0286

Sound Publishing
126 W. 14th St.
Owen Sound, Ontario, Canada

Source Communication, Inc.
P.O. Box A
Del Mar CA 92104
(619) 755-7431

Southam Communications Ltd.
1450 Don Mills Rd.
Don Mills, Ontario, Canada M3B
  2X7
(416) 445-6641

Southern Illinois University Press
P.O. Box 3697
Carbondale IL 62901
(618) 453-2281

Special Events Report, Inc.
213 W. Institute Pl., Suite 303
Chicago IL 60610

Special Libraries Assn.
1700 18th St., N.W.
Washington DC 20009
(202) 234-4700

Spon, E. and F.N., Ltd.
11 New Fetter Ln.
London, England EC4P 4EE
(01) 583-9855

Spon, E. and F.N., Ltd.
733 Third Ave.
New York NY 10017

Sporting News Publishing Co.
1212 N. Lindbergh Blvd., Box 56
St. Louis MO 63166
(314) 997-7111

Sports Ink Magazines, Inc.
P.O. Box 159
Fair Haven VT 05743
(802) 265-8153

Sportscape, Inc.
P.O. Box C9122
Brookline MA 02146
(617) 277-3823

Sportsguide, Inc.
P.O. Box 1417
Princeton NJ 08542
(609) 921-8599

Standard and Poor's Compustat
  Services, Inc.
7400 S. Alton Ct.
Englewood CO 80112
(303) 771-6510; (800) 525-8640

Standard and Poors Corp.
25 Broadway
New York NY 10004
(212) 208-8000

Standard Rate and Data Service, Inc.
3004 Glenview Rd.
Wilmette IL 60091
(312) 256-6067; (800) 323-4601

Statistics Canada
R.H. Coats Bldg.
Ottawa, Ontario, Canada K1A OT6
(613) 993-7276

Stoeger Publishing Co.
55 Ruta Ct.
South Hackensack NJ 07606
(201) 440-2700

Stuart, Lyle, Inc.
120 Enterprise Ave.
Secaucus NJ 07094
(201) 866-0490

TAB Books, Inc.
Monterey Ave.
Blue Ridge Summit PA 17214
(717) 794-2191

Talcott Communications Corp.
3405 Empire State Bldg.
New York NY 10018
(212) 629-0819

Tantivy Press
Magdalene House, 136-148 Tooley St.
London, England SE1 2TT

Taylor and Francis, Inc.
242 Cherry St.
Philadelphia PA 19106
(215) 238-0939

Taylor Publishing Co.
P.O. Box 597
Dallas TX 75221
(915) 949-3776

Technical Marketing Corp.
1460 Post Rd. E.
Westport CT 06880
(203) 255-9997

Texas A and M University Press
Drawer "C"
College Station TX 77843
(409) 845-1436

Theatre Communications Group, Inc.
355 Lexington Ave.
New York NY 10017
(212) 697-5230

Theatre Craft Associates
135 Fifth Ave.
New York NY 10010
(212) 677-5997

Thomas, Charles C., Publishing
2600 S. First St.
Springfield IL 62794-9265
(217) 789-8980

Thompson, J. Walter, Co.
401 Lexington Ave.
New York NY 10017
(212) 210-7000

TL Enterprises Inc.
29901 Agoura Rd.
Agoura CA 91301
(818) 991-4980

Touche Ross and Co.
1633 Broadway, Ninth Fl.
New York NY 10019
(212) 489-1600

Tower Books
Book Tower
Detroit MI 48226
(333) 961-2242

Trailer Life Publishing Co., Inc.
29901 Agoura Rd.
Agoura CA 91301
(213) 991-4980

Transatlantic Publishing
342 Madison Ave.
New York NY 10017
(212) 661-0656

Travel Concepts, Inc.
11510 Second Ave., N.E.
Miami FL 33161
(305) 759-8002

Travel Marketing
P.O. Box 2781
Culver City CA 90230
(213) 204-0673

Travel Text Associates
12605 E. State Fair
Detroit MI 48205
(313) 527-6971

Travel Trade Publishing Co.
Six E. 46th St.
New York NY 10017
(212) 883-1110

Trinet, Inc.
Nine Campus Dr.
Parsippany NJ 07054
(201) 267-3600; (800) TRINET-1

Turner, John S., And Associates
   Ltd.
41 High St.
Cambridge, England CB4 2NB

Twayne Publishers
70 Lincoln St.
Boston MA 02111
(617) 423-3990

Unique Golf Resorts of the World,
   Inc.
4501 Camden Dr.
Corona Del Mar CA 92625
(714) 760-0208

U.S. Bureau of Labor Statistics
Washington DC 20212
(202) 523-1364

U.S. Coast Guard
400 S.W. Seventh St.
Washington DC 20590

U.S. Department of Commerce
14th St. between Constitution Ave.
   and N.W. E St.
Washington DC 20203

U.S. Dept. of the Treasury, Bureau
   of Alcohol, Tobacco and Firearms
N.W. 15th and Pennsylvania Ave.
Washington DC 20224

U.S. Forest Service
U.S. Department of Agriculture
Washington DC 20250

U.S. Government Printing Office
N. Capitol and H Sts. N.W.
Washington DC 20401
(202) 275-2051

U.S. International Trade Commission
701 N.W. E St.
Washington DC 20436

U.S. Maritime Administration
GAO Bldg., Fifth and N.W. 6 Sts.
Washington DC 20235

United States Tennis Association
729 Alexandria Rd.
Princeton NJ 08540
(609) 452-2580

University of California Press
2120 Berkeley Way
Berkeley CA 94720
(415) 642-6683; (800) 822-6657

University of Colorado Business
   Research Div.
Campus Box 420
Boulder CO 80309
(303) 492-8227

University of Kansas Publications
Exchange and Gift Dept., Watson
   Library
Lawrence KS 66045

University of Minnesota, Dept. of
  Ag. Economics
260 Coffey Hall
Saint Paul MN 551-5366

University of Minnesota, Duluth
Bur. of Business and Economic
  Research
Duluth MN 55812
(218) 726-7256

University of Nevada Press
Reno NV 89557
(702) 784-6573

University of Tennessee Press
293 Communications Bldg.
Knoxville TN 07996-0325
(615) 974-3321

University of Toronto Press
Front Campus, University of
  Toronto
Toronto, Ontario, Canada M5S 1A1

University of Wisconsin Press
114 N. Murray St.
Madison WI 53715
(608) 262-4928

University Press of America, Inc.
4720 Boston Way
Lanham MD 20801
(301) 459-3366

Urban Land Institute
1090 Vermont Ave., N.W.
Washington DC 20005
(202) 289-8500

Vacation Work
Nine Park End
Oxford, England

Value Line, Inc.
711 Third Ave.
New York NY 10017
(212) 687-3965

Van Dahl Publications
520 E. First St., Box 10
Albany OR 97321
(503) 928-3569

Van Nostrand Reinhold Co.
135 W. 50th St.
New York NY 10020
(212) 265-8700

Van Zevern Publications, Inc.
3949 Oakton
Skokie IL 60076
(312) 982-1810

Variety, Inc.
475 Park Ave., S.
New York NY 10016
(212) 779-1100

Venture Publishing, Inc.
1640 Oxford Circle
State College PA 16803
(814) 234-4561

Video Marketing, Inc.
1680 Vine St., Suite 820
Hollywood CA 90028
(213) 462-6350

Viking Press
625 Madison Ave.
New York NY 10022
(212) 755-4330

Wakeman/Walworth, Inc.
P.O. Box 1939
New Haven CT 06509
(203) 562-8518

Warner Books, Inc.
666 Fifth Ave.
New York NY 10103
(212) 484-2900

Washington Researcher Publishing
2612 P St., N.W.
Washington DC 20007
(202) 333-3533

Weise, Michael, Film Production
P.O. Box 406
Westport CT 06881
(203) 226-6979

Western Marine Enterprises, Inc.
P.O. Box Q
Ventura CA 93002
(805) 644-6043

Wheatland Journals Ltd.
Penn Place
Rickmansworth, Hertfordshire,
   England W03 1SN

Whitney Communications Co.
840 Third Ave.
New York NY 10022
(212) 715-2600

Wiley, John, and Sons, Inc.
605 Third Ave.
New York, NY 10158
(212) 850-6418

Wilson, H.W., Co.
950 University Ave.
Bronx NY 10452
(212) 588-8400

Winter Sports Publishing, Inc.
11812 Wayzata Blvd., Suite 100
Minnetonka MN 55343
(612) 545-2662

Woodall Publishing Co.
11 N. Skokie Hwy., Suite 205
Lake Bluff IL 60044
(312) 295-7799

World Publishing Co.
1020 Church St.
Evanston IL 60201
(312) 491-6440

Writer's Digest Books
9933 Alliance Rd.
Cincinnati OH 45242
(513) 984-0717

Zanny Ltd.
186 Main St.
Unionville, Ontario, Canada L3R
   2G9
(416) 477-2922

Zoetrope, Inc.
80 E. 11th St., Suite 516
New York NY 10003

Index

References are to entry numbers rather than page numbers.

231